CW00536499

Airmen's Incredible Escapes

By the same author and in print with Pen & Sword Books:

With the East Surreys in Tunisia, Sicily and Italy 1942–1945: Fighting for Every River and Mountain (2012)

The Decisive Campaigns of the Desert Air Force 1942–1945 (2014)

Air Battle for Burma: Allied Pilots' Fight for Supremacy (2016)

Airmen's Incredible Escapes

Accounts of Survival in the Second World War

Bryn Evans

Pen & Sword
AVIATION

First published in Great Britain in 2020 by
Pen & Sword Aviation
An imprint of
Pen & Sword Books Ltd
Yorkshire – Philadelphia

Copyright © Bryn Evans 2020

ISBN 978 1 52676 172 9

Typeset by Mac Style
Printed and bound in the UK by TJ Books Limited,
Padstow, Cornwall.

Pen & Sword Books Limited incorporates the imprints of Atlas,
Archaeology, Aviation, Discovery, Family History, Fiction, History,
Maritime, Military, Military Classics, Politics, Select, Transport,
True Crime, Air World, Frontline Publishing, Leo Cooper, Remember
When, Seaforth Publishing, The Praetorian Press, Wharncliffe
Local History, Wharncliffe Transport, Wharncliffe True Crime
and White Owl.

For a complete list of Pen & Sword titles please contact

PEN & SWORD BOOKS LIMITED
47 Church Street, Barnsley, South Yorkshire, S70 2AS, England
E-mail: enquiries@pen-and-sword.co.uk
Website: www.pen-and-sword.co.uk

Or

PEN AND SWORD BOOKS
1950 Lawrence Rd, Havertown, PA 19083, USA
E-mail: Uspen-and-sword@casematepublishers.com
Website: www.penandswordbooks.com

Dedication

In memory of all those Allied airmen of the Second World War, on whom fortune did not smile, who were unable to make an incredible escape.

There is no certainty of victory in war, even when the equipment and numerical strength that cause victory exist. Victory and superiority in war come from luck and chance.

Ibn Khaldūn, fourteenth-century Arab historian

Contents

List of Maps

List of Photographs

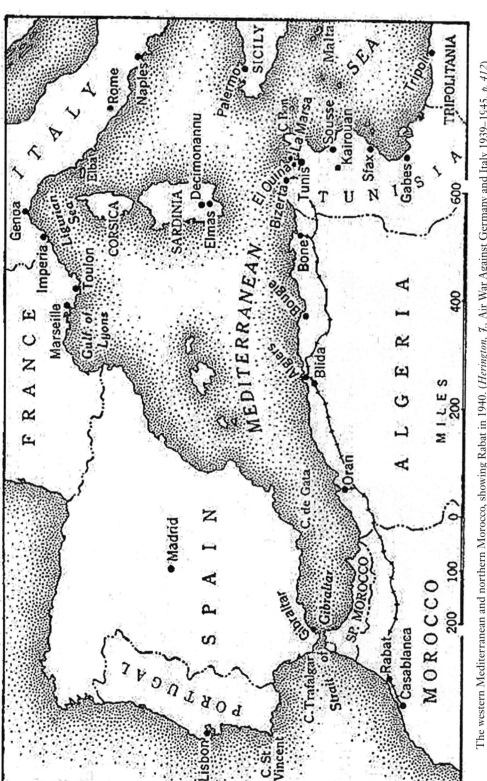

The western Mediterranean and northern Morocco, showing Rabat in 1940. (*Herington, J.*, Air War Against Germany and Italy 1939–1945, *p. 412*)

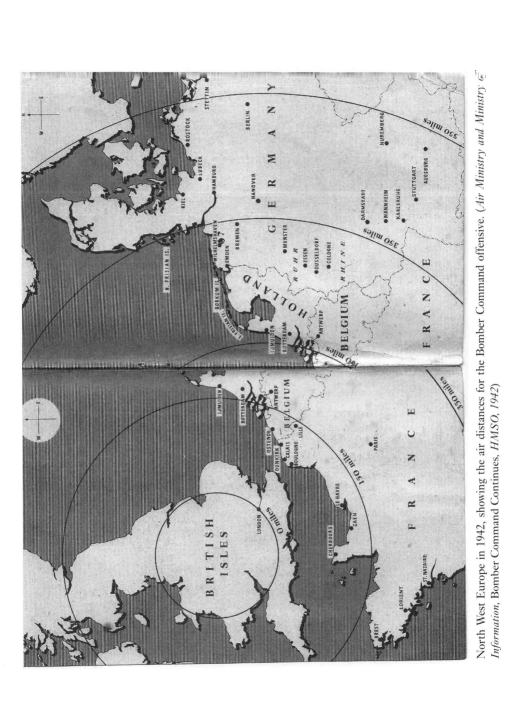

North West Europe in 1942, showing the air distances for the Bomber Command offensive. (*Air Ministry and Ministry of Information, Bomber Command Continues, HMSO, 1942*)

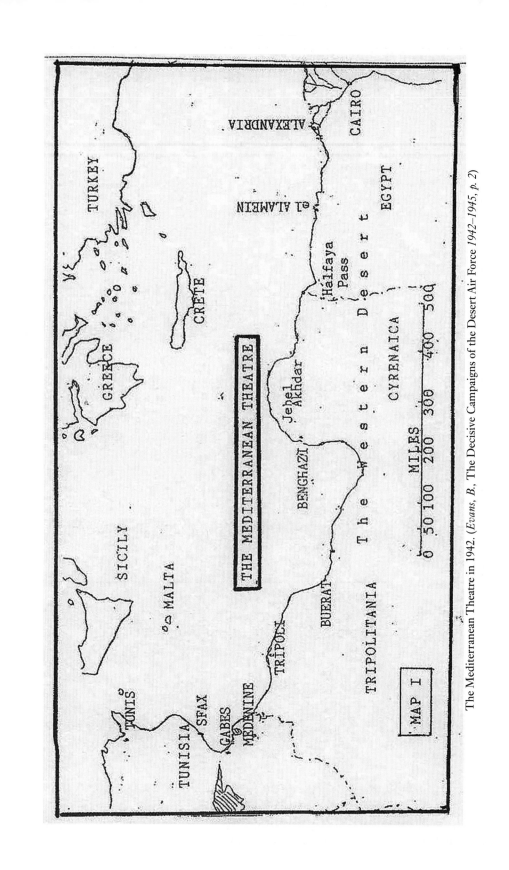

The Mediterranean Theatre in 1942. (*Evans, B., The Decisive Campaigns of the Desert Air Force 1942–1945, p. 2*)

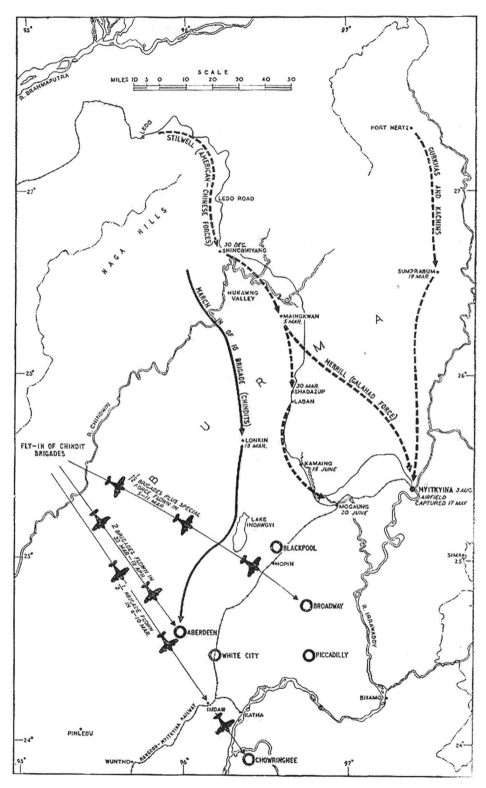

The second Chindit expedition Operation THURSDAY, showing the 'Broadway' base in Japanese-occupied Burma. (*Evans*, Air Battle for Burma, *p. xviiii*)

New Guinea and northern Australia 1944. (*Vincent, D, Catalina Chronicle – A History of RAAF Operations, inside cover map*)

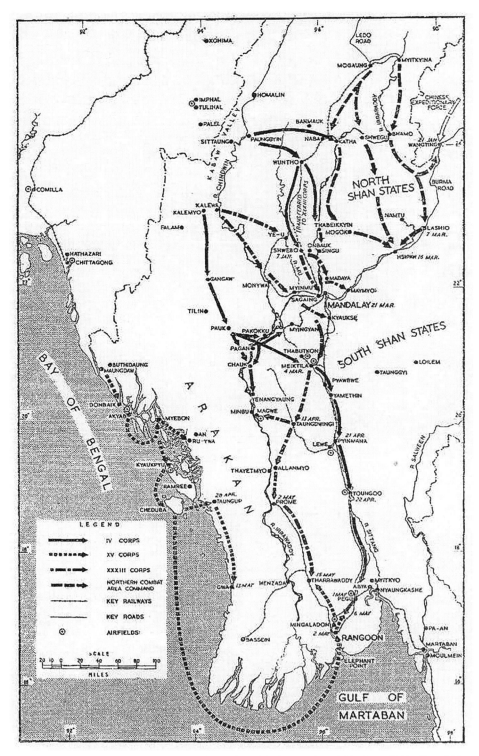

The reconquest of Burma 1944–45. (*Saunders,* The Fight is Won, Royal Air Force 1939–45, *p. 354*)

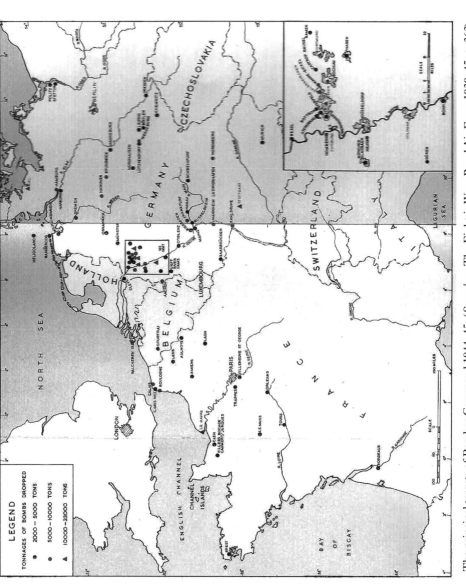

The principal targets of Bomber Command 1944–45. (*Saunders*, The Fight is Won, Royal Air Force 1939–45, *p. 262*)

Acknowledgements

In San Antonio, Texas, at the Day of the Dead Festival 1–3 November 2019, there was a shrine for families' loved ones who had passed away. One dedication read,

> When do the dead die?
> .....when we forget them.
> When do they continue living?
> ....when we continue remembering them.

It is a philosophy as old as the ancient Egyptians, perhaps older. In the course of writing the stories in *Airmen's Incredible Escapes*, there were many airmen, named or inferred, who did not live to recount their ordeal. Above all, this book is dedicated to all those who were unable to make an incredible escape. They will never be forgotten.

It is nearly impossible, seventy-five years since the end of the Second World War, to have any real understanding of what Allied servicemen faced. They were pitted in a life or death struggle against Germany, Japan and their Axis alliance countries, whose power-hungry regimes were waging total war against any nation and its people, who did not bow to the Axis goal of world domination. Men enrolled, or were conscripted into a war where the underlying ethos was 'kill or be killed'. There could be no negotiated peace.

Yet those servicemen, a majority being teenagers or young men in their early twenties, came from all walks of life just like you or me. No amount of training could ready them for facing an enemy who was out to kill them. As one veteran from Bomber Command described his wartime experience, the customary feeling of fear and dread before taking off on an operational flight can be understood only by those who experienced it. In many other veterans' accounts that constant and accumulating fear can be discerned.

The stories of amazing survival in *Airmen's Incredible Escapes* have only been made possible through the contributions and research material provided by veterans, their family members and friends. Their enthusiasm and interest, as in my previous books, has inspired me. The genesis of the book occurred eight years ago with a request by a veteran of Bomber Command, Lloyd Leah. I met Lloyd while researching *The Decisive Campaigns of the Desert Air Force*

1942–1945 when he told me his extraordinary experience of being shot down over Germany. He asked me not to write an article of his experience, but to put it in a book with others of incredible survival and it was an obligation that stayed with me.

Some veterans have been especially helpful in engaging with me, and sustaining my motivation, namely Keith Campbell, Alan Peart, John Jay, John McManus, Bill McRae and John Ulm. For all contributors, the book has only been possible because of their input. I can only offer my sincerest thank you, and hope that the result is worthy of their time and support.

Once more I am deeply grateful to Brigadier Henry Wilson, Publishing Manager at Pen and Sword, for his understanding of my concept proposal for *Airmen's Incredible Escapes* and his trust in me to deliver on time. Also I have been blessed to again have the renowned historian Richard Doherty as my editor, with his in-depth knowledge of the Second World War adding so much value to my writing.

A number of books provided me with a rich source of reference material, most notably those of Martin Middlebrook and John Terraine. Middlebrook's books on Bomber Command, such as *The Nuremberg Raid*, have been described as the finest on the RAF's bombing operations over Germany and occupied Europe, and inspirational for any writer of military history. Terraine in *The Right of the Line* wrote an encyclopaedic yet absorbing history of the role of the RAF in the Second World War.

Among the many research sources to acknowledge, I am as always particularly grateful to the National Archives of the UK in Kew, and the Imperial War Museum in London. The most influential research sources which I have consulted are listed in the Bibliography and Sources section, and I apologise if I have inadvertently omitted any.

Finally, as always, my deepest thank you is to Jean, not only for reviewing and advising on my concept, proposal and manuscript, but also for enduring my obsession, year in year out. Without her constant love, it would not have been possible.

Bryn Evans
March 2020

Foreword

Airmen's accounts of survival against all probability in the Second World War are also stories of the resilience of the human spirit. The war in the air was largely unseen except by individual airmen. Death in the sky or in an aircraft crashing to the ground could come suddenly and in terrifying ways. It was the first ever major war where the conflict in the air had a decisive influence on many battles and campaigns around the world.

Allied air forces' aircraft and their crews in all theatres were lost in innumerable encounters and circumstances, and in numbers never seen before or since. New weapons and technologies have made an air war on the scale of the Second World War, with such large numbers of aircraft and airmen on all sides, unlikely to be seen again.

Those airmen who did survive being shot down and who tried to evade capture were sometimes murdered by enemy forces or civilians. Deaths occurred in all kinds of ways; yet some airmen endured the most hostile circumstances. Some evaded capture to journey back to their base over several months. Accounts of such extraordinary survival were often not made known until after the end of the war. Many are known only by veterans, and their families, and have never been recorded or published.

The celebrated author Paul Brickhill was a fighter pilot and experienced his own incredibly fortunate escape. On 17 March 1943, flying a Spitfire in No. 92 Squadron RAF against Axis forces in Tunisia, he was shot down by an enemy fighter. Trapped in the cockpit of his Spitfire as it went into a death spin, he struggled to get out until, when only about 1,000 feet from the ground, he was thrown clear. Brickhill's parachute opened only seconds before landfall. Despite being dragged by the parachute across a minefield, and suffering serious injuries and wounds, he survived.

Brickhill was captured and sent to Stalag Luft III PoW camp south of Berlin, where he helped organise an escape plan for a large number of the PoWs. Secretly he documented what would become in 1950 a worldwide bestseller book, *The Great Escape*, and subsequently a similarly very successful film of the same name. He also wrote two anthologies of escape stories, *Escape to Danger*, and *Escape or Die*. Clearly the experiences of so many airmen's miraculous escapes were close to Brickhill's heart.

A true appreciation of the ordeals endured by survivors, and of the losses and sacrifices paid by Allied airmen, is difficult to fully comprehend. When so many of us today experience passenger plane travel, it is perhaps possible to imagine, if only with a fleeting sensation, the fear and terror of airmen in an aircraft fatally damaged by enemy fire. The accounts of those who came through the battles in the skies also give us an insight into the tumult and horrific death inflicted on those who did not survive. Eyewitness accounts paint a vivid picture of those surreal battles in the air, and how some airmen found a way to stay alive.

In the Second World War in RAF Bomber Command alone of approximately 125,000 aircrew who served more than 73,000 became casualties. The average losses per operation in Bomber Command were approximately 4 per cent per operation.[1] This meant that on or before an airman's twenty-fifth operation the odds were that he should be dead. To complete a tour of thirty operations and be eligible for transfer to a less lethal role was deemed to be unlikely.

A large number of aircrew did survive 'narrow escape' experiences. There is no known record of how many this might be, and it is probably impossible to know. However, anecdotal evidence suggests it is significantly higher than the number of casualties.

Although over the years many such stories have been published, it is likely that thousands have not. My research has shown that indeed a very large number of veterans' amazing survival experiences have only ever been known to themselves and their families. By publishing a request for such stories in the media, an unexpected wealth of unpublished accounts from veterans and their families was received.

In an air war largely unseen except by individual airmen, only these firsthand accounts by surviving aircrew can tell us what they endured in both accident-strewn training and operations against the enemy. Why is this important? The recording of more of these veterans' untold stories provides a more comprehensive understanding of their service and sacrifice – and the human costs.

They reveal the accumulating fear, terror and stress endured by airmen. Being shot down, making a crash landing, ditching in water or baling out was often only the beginning of an unknown ordeal to come. Evading capture by the enemy, staying alive in an inhospitable terrain, in sea or inland water, enduring the worsening pain from horrendous injuries or wounds, exhaustion, thirst, hunger, followed by the deprivations and cruelties of enemy PoW camps – these were the nefarious companions for airmen trying to stay alive.

Fate, fortune, good or bad luck was seemingly random, and ever present. Flying on operations in the Second World War was, as one veteran described it, 'dicing with death'.

But unless airmen took to the sky, and were prepared to die, the strategies and grand plans of the Allied high commands were worth nothing

It is said that for every participant in a battle, their experience and perspective is different and unique. That is certainly the case for aircrew in the air battles of the Second World War. *Airmen's Incredible Escapes* recounts just a few of those solitary and unique survival stories in the air war that was essential for the Allied victory.

Bryn Evans
January 2020

Prologue: Ditched and broken in half

For an operation to attack Berlin on the night of 22/23 November 1943, Bomber Command despatched 764 aircraft, fifty of which were Stirling bombers. This operation was one of nineteen major raids between August 1943 and March 1944 by Bomber Command in the Battle of Berlin. From 17.05 to 17.10 hours on 22 November seven Stirlings took off from RAF Chedburgh in Suffolk. One of those aircraft was a Stirling Mk III, No. EF445 of No. 214 Squadron, piloted by Flight Sergeant C.A. Atkinson. At 20.06 hours over the Berlin target area, Atkinson began his bombing run.[1]

The following is an edited summary of the combat report of No. 214 Squadron,[2] relating to the fate of Flight Sergeant Atkinson and his crew in the operation of 22/23 November to Berlin:

Flight Sergeant Atkinson and his crew bombed the Berlin target on a red sky marker with green stars. The glow of fires could be seen beneath the clouds. On the way back twenty miles east of Hanover the aircraft was hit by flak, causing the port outer engine to fail, and a loss of fuel. The rear gunner was wounded in his right leg by the attack, but refused to leave his gun turret. Loss of power from only three engines together with icing on the wings forced Atkinson to descend to between 1,500 and 2,000 feet.

Rather than ordering the crew to bale out over Germany, Atkinson was determined to bring the Stirling and his crew back to the Dutch coast, or ditch it in the sea as near to the coast as possible. While flying onward on three engines at this 'deck level' over western Germany and Holland, the mid-upper gunner and the rear gunner returned the fire of several flak positions, and claimed their gunfire damaged and shut down between fifteen and twenty searchlights. Over the Zuyder Zee a FW190 fighter was shot down by the rear gunner.

An SOS message was sent out at 22.31 hours reporting the loss of an engine and fuel. Sometime after crossing the Dutch coast the starboard outer engine cut out because of lack of fuel. In a rapid descent on the remaining two engines, Atkinson made a successful ditching at approximately 00.10 hours on 23 November in the North Sea. However, the impact with the water caused the Stirling to crack in half, breaking in two behind the mid-upper gunner's turret. The tail half of the aircraft's fuselage disappeared immediately below the waves. Atkinson was trapped in the nose of the Stirling as it also sank rapidly into the sea.

In winter months the average water temperature of the North Sea is around 4–6 degrees Centigrade. Even if crew members were able to extricate themselves from the rapidly sinking two halves of the Stirling's fuselage, then inflate their Mae West life vests or a rubber dinghy, they could not expect to survive for long. With sodden clothes, exposed to wind and rain, hypothermia was now the enemy.

> The wounded rear gunner struggled out of his rear turret, and was heard by other crew members somewhere amongst the waves, shouting that his Mae West life-vest was not supporting him effectively. Between 12.15 and 13.15 hours on 23 November five members of the crew were found and picked up by an Air Sea Rescue launch. The rear gunner could not be found despite a long search. Atkinson was presumed drowned with the aircraft. This quick rescue just twelve hours since the bomber went into the sea, was due entirely to the signals and accurate W/T procedure followed by the wireless operator who remained at his post in the aircraft right to the end, when the Stirling bomber ditched in the sea.

*   *   *

Of the total 764 aircraft despatched by Bomber Command twenty-six were reported missing. These comprised eleven Lancasters, ten Halifaxes and five Stirlings, which was 3.4 per cent of those sent to Berlin and, being below 5 per cent, were seen by Bomber Command as routine and acceptable.[3] Losses of aircraft were routinely recorded as 'Missing' or 'Did not return', or in similar non-specific remarks since the fate of the aircraft and crew was usually not known.

In most instances this remained the case until the end of the war, when any survivor of a missing aircraft who had been made a prisoner of war (PoW), was able to recount their experience. The report on the fate of Flight Sergeant Atkinson's Stirling bomber and its crew was uncommon, and only possible because five crew members were rescued, and able to recount the events. For the large majority of aircraft lost, no report of the circumstances was possible.

Part I

1939–40

Chapter 1

'Friendly Fire' is just another enemy

Flying Officer Paul Richey DFC and Bar

In quick succession anti-aircraft shells ripped into the plane's fuselage. Capitaine Casanova of the *Armée de l'air* (French Air Force) wrenched the controls away from his co-pilot, Flying Officer Paul Richey of the RAF,[1] and heaved the heavy Wibault T.12 transport aircraft into evasive action. Casanova's fast reactions saved them from more damaging hits, and he led the other three transports back to their airfield at Norrant-Fontes which was situated about halfway between Calais and Lille. On 9 October 1939 the French Wibaults had been transporting men, equipment, stores and ammunition for the Hurricane fighters of Nos 1 and 73 Squadrons RAF in an advance party to Vassincourt airfield.

Flight Lieutenant Paul Richey DFC*. (*Public domain*)

If the four transport aircraft had been shot down, it would have wiped out Nos 1 and 73 Squadrons. It was a lucky escape from disaster. Once they landed back at Norrant-Fontes airfield, Richey learned that they had been fired upon by British anti-aircraft guns by mistake. It was little more than a month since war had been declared and the two RAF squadrons of Hawker Hurricane fighters had been ordered to move to Vassincourt some fifty miles east of Rheims. Vassincourt was located south-west of Verdun and Metz, and closer to the French defences on the Maginot line and the front facing the threat of a German invasion.

*　*　*

On 1 September 1939 Germany had invaded Poland. As a consequence, on 3 September the British Prime Minister, Neville Chamberlain, declared that the

United Kingdom was at war with Germany. There followed a period of months that has often been described as the quiet or Phoney War. It was a misleading term. Two divisions were sent to France as part of the British Expeditionary Force in October and two more in November. As early as 2 September 1939 ten RAF squadrons of Fairey Battle light bombers had begun to be based in France, as part of the Advanced Air Striking Force (AASF) in anticipation of a German attack.[2] Two of those Fairey Battles were shot down on 20 September by Luftwaffe fighters. For Allied pilots the war had commenced.

On 8 September Flying Officer Paul Richey and No. 1 Squadron had flown their Hawker Hurricanes from their Tangmere airfield in Sussex across the Channel, to join the AASF at le Havre. Later they moved to the Norrant-Fontes airfield in northern France. Following the near disaster from 'friendly fire' on 9 October, No. 1 Squadron relocated successfully later in October to Vassincourt airfield which was laid out on high ground and ringed with woods. The squadron was billeted in the nearby small village of Neuville which was lower down and across a canal and railway line.

Richey was born on 7 May 1916 in Chelsea, London, while his father, Lieutenant Colonel George Richey CMG DSO and Bar, was serving in the First World War in France. He joined the RAF on a commission in 1937, training on Hawker Furies until he was posted in March 1939 to No. 1 Squadron at Tangmere in Sussex, where the squadron converted from Furies to Hawker Hurricanes.

In the afternoon of 16 October 1939 Flying Officer Richey took off from Vassincourt in Hurricane L1971 in a precautionary patrol to ward off any air reconnaissance by the Luftwaffe.[3] In preceding days an unidentified aircraft had been seen in the vicinity. For ten minutes, guided on radio by another pilot parked on the Vassincourt airfield, Richey flew westwards, saw nothing and turned back. During his return flight at 10,000 feet he saw six aircraft about three miles distant on his starboard side. Thinking them to be Hurricanes he closed towards them. While Richey gazed at the growing silhouettes of those

Hurricane of No. 1 Squadron RAF being refuelled at Vassincourt, France. (*IWM, public domain*)

aircraft, he suddenly realised the big mistake he had made to approach them without first gaining a height advantage. He was shocked. The aircraft were not Hurricanes. Were they a Luftwaffe formation?

As if Richey's thoughts had been transmitted by radio, the number two aircraft in the group saw him, waggled his wings at his leader, turned and headed in Richey's direction. This breakaway aircraft then dived and began to pull up towards him. From the *tricolore* on its tail he saw that it was a French Morane fighter. It seemed that their French pilot allies were in an aggressive frame of mind towards any unidentified aircraft.

The Morane-Saulnier MS.406 fighter, although inferior to Luftwaffe fighters, was not so much disadvantaged against the Hurricane Mk I. The Morane's 860hp engine was not as powerful as the Hurricane's 1,030hp from its Rolls Royce Merlin. Yet the Morane's top speed was only 20mph less than the 324mph of the Hurricane. The Morane could climb to 16,400 feet in six minutes and thirty seconds, whereas the Hurricane climbed to 15,000 feet in six minutes and eighteen seconds. In firepower the Morane had only two machine guns but it also had a cannon that packed more punch than a Hurricane.[4]

The Morane came up in a battle climb approach towards Richey, and fired a deflection burst at him. Another French fighter quickly followed up in support. Richey was clearly outnumbered. Luckily he had already reacted, turning to the left in a climb, which took him over the top of the first Morane

> I then dived in a turn to the right, did an Immelmann to the left which took me above a small cloud, stood on my tail, stall-turned and dived in a vertical left-hand spiral at full throttle. One Morane got on my tail, but I reckoned he was out of range ....[5]

Although the Hurricane was less manoeuvrable than a Morane, Richey knew his plane was faster. He finally pulled out of his crazy spinning dive and levelled off at about 200 feet and, keeping the Hurricane at full throttle, headed for what he thought was a homeward direction. He soon shook off the French fighters but realised he was lost. Having taken off in haste from Vassincourt, there had been no time to find any maps.

Richey circled for a while, in doubt as to which way to head. When he saw that he had only twenty gallons of fuel left, he decided to make for a town that he had seen and look for somewhere close by to land. He spotted a field on high ground which ought to be dry and, on flying low over it, thought the surface looked reasonable. After dropping down twice in trial approach runs, with his flaps and wheels down, Richey decided to put the Hurricane down. With his fuel near empty he had no choice.

His landing turned out to be good despite being up a slight slope, coming to a halt near some trees. To his relief, some French air force officers, rather than German troops, were soon on the scene and took him back to their mess. There they treated him to a fine dinner and wine, and Richey learned that one of the French Morane fighters had made a forced landing and damaged its propeller.

The French pilot of that Morane fighter contacted the police, telling them to search for the German fighter which he thought that he had shot down. Once he was told that it had been an RAF aircraft, he was crestfallen. When Richey heard this it prompted him to ask that they invite the dejected pilot to their dinner. His new-found French colleagues decided to play along with their fellow pilot's distress. So as to give the appearance that Richey had been wounded, they wrapped him in bandages.

The pilot, Sergent-Chef Léo Boyer, duly arrived, and joined the party with a look of guilt. Richey stood up, decided the prank had gone far enough, laughed and proffered his outstretched bandaged hand in greeting. The wine was soon flowing once more, and Richey and Boyer engaged in convivial conversation. He learned that Boyer was an outstanding pilot of eight years' experience, and a member of the renowned *Formation Aérobatique* squadron of Dijon.

Richey also heard Boyer say that he had fired a minimum of 400 rounds and forty cannon shells at his Hurricane. That, in combination with Richey's spiralling dive earthwards, had convinced Boyer that he had shot down what he thought was a German fighter. Richey had indeed had a narrow escape. On the back of this fortuitous outcome Boyer and Richey became close friends. Nonetheless, in little more than a month since war was declared, Richey had twice escaped death from 'friendly fire'. The considerably more dangerous life or death encounters with German fighters and bombers were yet to come. Yet throughout the coming years of war 'friendly fire' would prove to be a continual and dangerous enemy.

*   *   *

From 30 October 1939 to 19 May 1940 Richey recorded in his notebook that he and his fellow pilots of No. 1 Squadron claimed to have shot down 140 enemy aircraft. Their own losses were only three pilots killed, two wounded, and one taken prisoner.[6] Although there would have been some degree of overclaiming, the statistics give an indication of the intense air fighting undertaken to counter and slow the German *Blitzkrieg* which, in its all-arms tactical doctrine, included integrated Luftwaffe support.

Chapter 2

Baling out at 200 feet – is not recommended!

Flight Lieutenant C.A.R. Crews and Leading Aircraftman T.S. Evans

The two airmen hung near motionless from two pine trees. Their crumpled parachutes hooked into the higher branches billowed intermittently catching any breeze. In the silence anyone walking through the forest would think the two men were dead. In a small clearing between the two trees another body lay lifeless, and acrid smoke permeated the air. A little farther off an aircraft's fuselage burned fiercely.[1]

*   *   *

Earlier on the morning of 11 May 1940, as German forces blitzed their way into Belgium and Holland, aircrew of No. 218 Squadron RAF at Auberieve-sur-Suippes airfield near Rheims in northern France were ordered into an attack on German troops in Luxembourg. At 09.30 hours Flight Lieutenant C.A.R. Crews, his wireless operator/gunner Leading Aircraftman T.S. Evans, and navigator Sergeant C.M. Jennings took off in a Fairey Battle light bomber.

With another Fairey Battle in support, Crews was flight commander, tasked with a low-level bombing attack on a key bridge which lay near St Vith close to the Belgian-German border and in the path of the advancing German army. At the outbreak of war in early September 1939, No. 218 Squadron had moved to France as part of the RAF Advanced Air Striking Force. In total on 11 May eight Fairey Battles were despatched against German forces advancing through Luxembourg.[2] Against the massed flotillas of the Luftwaffe it was insignificant.

At first Crews' route to the north-east over Champagne's flat plain and the Ardennes forests was calm, like a training flight. Some thirty miles from St Vith they came under anti-aircraft fire from German columns of army vehicles pouring into Belgium. Crews' Fairey Battle was hit, damaging his instrument panel. Luckily he and Evans were unscathed. To Crews the aircraft showed no ill effects, responding normally to his controls. The two Battles flew on through continuing flak, and within minutes Crews saw the bridge at St Vith.

Three Fairey Battles of No. 218 Squadron RAF, based at Auberives-sur-Suippes, on patrol over northern France. On 11 May 1940 Battle K9325 HA-D (on far right of the formation) went missing in an attack on German troops near St Vith. (*Public domain*)

Crews led the two aircraft into a turn and a bombing run to the bridge, only for an anti-aircraft shell to smash into his engine in the aircraft's nose. Glycol gushed out from a huge cavity, and blazing fuel surged back under the cockpit. Blistering heat hammered Crews. Although little more than 300 feet above the trees, Crews decided that the only option was to bale out.

Aircrew of the RAF were advised that baling out below an altitude of 1,500 feet was not recommended. Although there are many factors and circumstances that have an effect on what might be the lowest viable altitude for baling out, e.g. aircraft speed, the attitude of the plane, air temperature, weight of the person, any delay in pulling the ripcord etc., the absolute minimum was thought to be a height of around 300–400 feet. Below that the parachute was unlikely to have time to open.[3]

Very few have survived baling out from below this height without ejection seats since, without the time to open fully, the parachute is unable to arrest the fall before an airman hits the ground at terminal velocity with lethal result. Where the parachute has insufficient time to open fully, survival is usually only possible through the fall being checked by some other fortuitous means.[4]

None of these considerations were in Crews' mind. His aircraft was doomed. On one side he could see a wooded slope above them. They were losing power and height. He pulled the cockpit hood back and shouted to Evans and the navigator to bale out. The wind draft brought the fire roaring up through the floor, to lick around his body. Crews kept the control stick pressed back, hoping in vain to gain some height. To escape the flames writhing around him, he hauled himself upright, standing on his seat, so that his upper body was buffeted in the slipstream.

In that instant Crews knew that he had to jump and accepted that at this height of little more than 200 feet, he was going to die. Behind him, Evans and their navigator were also struggling out as the Fairey Battle slowed and was about to stall. Crews lowered himself onto the starboard wing where it joined the fuselage and dropped away. Simultaneously, he pulled his parachute

Wreckage of a Fairey Battle shot down in May 1940 by the Wehrmacht in northern France. (*Public domain*)

ripcord handle, just hoping that the canopy would not be caught by the aircraft's tailplane.

Crews glimpsed Evans also falling, as a blanket of green foliage rushed up towards them. He was unsure whether his parachute had opened as he closed his eyes, instinctively tensing himself for impact. Within two or three seconds he was into the trees. Pine tree branches tore at his body, ripping at exposed skin, before a sudden jolt halted his fall.

In an instant all was quiet, and Crews opened his eyes. The ground looked to be about six feet below. He was hanging from his half-opened parachute, which was snagged in higher branches of the pine tree. Only a few feet away Evans was dangling in a similar fashion. It appeared that their parachutes had streamed out, but had not had sufficient time to open fully. Simply because the trailing canopies had been caught up in the trees' branches, the two airmen were alive.

Crews and Evans, battered and scarred, stared dumbly at each other in shock. Evans remembered that he had for the first time forgotten to bring his lucky mascot, a small white elephant on the flight. They released themselves from their parachute harnesses and dropped to the ground. Crews and Evans were doubly fortunate to avoid being seriously injured, or even impaled by a tree branch, and not to have been left suspended twenty feet or more from the ground, and facing a back-breaking drop.

They walked over to the still body lying close by. It was their navigator; he was dead. His parachute, like theirs, had streamed, but not had time to open. Crews and Evans were uninjured apart from cuts and scratches. Their navigator had hit the ground just some fifteen feet away, in a narrow clearing where there were no trees to snag his parachute and had been killed on impact.

Thirty feet away the wreck of the Battle continued to burn amongst the trees, confirming that baling out had been their one chance. It seemed that fate had arbitrarily decreed who would live and who would die. Subsequently Crews and Evans attempted to walk back to Allied lines but were captured and spent the rest of the war as PoWs.[5]

Of the eight Fairey Battles sent out on 11 May 1940, only one returned.[6] In attempts to halt the enemy columns No. 218 Squadron suffered heavy casualties, and by early June 1940 it had lost all its aircraft. The remaining squadron aircrew and ground personnel were evacuated to the UK.[7, 8]

Chapter 3

Flight from the German Blitzkrieg – on land and sea

Sergeant Ricky Dyson[1]

In May 1940 aircraftsman Richard 'Ricky' Dyson with No. 59 Squadron RAF in France flees with other ground crew and staff on foot from the German Blitzkrieg, and makes for the port of Boulogne along with retreating troops of the British Expeditionary Force (BEF) and tens of thousands of refugees. The Luftwaffe's fighters and bombers are dominant. Troops and civilians are being bombed repeatedly by enemy dive-bombers.

*   *   *

In the face of the German armies' invasion into the Low Countries in May 1940, fear spread through the civilian life of Belgium and northern France like a contagion. A million or more people clogged the roads seeking a safe haven, 'in a honking, shouting, earsplitting cavalcade … whole families in old rattletraps piled high with mattresses, their sole pathetic armour'.[2] French and British troops withdrawing towards Dunkirk on the coast were swamped and mixed up in this slow-moving tide of humanity. The fighters and dive-bombers of the Luftwaffe swooped on the columns, bombing and strafing without any regard for collateral damage to innocent civilians.

By 21 May all but three squadrons (Nos 1, 73 and 501) of the Advanced Air Striking Force (AASF) in France had been withdrawn with any remaining aircraft, or were in the chaotic process of doing so in the confused evacuation.[3] Pilots flew their aircraft back to airfields in Britain, leaving their ground support staff and groundcrew to retreat as best they could by land and sea. One of those RAF groundcrew airmen was Ricky Dyson.[4]

Dyson was born in Windsor, the Royal Borough west of London, educated at the London Choir School, and was only seventeen when, in 1935, he left his job as a furniture salesman in Maidenhead and joined the RAF. In 1935

Sergeant Ricky Dyson – back row extreme right. (*Private collection, M. Dyson*)

pantaloons, puttees, swagger sticks and tunics buttoned to the neck were still in military vogue. Dyson's father was Commandant of the Windsor Special Constabulary and his grandfather was Sir Frederick Dyson, mayor of Windsor for three years.[5]

After training at Uxbridge and Cranwell, Dyson was posted to No. 108 Squadron as an aircraftsman, where he learned to fire a Lewis gun from the back seat of a Hawker Hind light bomber's open cockpit. Next followed a transfer to the Fleet Air Arm (FAA), which at that time was part of the RAF, with No. 852 Naval Air Squadron aboard the aircraft-carrier HMS *Glorious* in the Mediterranean. In May 1939, when the FAA became part of the Royal Navy again, Dyson was transferred back to Britain and No. 59 Squadron RAF at Andover.

I was still at Andover in September 1939 when war was declared, and shortly after No. 59 Squadron was sent to France as part of the British Expeditionary Force. We were equipped with the long-nosed Blenheim for photo-reconnaissance work. Our airfield was situated on a plateau above the town of Poix a few miles from Amiens, and we were billeted on its outskirts in barns, in which we slept on straw palliasses in the loft – cows below! Christmas came and went, as did the 'phoney war'.

In the Spring Hitler attacked the Low Countries on all fronts. The German advance was so rapid that by May 15 the Dutch had capitulated, and the Belgians surrendered shortly after. We moved back to Arras and soon after began a full evacuation, in which all airworthy aircraft were to be flown back to England. Ground crew and staff had to carry out a 'scorched earth policy' of burning all stores and equipment. We then had to make for the Channel ports as best we could.

It was a case of every man for himself, so with three other airmen I left Arras on a tractor. We ditched this later as the roads were choked with refugees. They were using all types of transport, cars, lorries, horse-drawn vehicles, bicycles etc. There were also hundreds on foot with prams and push-carts stocked with their worldly goods. The columns stretched for miles, making them an ideal target for German dive-bombers. At night we slept in ditches along the roadside, or when safe beneath cars and lorries.[6]

In the chaotic stream of civilians and troops fleeing for their lives, Dyson and his three companions walked westward towards the coast. When the Stuka dive-bombers attacked, they joined the lottery of diving into hedges and ditches by the roadside. The English Channel and a boat, any boat, seemed to be the only possible hope of escape and staying alive for Dyson – and a few hundred thousand other souls, both civilians and troops. It appeared a forlorn hope.

It took us three days to reach Boulogne on 19 May, which was my twenty-second birthday. The next day, together with hundreds of other servicemen, I was very lucky to get aboard a cross-channel paddle-boat, and made the crossing to England. I was much relieved at still being alive and in one piece! [7]

It was no less confusing and dangerous for pilots and aircrew trying to withdraw, with or without their aircraft. On the night of 18/19 May Pilot Officer C.R. Wylie and his aircrew of No. 59 Squadron slept beside their grounded Blenheim bomber, which was nearly out of fuel. Wylie awoke at 03.00 hours on 19 May.[8]

When we were all awake we walked to the village of St Vast, six miles west of Amiens, on which I witnessed a bombing raid by more than forty German dive-bombers. Some enemy aircraft were machine-gunning ground targets. As we hurried to the shelter of some woods, my air gunner fell and hit his head, knocking him unconscious for more than ten minutes. Once he recovered we returned to our aircraft. I removed maps, other documents and the observer's compass, then taxied the Blenheim to the lee of a wood.

We set off walking with the intention of reaching Crecy, to try and obtain some fuel for the Blenheim. But at Picquigny we were forced to join fleeing traffic and people being diverted from Abbeville. Enemy aircraft appeared to be bombing Abbeville and Dieppe. We walked about another thirteen miles until we were lucky to be given a lift in a French air force lorry, which took us through Airaines, Hornoy and Aumale, where we joined up with a convoy of 52 Wing RAF.[9]

Wylie and his crew arrived at Rouen on 20 May at 19.00 hours, before reaching the port of Cherbourg on 21 May at 07.30 hours. Their luck held and they were able to board an evacuation vessel across the Channel, enabling them to disembark at 22.30 in Southampton.

*   *   *

Dyson and Wylie were just two airmen who were lucky to survive the withdrawal and evacuation from France in May 1940. In a way Dyson was doubly fortunate to still be alive, for two weeks later on 8 June the aircraft-carrier HMS *Glorious*, which he had left a year ago, was sunk by the German battle-cruisers *Scharnhorst* and *Gneisenau*. Of some 1,500 sailors and airmen on HMS *Glorious* only forty-six survived. Back in England, having survived the evacuation from Dunkirk, Dyson re-joined No. 59 Squadron, and commenced training for aircrew and practice at Gunnery School. For Dyson and Wylie, like all Allied forces, this was just the beginning of gambling with death, and fate had much more in store for Dyson in particular.

Chapter 4

Secret flight to a Moroccan River – to save Britain and France?

Flight Lieutenant Julius A. Cohen DFC

In early June 1940, despite many French politicians wishing to make peace with Germany, the French Premier M. Reynaud was prepared to continue the fight against the German invasion. Reynaud and his government had retreated to Bordeaux, and yet the French armed forces still had considerable resources with which to fight on. Churchill, the new British prime minister of only a few weeks, made an incredibly generous offer to Reynaud. This was to establish a free alliance of France and Britain against Germany, in which the French people would also become citizens of Britain, and British people would become citizens of France. Reynaud was very supportive of the proposal, but was unable to garner enough support from members of his government.[1]

Flight Lieutenant Julius A. Cohen DFC (Virtual War Memorial, www.vwma.org.au/ explore/people. (*Public domain*)

It left Britain in a dire situation. If Germany was able to take possession of the French naval fleet, which had taken refuge in France's North African colonies, Britain would face overwhelming odds against her survival. In a desperate attempt to prevent this, on 24 June 1940 a Sunderland flying boat and its crew of No. 10 Squadron RAAF was ordered to fly in a top-secret mission from its base at Plymouth to Southampton, where its pilot, Flight Lieutenant Julius A. Cohen, would receive further secret instructions. At 07.10 hours on the morning of 25 June, Lieutenant Cohen landed Sunderland P9602 on Southampton Water at Calshot.[2]

Flight Lieutenant Julius A. Cohen[3] was born in Moree, New South Wales, Australia, in 1916 and joined the RAAF in 1935. He was twenty-four, still wore the dark blue of the RAAF uniform, and flew the Sunderland on daily patrols of surveillance and protection for convoys, and searches for German U-boats. He was six feet tall, with dark eyes and a temperament that exuded a calmness and a professional approach to his role. In July 1939 Cohen had arrived in Britain to train on the Short Sunderland flying boat, before he and other pilots would ferry nine of them back to Australia.

At 09.00 hours on 25 June 1940 on Southampton Water with his second pilot, Pilot Officer Stewart, he lifted the Sunderland into the air with orders to fly to Rabat, capital of French Morocco on the Atlantic Coast, and land on its Bouregreg river. Two important government passengers were aboard, General Lord Gort VC, and the Right Honourable Alfred Duff Cooper, Minister of Information. Theirs was a desperate mission, to persuade certain French statesmen in Rabat, to carry on the war, and not seek peace with Germany. [4]

For twelve hours Cohen flew the flying boat south at around 500 feet above the waves to avoid enemy fighters until, a little before 19.00 hours, he sighted Rabat.[5] As he circled the city on the banks of the Bouregreg river to assess a suitable stretch of water for landing, he could see that the river was no more than 150 feet wide at most. Since the Sunderland's wingspan was approximately 113 feet, even if he managed to put down precisely midstream that would only leave about eighteen feet clearance at best for each wingtip. Yet the situation was actually worse. On both riverbanks the moored boats of the local population reduced the clearance margin further, while bends in the river made a descent and landing even more hazardous.

In normal times no one would attempt to land a Sunderland in such a restricted space. The two VIP passengers, Lord Gort and Duff Cooper, could see with their own eyes the great difficulty facing the pilot as he circled around. After Cohen came back and explained to them the severe constraints and narrow margin of error in stark detail, he asked Lord Gort if he still wished to attempt a landing on the river. Calmly the VC holder gave the go ahead. He knew that their mission, if successful, could change the course of the war.

Cohen brought the twenty-two ton Sunderland around over the sea before commencing his approach to landing on the river. He began to lose height and speed. A 10mph cross-wind, ordinarily of little consequence, accentuated the need for him to find the precise centre of the river. The two VIPs had put their trust in him. Unaware of his tightening breath he touched down the flying boat's hull as near as he could judge midstream, and for some 300 yards he held the aircraft steady as it slowed, using the rudder to guide it around a bend. As a crew member dropped anchor, Cohen saw a boat of French officials set out to meet them.

Escorted by French air force officers Cohen went ashore with Lord Gort and Duff Cooper, and after being allowed to send off a signal to London of their arrival in Rabat, he returned to the Sunderland. While Lord Gort and

Duff Cooper remained ashore in talks with the French authorities, in the early evening Cohen received a secret signal from London for the two emissaries. At first he was prevented from disembarking to take the message to Lord Gort by the French police boat.

Only when Cohen and his crew threatened the police at gun point was he able to get ashore. Once on land he had to talk his way carefully through delicate red tape and difficult negotiations with more police, and draw his revolver as a threat, before he was able to make his way to Lord Gort with the important communication. It is probable that the coded signal from London was to warn Lord Gort and Duff Cooper that the French authorities in Africa were moving towards an agreement with the pro-German Vichy Government in France.[6]

Whatever the content of the message might have been, there was some kind of confrontation with guns drawn, and it was not until around 03.00 hours that Lord Gort, Duff Cooper and Cohen returned to the Sunderland. A favourable outcome to the talks did not look hopeful, and the French police boat continued to circle and closely guard the flying boat as it drifted at anchor. Cohen was determined that they would not fall into the clutches of the French, and be detained in Rabat.

He placed all his crew on duty for the rest of the night with guns manned. He knew that the Sunderland, endowed with two 0.303in machine guns in the bow turret, four of the same in the tail turret, and one in each of the port and starboard beam positions, was far from defenceless.[7] The French authorities and police in Rabat had been antagonistic from the moment of their arrival and, if their political masters were still considering making peace with Germany, anything might happen.

Shortly before first light on 26 June Cohen gave the order to cast off, and began to taxi towards the ocean. To attempt to take off from the constricted river in the dark was too dangerous. The French police boat, which wisely did not open fire or try to obstruct the Sunderland's path, was ignored. When they reached the opening to the sea, Cohen saw that they faced a long rolling swell. To attempt a take off in those conditions risked losing one or both floats, and other damage, which could cripple the flying boat and prevent take off, or endanger an eventual landing.

Once again, after discussion, Lord Gort gave Cohen approval to take the risk. Turning back to Rabat and being detained by the French was not an option. Cohen turned on the power, bounded the Sunderland across the tops of a couple of swells and, at 06.10 hours, lifted the aircraft unscathed into the air. By 07.30 hours they splashed down in Gibraltar, and after leaving there next morning they reached Southampton by 18.10 hours on 27 June.[8]

*   *   *

The selfless efforts of Lord Gort, Duff Cooper, Cohen and his crew proved subsequently to be in vain. The French government spurned Churchill's offer and made a humiliating peace with Hitler. This resulted in the Royal Navy attacking the French fleet, and sinking a number of its ships on 3 July 1940 at Mers-el-Kebir, Algeria, so as to prevent it falling into the hands of Germany.

The skill, judgement and courage of Flight Lieutenant Cohen were recognised when he was immediately awarded the DFC. In a distinguished record of service for the rest of the war, including senior command appointments in the Far East theatre, Cohen attained the rank of wing commander. Later, post-war, he changed his name, and was knighted as Sir Richard Kingsland AO CBE DFC and led an eminently successful career in both business and public service. He married Kathleen Adams, a WAAF officer, and they had a son and two daughters.[9]

Part II

1941

Chapter 5

Down the gangplank, and across Africa

Flight Lieutenant Lewis Bevis[1]

Flight Lieutenant Lewis Bevis walked down the gangplank of an old Irish Sea cattle-boat in the port of Takoradi. It was September 1941 and he was ashore in the Gold Coast, West Africa. He had sailed from Greenock, Glasgow, a first stage in a passenger liner to Gibraltar, before his second voyage south in a cattle freighter. Bevis, who was from London, had joined the RAF in 1940, gained his wings earlier in 1941 at Brize Norton and then trained on Tomahawk fighters. Now he had to report to the Takoradi RAF base, and fly a Hurricane fighter thousands of miles across Africa to the Desert Air Force of RAF Eastern Command in Egypt.

* * *

The Desert Air Force (DAF), in its air war against the Axis air forces, and in support of the embattled Eighth Army in the desert war against Rommel, was continually short of planes. During 1941 in the North African campaign there were only three routes by which aircraft could be delivered to Egypt and the Middle East. Although an itinerary by ship around the Cape of Good Hope, South Africa, then north to Port Sudan on the Red Sea, or Port Tewfik at the southern end of the Suez Canal, was the most secure it was the longest duration. Flying aircraft over occupied France and through the Mediterranean was extremely hazardous. The Luftwaffe and the Regia Aeronautica had fighters based in North Africa, Sardinia, Sicily, Crete and other islands such as Pantelleria.

Irrespective of the threat of interception by Axis aircraft, RAF fighters from Gibraltar did not have the range to even reach Malta, although in early 1942 some did so by flying from aircraft carriers in the western Mediterranean, when they were within one-way-flight range of the besieged island. By ship to Malta or Cairo through the Mediterranean was far too dangerous to consider. Cargo ships were being sunk at an alarming rate either by Axis aircraft or naval vessels.

Wreckage of an RAF aircraft at Takoradi airport, 12 December 1942. (*Public domain*)

The third route, flying via Gibraltar and the west coast of Africa across the Sahara to the Sudan and then north to Cairo, became the most dependable. Opened as a civil aviation route in 1937, it became a vital lifeline for delivering aircraft to the Middle East and in particular to the RAF in Egypt. In early 1941 the numbers of aircraft delivered on the cross-Africa route were, for example, forty-nine in March, 134 in April, 105 in May and 151 in June. The total flying distance for these aircraft was around 4,000 miles, broken into stages for refuelling, before they reached RAF Eastern Command in Cairo.

It may have become the most reliable and quickest route to ferry aircraft to Egypt, but it still presented both foreseeable and unpredictable dangers to pilots. The cross-Africa route was a daunting first-time flight across unknown terrain and skies, especially for the large numbers of inexperienced and recently trained pilots.[2]

After a week or two of training and acclimatisation at Takoradi, Bevis took off in a flight of six Hurricanes on the first leg of the long haul to Egypt. The first day they followed a Bristol Blenheim, which was in the lead for navigation, south to Lagos in Nigeria where they spent the night. Next morning, with the other five Hurricanes, Bevis lifted off on a four-hour flight to Kano in Northern Nigeria.

In the group with me was another Londoner, Rick. Petrol economy was important and we were instructed to fly at low revs and high boost to achieve this. After a little over an hour's flying, I developed engine problems with a loss of performance. I fell behind the flight and was advised by the leader to make my own way.

However, Rick decided to stay with me. We were at 12,000 feet over thick cloud when I explained to him over the R/T that if I descended below the cloud I would not have enough power to regain height. He suggested that he should go down below the cloud and advise me of the terrain. Checking the course on my map, I saw that we could possibly be over mountains up to 5,000 feet, so I told him to wait.[3]

Rick did not wait. Ten days later he was found dead, having descended into the cloud and crashed into a mountain face.

I continued on, and no longer being in touch with Rick, decided I had to try to get below the cloud cover. I broke cloud at about 3,000 feet over high ground coming out just above the treetops, luckily to a landscape falling away in front. Being on course I was able to pick up the Niger river and, in time, landed at Minna where petrol reserves in 4-gallon cans were available.

The next day Bevis, with a full tank of fuel, was able to reach Kano. The ground crew there found that the Hurricane's engine required maintenance on its plugs, caused by the necessary over-boosting during the flight. This meant that he had to wait to join the next ferry flight of Hurricanes. When they arrived three days later, Bevis set off with them on the various stages via Maiduguri, El Geneina, El Fasher and Wadi Seidna across the southern Sahara and Sudan. At the Wadi Seidna airfield, despite Bevis and the other pilots having been flying since 05.45 hours that morning, the station officer made them refuel and take off again on a seven-hour flight north to Luxor in Egypt.

During the flight from El Fasher, Bevis had dropped his maps on to the floor of the Hurricane, intending to recover them on landing at Wadi Seidna. Distracted by the orders of the station commander, he forgot to do so. Once airborne, Bevis found himself thinking it would be easy to follow the other five Hurricanes without his maps: 'After nearly an hour, we ran into a sandstorm, reducing visibility to nil. We got split up and now I was on my own.'

He needed those maps, but would need to land in order to find them, wherever they had lodged in his cockpit. He made several attempts to land in the desert, pulling away at the last moment from rock-strewn areas.

Finally I noticed a native village with a clear area nearby on which I landed. I was then able to recover the maps. While I was doing this, I was descended upon by a crowd of natives from the nearby village, riding donkeys and camels. While they gathered round, I pointed to place names on the map to establish my position. The name Abu Ahmed rang a bell with them, and that apparently was where I was.

The village headman gave Bevis a bed for the night made out of ropes, and he slept surprisingly well. In the morning, by using sign language and pointing at chickens, he managed to get boiled eggs for his breakfast. However, when he reached the Hurricane, he found that the villagers had stripped it of the leather gun covers, his parachute and, among other loose items, his Very pistol, which was his only means of defence.

> I started up the motor, surrounded by donkeys and camels. I had checked my fuel and the distance from Abu Ahmed to Luxor, and I reckoned I still had enough to get me there. I climbed to 8,000 feet and set course.
>
> At a point some forty miles south of Luxor, where a low mountain chain crosses the Nile and there are river cataracts, the red fuel-warning light came on. I was shocked, very short of fuel, and wondering whether the gauges were accurate. Looking around, I saw what appeared from high up to be a roadway.
>
> However, when I got down to about 1,000 feet what had looked a suitable road from higher up was, in fact, a doubtful surface with banking on each side. Committed I made a good landing, but unfortunately hit a large boulder. This turned the aircraft off the road and onto its back, and I passed out.
>
> Although unconscious for a while I was not seriously hurt. Eventually an Egyptian, an educated engineer working on the Nile, came to help me. He took me to a telephone. After some hours a truck arrived from Luxor with airmen seeing what they could recover from the Hurricane.

Bevis then returned to Luxor with the recovery crew, and in a few days was allocated another Hurricane in a group flight to go on to Cairo.

> On this last leg of the journey I flew into a khamsin sandstorm. The desert sands are lifted by gale-force winds to heights of 10,000 feet. It gives you the impression of being just above the ground temporarily raised to 10,000 feet.
>
> In the poor visibility once again I became separated from the rest of the flight. I climbed above the sandy murk to work out a plan, knowing that I required sufficient fuel to make a precautionary landing if necessary. With this in mind I decided that the best course was to try to land while I still had petrol in hand.

Bevis dropped the Hurricane down into the sandstorm's higher clouds. Immediately he could not see anything at all. There were no breaks in the cloud at all. All he could do was to continue to descend steadily by circling turns, all the while watching the air speed, gyro instruments and altimeter.

At around 800 feet I suddenly noticed the colour around me changed from a reddish-brown to grey. This turned out to be the ground coming up! I levelled off, and landed into a 40mph wind. I rolled no more than a few hundred yards before coming to a stop.

I began to get out of the aircraft to look around, but as I was dressed only in shorts and a sleeveless shirt, I found the gritty wind stung too much, so I stayed in the cockpit. It was about 15.00 hours. As the evening drew on, the storm abated as is usual in a *khamsin*. I took a look around in the dark, returning to the aircraft to try and get some sleep sitting up.

In the morning Bevis was able to walk around and inspect the area where he had landed. The storm began to regain its tempo, and he knew he needed to take off again soon.

I had landed in a small wadi with soft sand scattered through it. I started the engine and taxied to the far end. Several times the wheels sank ominously into the sand, making it feel as if the aircraft must go up on its nose. I then realised I would have to prepare a path. I began laying flat stones to try to make a firmer surface for take-off.

It was tedious backbreaking work. The temperature rose above 100. What little water I had in my flask I sipped economically throughout the day. By evening my confidence was slipping. I knew I was in for another night in the cockpit. I continued to gather stones for the take-off that I had put off to the following morning. I also knew I was beginning to dehydrate.

Bevis spent another night sat upright in the Hurricane's cockpit. When he woke in the morning he realised his situation was desperate. His water was nearly all gone, and it was doubtful that he could last another day in the heat with no shelter. He had to get away at once. Otherwise he would die in this desert.

Then another blow struck me. When I pushed the starter button the engine wouldn't turn fast enough to fire. I now seemed to lose my power of reason. My mind started to wander back over past years. I thought of my early training – of school, Sunday school and God. Although I had been brought up strictly in the Church of England, I had in my late teens decided to be an agnostic. I reasoned this was the only way to be free and unencumbered with mythology. Yet now in my despair, I sought an answer from God.

Exhausted, demoralised, his lips burnt and tongue swollen with thirst, Bevis sank to his knees. He prayed for divine intervention.

I saw the faces of all those with whom I had argued and discussed religion. They seemed to scorn my present weakness, which drove me to my feet. I summoned the strength to unpack part of the tool kit and remove the engine cowling. I took out several plugs and, using my shirt dipped them into the petrol tank, I squeezed fuel directly into the motor.

Bevis knew that what he was doing was his last chance. Somehow his training kicked in and he concentrated on what he was doing, readying himself for the opportunity to fire up the Hurricane's engine, and lift the aircraft into the sky. He removed the copper wire on the throttle, intended only for emergency use, and then pressed the starter button. The engine turned, fired, but would it hold? For a few seconds the tension was unbearable. If the engine died, he was done for.

But the motor caught properly. The airscrew was spinning. I put down 30 degrees of flap, held the stick back into my lap, and opened the throttle wide. The power was surging now, and the aircraft began to roll forward. Slowly, then faster, and faster. For the first 200 yards or so it was touch and go. The Hurricane bucked, but with the tail still held down I was airborne, hanging precariously on the prop.

Soon I was gathering flying speed. I kept the hood back and climbed into the still, clean air above the sandstorm. After heading east for some forty minutes, I saw a town on the banks of the Nile. It appeared to be a military barracks and a landing strip beside it. It was Asyut, and I put down, and was taken to the Egyptian base hospital for a check-up.

Next day Bevis flew on to Kilo 8, his planned destination close to Cairo. He had faced down unimaginable hazards and predicaments – another Hurricane fighter and pilot had arrived for the Desert Air Force.[4]

Chapter 6

The nightly 'Mail Run' comes to an end

Pilot Officer Allan Simpson[1]

As the bombs dropped away down onto a target in Axis-held Benghazi, the Wellington bomber was bathed in the glare of anti-aircraft searchlights. Relieved of the bomb load the aircraft surged upward, moments before Pilot Officer Andy Anderson heeled it over into a spiralling dive to escape the flak. It was too late. An anti-aircraft shell burst through the cockpit floor blinding Anderson and his navigator Pilot Officer Allan Simpson[2] in a deafening and mind-numbing explosion.

* * *

In the second half of 1941 both the Axis forces in western Libya and the British Army to the east, coveted Libyan ports so as to maintain critical supplies. From 1 June until the end of October 1941, the RAF and the Fleet Air Arm sank more than half the 220,000 tons of Axis shipping bound for the enemy ports of Tripoli and Benghazi. While Malta-based Wellington bombers concentrated their attacks on Tripoli, Wellingtons based in Egypt mainly targeted Benghazi.

On 23 October 1941 Wellington IC T2832 of No. 108 Squadron RAF was in a night raid on the port of Benghazi.[3] Squadrons such as Nos 37, 38, 70, 108 and 148, using airfields in Egypt, attacked Benghazi in 102 operations in the second half of 1941. At times there were operations to bomb Benghazi nearly every night, prompting aircrew to name a Benghazi raid as 'The Mail Run', and compose mournful squadron songs in recognition of their likely fate. One such ditty included two typical lines to the tune of 'Clementine':[4]

> *We must do the ruddy mail run*
> *Every night until we die*[5]

The target on 23 October was an Italian convoy that had run the Royal Navy's blockade, and was reported to be in the Bay of Sirte awaiting daylight to enter the harbour. Pilot Officer Allan Simpson had only recently arrived in Egypt with another Wellington crew.

On his first operational flight, Simpson had flown a Wellington on a route over German-occupied France to Malta, an eleven-hour first leg, and then on to Egypt. Of nine Wellington aircraft which left the UK, Simpson's Wellington was one of only a fortunate three to survive the hazardous journey.

In his first operation with No. 108 Squadron against Axis targets, he was placed as navigator to the captain, Pilot Officer Anderson, for experience. Simpson had plotted a course so that they crossed the coast just south of Benghazi before the final bombing run. From the Wellington's astrodome he peered into the night to catch sight of the enemy ships. 'Away to the north we could see parachute flares being dropped over the sea as the other Wellingtons searched for the Italian ships.'[6]

One after another the Wellingtons exhausted their flares, gave up their search for the ships, then turned in to bomb the secondary target, which was a number of warehouses along the Cathedral Mole of Benghazi's docks. Simpson watched as searchlights fastened on to an approaching bomber, while the port's anti-aircraft guns launched a hail of flak against each aircraft on its bombing run.

> We began our search at about nine thousand feet. That was the effective ceiling in North Africa for our 'Peggy Wimp', a Wellington powered by Pegasus engines. We decided to search south of the harbour, which at first

Wing Commander R.J. Wells, CO of No. 108 Squadron RAF, addresses crews of Wellington bombers at RAF Fayid, Egypt 1941. (*Public domain*)

I thought was lucky. With our first flare we saw the convoy of ships. Andy executed a tight turn, but before we could get into an attacking position the flare went out.

They repeated the dropping of a flare again and again but, although the ships could be seen each time, the flare did not last long enough, and on a moonless night the convoy was then swallowed up in the blackness of the sea. Each time a flare was released Anderson took the bomber a few hundred feet lower, but Simpson was unable to sight the ships.

As the last of our flares went out, we were down to under five thousand feet with barely enough fuel remaining to get us back to our advanced landing ground, LG104 in Egypt. Andy turned us to go straight across Benghazi to attack the secondary target, Cathedral Mole. All this time I had been in the astro-dome acting as lookout. As we approached the Mole, I spotted fighters – the exhausts of two aircraft, probably Bf.110s which crossed our path, almost colliding with us.

At that moment the ground defences, searchlights and guns, took over. They had been well and truly alerted by earlier Wellingtons, and the searchlights at once zeroed in on us. Flak began to explode around us, below, above and on all sides, as we continued in towards the mole, with our bomb doors open. All the time we were being held fast in the blinding glare of converging searchlights.

An anti-aircraft shell burst through the floor of the Wellington, blinding and deafening Simpson and other crew members. The aircraft had gaping holes in its fuselage; its hydraulics were out of action, the undercarriage had dropped, flaps forced down, and the bomb doors jammed open.

After the flak shell hit the Wellington and exploded through the aircraft's fuselage between the cockpit and Simpson, he was temporarily blinded.

By the time I could see again we were out of the searchlights' cone, beyond the range of the anti-aircraft guns, and down to around four thousand feet. We still had flaps out, undercarriage down, and bomb doors open, yet by some miracle the aircraft still flew, despite huge holes in the fuselage. Shell fragments had torn out whole sections of the aircraft's geodetic airframe. I was saturated in hydraulic oil.

The hydraulic system was destroyed, preventing any operation of the flaps, undercarriage or the open bomb doors. Yet incredibly Simpson and the rest of the crew were all unscathed.

We set course to return to our advanced landing ground LG104, but because of our jammed undercarriage, flaps, open bomb doors, and damaged fuselage, we could do no more than 80 knots. At this speed and [with the] limited fuel remaining our chances of getting out of enemy airspace, let alone reaching our own airfield, were slim. With our engines labouring against the extra drag, we lost height gradually. Eventually, south of Sollum, we were down to about two thousand feet, as we crossed over into unoccupied territory between Axis forces and our lines.

Simpson and the others began to hope the fuel would get them back. It was not to be. Suddenly at under a thousand feet the fuel ran out. The engines were suddenly silent, and the Wellington pitched into a steep death dive.

Andy gives the order to bale out. Never have I moved so fast. I clip on my parachute and dive aft to the mid-under hatch, with our bomb aimer close behind. We open the hatch, sit on the edge, he forward and myself aft, with our feet dangling in the slipstream. It is not a time for politeness, but we each shout, 'After you!' We are very low, too low to delay, and he somersaults out and I follow.

Simpson had no idea how close they were to an impact with the ground. Only a few seconds remained before the desert would swallow up both aircraft and airmen.

As I tumble out I pull the rip-cord. There is a heart-stopping pause then with a violent jerk the parachute opens, and the dark shadow of the aircraft disappears above me. Within a few seconds – thump! I have hit the ground, jarring, and maybe breaking every bone in my body.

Five of the crew, the two air-gunners, the wireless operator, the bomb aimer and Simpson, landed within yards of each other, in a rough, rocky boulder-strewn patch of desert. Despite baling out at near zero height and landing in such dangerous terrain, there were, miraculously, no broken bones.

We were a battered, bruised lot, and did not know whether our two pilots had been able to abandon the aircraft. We rolled up our parachutes and harnesses, anchored them with rocks, and set off walking north towards the Mediterranean coast. We each had a primitive survival kit, which comprised a bottle of water and a revolver! We were I believed fifteen miles or so south of the coast road, about halfway between Sollum and Mersa Matruh.

I thought we were east of German and Italian forces, and with luck there may be British vehicles on the coast road. We trudged through the remainder of the night, keeping the North Star ahead, stumbling in the darkness up and down rough, rock-strewn slopes.

Shortly after dawn they reached the coast road. They turned east and at the same time began looking for somewhere to shelter from the heat of the day. Thirst, hunger and tiredness were taking their toll. And they also needed shelter from the enemy for, as the sun rose, they would become on this road, easy prey for Axis patrols of troops or fighter aircraft.

> The road was deserted, and this seemed to confirm our belief that we were in a no man's land. We trudged on, reluctant to halt. Eventually when we did hear a vehicle approaching, we took cover among the rocks along the roadside.

No doubt on account of their tiring trek through the night, around fifteen to twenty miles over rugged terrain, the five men were not quick enough in seeking cover. They had been seen.

> A staff car stopped at some distance from us. Four occupants got out of the car, and aimed rifles at our positions. We could see that all four were wearing side-arms, then we saw that our luck was in once again. The four men were wearing British battle-dress! We stepped out, hands in the air, and shouted out that we were RAF aircrew.

The four men were South African war correspondents on an unofficial, and unauthorised reconnoitre ahead of forward British positions. They were nervous and trigger-happy.

> They probably shouldn't have been armed, and they certainly shouldn't have been driving along that road in no-man's land. However most of all, they were very, very welcome!

It was a chance encounter. Otherwise Simpson and his fellow crew faced dehydration in the desert heat, increasing hunger and fatigue, and the likelihood of being killed or captured by enemy forces. The South Africans crammed the five of them into the one car, turned it around and drove them back down the road east to their airfield LG104 some twenty miles away and closer to Alexandria. 'We were lucky again. One of our Wellingtons had been delayed at LG104, and soon we were on our way back to our main airfield at Fayid.'

In the Fayid mess that evening the CO said to Simpson, 'Nice trip last night? Don't expect them all to be so easy. I'll see you at briefing in the morning. You will be flying with me tomorrow night.'

> So on 25 October there I was stiff and sore, spreadeagled over the bombsight in the nose of a Wellington bomber, watching tracer come up

from Benghazi. I pressed the toggle to drop a stick of bombs along the Cathedral Mole.

Simpson later learned that the pilot Anderson and his co-pilot had not had enough time to bale out. Quite unbelievably, however, Anderson crash-landed the Wellington in the dark, into possibly the only stretch of desert in that area which was not strewn with boulders. The two pilots were found alive and well a day or so later. It meant that the whole crew of their Wellington had survived. To cap it all, some months after, Anderson took an RAF recovery team to the downed aircraft, repaired and serviced the bomber, cleared a rough landing strip and flew it out.

Part III

1942

Chapter 7

The Audacious Augsburg Raid

Wing Commander John Dering Nettleton VC

By April 1942 the new Avro Lancaster bomber was beginning to be delivered in ones and twos to various Bomber Command squadrons. Its performance was being viewed with glowing appreciation. Yet only a few Lancasters had flown on active bombing operations, within squadrons of other aircraft types, and there was a desire to test out its capabilities in full.

On 17 April 1942 twelve Lancaster Mk I bombers, six each from Nos 97 and 44 Squadrons RAF, were ready to leave on an audacious daylight operation to bomb a German manufacturing plant, Maschinenfabrik Augsburg-Nürnberg (MAN), the U-boat diesel engine factory at Augsburg. During 1941 and 1942 the U-boats of the *Kriegsmarine* (German Navy) were enjoying great success in sinking Allied ships and exacting heavy losses on merchant ships of both the UK and the USA.

In February 1942 the situation had worsened considerably. The Kriegsmarine modified their Enigma code, and Britain's codebreakers at Bletchley Park were unable to decipher the code change for a number of months. In 1942 some 1,100 Allied merchant ships would be sunk, reaching a peak of 173 in June. To bomb the factories in Germany which were building the U-boats and their engines, was one of a range of actions pursued to curtail the shipping losses.[1]

By the end of March 1942 for a bombing raid on the U-boat engine factory at Augsburg, Bomber Command planned for the outward flight and approach to the target to be at low level. For a week before the operation, bomber crews of Nos 97 and 44 Squadrons trained in low-level flying to make a round trip of an estimated 1,250 miles. Not only would the Lancasters be flying to the limit of their estimated range, at treetop height in daylight, they would also be expected to defend themselves without any fighter escorts.[2]

The six bombers of No. 44 Squadron, led by twenty-four year-old Squadron Leader John Nettleton in Lancaster R5508B, were fuelled to capacity and were the first to take off at 15.12 hours from RAF Waddington in Lincolnshire.[3] Nettleton led the six bombers south, passing over Selsey Bill before crossing the English Channel at only fifty feet above the waves to avoid German radar.

Squadron Leader John Nettleton VC (seated second from left) and his crew, after the ill-fated raid on 17 April by No. 44 Squadron RAF to Augsburg. Nettleton's Lancaster was the sole aircraft to return. (*Public domain*)

John Nettleton was born on 28 June 1917 at Nongoma, Natal in South Africa. His family had a naval tradition, that included his grandfather Admiral A.T.D. Nettleton of the Royal Navy, that led to Nettleton spending some time in his teens as a cadet and junior officer in a South African merchant shipping line. Following that he became an apprentice civil engineer with Cape Town City Council.

In 1938, while making a visit to Britain with his mother, he decided to join the RAF. After completion of elementary pilot training at RFTS Reading, in December 1938 he was accepted on a short service commission. In July 1939 Nettleton graduated as a pilot, and then saw service with Nos 207, 98 and 185 Squadrons flying Hampden bombers, before he joined No. 44 Squadron at Waddington, where in July 1941 he was promoted to squadron leader. In December 1941 he was Mentioned in Despatches for his leadership of bombing operations over Europe. By April 1942 he was a very experienced bomber pilot and squadron leader, and nearing completion of his tour of thirty operations.[4]

No. 44 Squadron had an illustrious RAF history. First formed in 1917 as part of the London Air Defence Area, it was disbanded in 1919 before being reformed in 1937 as a bomber squadron. In 1941 it was renamed No. 44 (Rhodesia) Squadron in honour and recognition of the African colony's contribution to the war effort, and of a high proportion of Rhodesian ground and air crew. The squadron badge is based upon the seal of a Matabele chief in Rhodesia (now Zimbabwe). It would become one of the very few squadrons to operate continuously throughout the war.

When the six Lancasters of No. 44 Squadron were well past the French coast on 17 April 1942, still flying at around fifty feet, they were unluckily sighted. Nettleton was the first to see two or three German fighters.

> They were about 1,000 feet above us, and the next thing I knew they were all around us. The first casualty I saw was Sergeant Rhodes' aircraft. Smoke poured from his cockpit, and his port wing caught fire. He came straight at me out of control, and I thought we were going to collide. We missed by a matter of feet, and he crashed beneath me. Two others went down almost at once, and I saw a fourth Lancaster on fire. During the fighter attack the rear guns on our aircraft seized up after firing some 800 rounds.[5]

Nettleton and Flying Officer Garwill, pilot of the remaining Lancaster (R 5510 A), were undeterred, and continued on their course. Both aircraft, however, had also suffered numerous hits from the fighters' gunfire and the odds were against them surviving any further attacks. Then, without warning, the German fighters broke away, possibly because of low ammunition or fuel. Nettleton's Lancaster was riddled with holes, and particularly vulnerable without its rear guns, yet despite this he and Garwill flew on.

The two pilots mostly kept to fifty feet above the ground across northern France, then along the Swiss border until reaching Lake Constance. There they turned north-east towards Munich before, on sighting the Ammersee, they headed due north for Augsburg. On their approach to the target, still at about only fifty feet, the two Lancasters encountered intense anti-aircraft fire. Nettleton led the two aircraft in a bombing run low over the town's rooftops.[6]

> The light flak was terrific. At 19.55 hours we dropped four 1,000lb bombs on the target. Both the rear gunner and myself saw them burst. Flying Officer Garwill's aircraft was hit and caught fire. He made what appeared to be a successful forced landing, and I thought the crew would most probably have been safe.[7]

In a Lancaster riddled with holes, Nettleton climbed for height and set course for their return to Waddington; it was impossible for him to make the return

Lancaster Mk 1 bombers of No. 44 Squadron RAF, 1942. (*Public domain*)

flight at low level in the dark. Nettleton's damaged aircraft with no rear guns was on its own, and would be easy prey if found by Luftwaffe night-fighters. Radio silence was imperative, the crew could only hope that German radar did not detect them. The solitary Lancaster pressed on westward, hopefully cloaked by the night.

When Nettleton and his navigator estimated that they had finally crossed the North Sea, and radioed their base at Waddington to request navigation assistance, they found that they had overshot and were still heading west over the Irish sea. Nettleton turned the Lancaster around and landed close to 01.00 hours on 18 April at Squires Gate airfield near Blackpool in north-west Lancashire. After some ten hours in the air, Nettleton's Lancaster was the sole surviving aircraft of the six which had set out from No. 44 Squadron. Eleven days later the award of the Victoria Cross to Nettleton was announced in the *London Gazette*.[8]

Of the second wave of six bombers from No. 97 Squadron, two were shot down. Squadron Leader Sherwood's Lancaster was hit by flak and set on fire. Despite this, he continued to lead the six aircraft in their bombing run until the fire caused a wing to fall off. The bomber fell straight down, and on impact with the ground burst into a massive explosion.[9] Miraculously, Sherwood was catapulted still strapped in his pilot's seat out of the inferno and was the only survivor. Sherwood, although nominated for the Victoria Cross, was awarded the DSO.

Overall the raid by the twelve Lancasters of Nos 44 and 97 Squadrons inflicted serious damage to the MAN factory buildings, but little to the manufacturing machinery and capability. Production of the U-boat diesel engines was hardly affected. Too a high price was paid. Bomber Command lost seven of its twelve new Lancaster bombers, and forty-nine experienced aircrew. It was later learned that, of seventeen bombs that hit the factory, only five exploded. The lesson learned was that daylight bombing raids on Germany would result in too great a loss of aircraft and airmen to be justified.[10] From then on, Bomber Command would concentrate the bulk of its operations on night raids against Germany and occupied Europe.

*   *   *

On 24 April 1942 the *London Gazette* announced the award of the Victoria Cross to Squadron Leader Nettleton. The citation concluded: 'Squadron Leader Nettleton, who has successfully undertaken many other hazardous operations, displayed unflinching determination as well as leadership and valour of the highest order'.[11]

In July 1942 he married Section Officer Betty Havelock, WAAF, in Lincoln and, after a spell of other duties, was promoted in January 1943 to wing commander, returning to command No. 44 Squadron at Waddington. On the night of 12/13 July 1943 he led fourteen Lancasters in a raid on Turin. His Lancaster did not return and was listed as 'Missing'. Nettleton's aircraft, his body and those of his crew have never been found.

John Nettleton and his wife Betty had been married for just a year. His presumed death was not announced until 23 February 1944, when on the very same day, in a tragic coincidence, the birth of his son a few days earlier was announced – the son he never saw.[12]

Chapter 8

Falling into the jungles of New Guinea ...
death seems certain, quick or slow

Lieutenant Colonel Harvey E. 'Gene' Rehrer[1]

In June 1942 Lieutenant Gene Rehrer of the 39th Pursuit Squadron of the USAAF took off from the squadron's airfield near Port Moresby in New Guinea. In a scramble to meet fighters of the battle-hardened Imperial Japanese Air Force and, in his first combat encounter, the probability was high that his inexperience might prove fatal. As if pre-ordained, an enemy fighter attacked Rehrer, sending his P.39 Airacobra fighter into an inverted spin. His aircraft pitched into a death dive towards the blanket of the thick New Guinea jungle.

*   *   *

On 7 December 1941 the Japanese had attacked Pearl Harbor, which changed everything. The USA's reactions to the Pearl Harbor disaster were widespread and rapid. The US Army Signals Corps, in some respects a forerunner of the US Army Air Forces, immediately changed its plans so as to fight a war in the Pacific against Japan. Newly-trained pilots including Lieutenant H.E. 'Gene' Rehrer were sent by train to a hastily arranged and temporary staging post at Hamilton Field, San Francisco, arriving there on 19 December.

Gene Rehrer was born on 26 December 1916 at Reading, Pennsylvania, where he attended high school. Later he worked as a milkman, and a car mechanic, before enrolling as a student at Wyomissing Polytechnic Institute. Sensing that war was looming he enlisted in September 1939 in the Army Signal Corps, and trained at a new air base in Puerto Rico, gaining his pilot's wings in November 1941.

At San Francisco on 11 January 1942 Lieutenant Rehrer with other pilots embarked aboard a converted luxury liner, the SS *President Coolidge* which, on the next day, was part of the first large convoy to sail for Australia after

Pearl Harbor, carrying troops, supplies, ammunition and weapons, as well as fighter aircraft.

After a voyage across the Pacific the SS *President Coolidge* docked on 2 February 1942 at Melbourne, Australia. From there the contingent moved to Sydney's Bankstown airfield, then to an airfield at Mount Gambier in South Australia where Rehrer was assigned to the 39th Pursuit Squadron flying Bell P-39 Airacobra fighters. After further relocations the squadron moved in late May 1942 to Woodstock, close to Townsville in far north Queensland, where the squadron lost its first pilot in a training flight accident.

Lieutenant Colonel 'Gene' Rehrer, 39th Pursuit Squadron, USAAF. (*Private collection, Larry Rehrer*)

During May and June pilots transferred progressively from Woodstock to Port Moresby in New Guinea to confront Japanese air raids. Rehrer met a local Australian girl, Norma Cox, in Townsville, with whom he quickly struck up a relationship and became engaged. This meant that he relished being one of the last pilots to be given orders to leave Woodstock. In early June he arrived at the Lalokie airstrip about sixteen miles outside Port Moresby, one of two airstrips assigned to 39th Pursuit Squadron.

The second airstrip, which was known as 'Twelve Mile', was situated on the other side of the Lalokie river, across which the only means of transport was by barge. In the squadron's camp on the side of a hill near the Lalokie airstrip, Rehrer could see the dust rise from the planes taking off on the Twelve Mile strip. Despite the remote location, Rehrer thought the camp's facilities to be fairly comfortable.

> While we were there for a grim job, the food was good, and we had some good times. About three weeks after my arrival our flight was called out to intercept some enemy fighters, that were approaching our general vicinity.[2]

When Rehrer took off in P-39 Airacobra 41-7204, it was to be his first experience of combat flying in an encounter with the experienced and ruthless Japanese Naval Air Force (JNAF). Statistically his chances of survival were not high. 'Lieutenant F.L. Faurot and I took off from Lalokie to take up number three and four positions in the first flight of four aircraft.'

Unbeknown to Faurot and Rehrer, however, some confused communications between the two airstrips meant that two fighters from the Twelve Mile strip had already taken off, and slotted into the three and four positions of a four-aircraft flight formation.

This of course left us searching for a position in a six aircraft formation. We were at about 21,000 feet when the gas pressure dropped on my aircraft, since I was still using my belly tank. The engine coughed and almost died before I was able to switch to a wing tank. All this caused me to be left far in the rear of what was already a poor formation.

Once I had everything righted again and all instruments checked, I again looked around for enemy planes. In that instant tracer bullets were flying past me on both sides of the cockpit. Within split seconds these bullets penetrated the aircraft's belly tank, causing it to begin to burn vigorously.

Rehrer tried to jettison his 300-gallon extra fuel tank. It was stuck, probably already damaged. Next, he tried the doors. They wouldn't budge. By this time the plane was in an inverted spin, the death spin. Rehrer thought he was going to die, so he wrenched off his seat harness. Thrown up into the roof of the plane by centrifugal force, he inched painfully toward one of the doors to try and force it open. He knew that he only had seconds before impact with the ground, or before the fire enveloped him first.

Next thing I am falling through space with my parachute still in the pack on my back. I am feeling so terribly light and wondering if I really do have a chute on. While taking real large summersaults, I pull the rip-cord, which very suddenly lessens the speed of my descent. The jerk causes me to lose one flying boot and a glove, and a terrible pain shoots through my right shoulder.

Luckily the side door on the Airacobra must have burst open and the slipstream had dragged Rehrer out. Until his parachute opened he had fallen around 8,000 feet. That left him somewhere in the vicinity of 13,000 feet and still between two layers of clouds. The cloud layers, and the fact that he dropped a good distance before opening his parachute, probably explain why he was not strafed by Japanese fighters.

I was unable to steer the chute for I could scarcely use my right arm. The descent seemed very long but pleasant. The phase 'hanging in space' surely describes a wonderful sensation. It was no time before I was drifting through the lower layer of clouds. The layer seemed exceptionally thick but finally it became thin and I again saw earth below.

Oddly enough I saw my plane burning almost directly below me. In fact, I was rather worried with the thought of being directly above, especially so since I couldn't choose my landing spot. The last three hundred feet seemed rather fast, and very shortly, I found myself on the slope of a little hill. My chute hung entangled in the trees overhead. By looking down this slope, which was really one side of a ravine, I could see a tiny trickle of a stream.

Rehrer was fortunate that his parachute had not been hooked by higher branches which could have left him hanging helpless in mid-air. Since his plane was nearby, and burning rapidly, with its ammunition exploding, he lay quiet until all the cartridges were spent.

> The very first thing I did was to slip out of the chute and gain access to the kit contained in my backpack. Having done so, I made a crude shoe for my left foot out of my canteen cover. Then with great difficulty (for my shoulder hurt badly) I climbed to the top of the hill on which I had landed. This did not give me any advantage at all, so I climbed back to my chute and arranged my worldly belongings as best I could, and took all I could carry with me. I bathed my face in the cool water of the stream I had seen earlier.

Refreshed by the water, Rehrer trudged along by the stream and then beside a river that it had joined. Further on he saw a clearing in the jungle on the river's other bank, which offered easier terrain.

> I started to wade across and lost my footing and truthfully nearly drowned for, as well as the strong current, I was loaded heavily and hampered by my injured shoulder. Having 'just made' the opposite shore, I lay there for some time breathless. Foolish though it seemed, I had to get to this clearing because it wasn't too far from the scene of the crashed airplane, so, if a search party was sent out from Lalokie, I could better signal them. For this reason I stayed at this spot the remainder of the day after having first spread my chute out on the rocks so that it appeared as a white dot from the air.
>
> I then tried to become comfortable so as to get a rest. Night came and I wrapped the now dry parachute about me and put my mosquito head net on, and stretched out on some leaves I had gathered. That night I was real warm but couldn't sleep for my shoulder pain prevented it. As soon as daylight came, and it was a terrible long time in coming, I got my pack together again and set out along the west bank of the river.
>
> Spiders, fish and birds were the only life I saw this day, but the day before I had seen a pretty red snake in the stream. I do not believe that I travelled more than six or eight miles this next day, a Wednesday, but

the route I took zig-zagging and up and down must have been twice that. This same afternoon I decided to cross the river again to gain access to a spot that I had seen as suitable for the night. It was slightly better than the last one, but I did narrowly escape drowning once again.

Inadvertently Rehrer found himself on an island once more. During the day he had discarded unnecessary items such as various flying accessories to lighten his load, so that he now carried only essentials with him.

The night was spent as before, restless and with a few scares, and again it seemed as though daylight would never again bless the land. The following morning, Thursday, since I was on an island I had to get wet from the start of the day. I resolved to try a new idea to possibly hasten my journey back to my home base. The river seemed to flow for the most part to the south-west and I definitely wanted to travel south-east, so I decided to follow the compass instead of the river.

The new direction took Rehrer far away from the river and climbing into mountainous terrain.

I remember seeing many trails made by wild pigs. I thought they could be wild boar trails and so I drew my already cocked gun several times when I heard a rustle in the nearby bushes. The trails made it somewhat easier to climb the mountainside and so I stayed on them as much as possible while trying to maintain my general direction. Finally, about noon, I reached what looked like the crest of the mountain and began to search for a ravine on the opposite side, thinking that this would lead me to another creek, then a river flowing south east.

I found a ravine and began to descend over rough ground. Within a few minutes I stumbled directly into a yellow-jacket hornet nest. The hornets swarmed over me and I had no other choice but to get going and the easiest direction was down the hill. I fell many times, always it seemed on my right injured shoulder, and finally was tripped by a vine, which entangled my left leg. The little devils were greatly thinned out by this time and I was able to brush the remaining ones off with the scarf I had made out of my parachute. These hornets had stung me on the forehead and hands so much that all my exposed skin except my chin, which was covered with a good beard, became extremely hot and painful from the stings.

After a short rest I took an inventory of myself and found my entire web belt was missing. On it was my gun, first aid kit and the coveted rip-cord from my chute. All of these were very important, so I decided to retrace my steps a short way back in an effort to regain my possessions.

My search was in vain and I turned around to again begin my journey in a seaward direction, feeling at quite a loss, especially without my gun.

Nevertheless, as he had hoped to do, Rehrer came upon a trickle of a stream which he followed so as to find eventually another river to lead him to the sea.

The sun was fast falling, and I began to feel terrible at the prospect of spending the night without a gun. Fortunately enough for me, I again stumbled upon a river just as I was about to give up for the day. I believe it was the same river that I left that morning. I tied a good sized rock in my scarf and was going to use this as a weapon if any animal should set itself upon me.

Ever since I had waded the stream earlier, my clothes had remained saturated, which made it seem the longest night ever. I am sure that I could not count the number of large bats that flew over. The night sky was just covered with them. When the daylight did finally come, I set out once more following the river's flow, and kept as close to its shore as the terrain and thick foliage would permit.

It was now four or five days since Rehrer had taken off and been shot down; he was losing count of the exact number. Every day, every minute of each day, the odds were lengthening against his survival. He needed to reach help before his dwindling strength gave out.

Upon taking stock of my situation I decided to make a raft from dead wood to float downstream. With parachute shroud lines that I had been saving, and eight or ten fallen tree logs, the size of which I could drag with the aid of my left arm and left hip, I made up my raft. It took about four hours to build, and finally I gave it a try.

Rehrer hauled his makeshift raft to the river's edge, pushed it in until it floated and clambered on board.

Hanging on to the raft was perilous because of the rough waters in stretches of the river. In other places the river would spread out until there was scarcely enough depth for my raft, even when I got off it. There were also wide and deep places, near stagnant pools, where I scarcely moved at all.

He was conscious that his condition was deteriorating and instinctively knew that he was running out of time. As he drifted along, he saw a crocodile but luckily it ignored him. Time passed along with the current and, somewhere in the back of his mind, Rehrer recognised something about his state of mind and health, and something about malaria symptoms.

Sometime during the afternoon I drew the raft up onto a sandy and rock covered shore, and slept about an hour for I was badly in need of sleep. The sun baked me and dried me and gave me new life. However, I had to get on and so I floated on the raft downstream until I could scarcely see for the darkness, and pulled up and tried to sleep on the raft. I was wet and cold and could of course not sleep nor even rest.

Just as soon as it was light enough to navigate, I got going on the raft again. I think I must have drifted about five miles this day before a very bad happening occurred. The water was treacherous in places and the further I went the worse it became. At one particular rough spot a great tree spread out into the current a good way.

It was unavoidable and blocking his course. He readied himself and, as the current sucked the raft out from under him, he grabbed onto the tree for dear life. He made his way to the shore and slumped to the ground, beaten and demoralised, trying to catch his breath, and prayed that his head would stop spinning.

I had lost my raft. It was wedged under the surface of this giant tree and no power of mine could dislodge it. The few supplies I did have were tied upon the raft, and I could not for the life of me get them loose. Really I do not think I tried very hard for I was exhausted, and getting to that stage of my journey and my physical deterioration, that I didn't care anymore.

After getting ashore again, Rehrer found himself in a flatter area and struggled as best he could through wild sugar cane, some of which extended to a height of twenty feet. In desperation, every so often he would utter a cry in despair. He was now into a fifth day at least without food and fresh water. He made the decision to break his silence and call for help. Now he really didn't care who heard, enemy or not. He called again and again, growing weaker and weaker, hoping to hear an answer.

While I was staggering my way along the west side of the river, after I had given a series of increasingly despairing shouts, I imagined I heard an answer. I was in a frenzy at the possibility that there was someone nearby, friendly or otherwise. I shouted again and again, and each time unbelievably, it was answered. The reply grew closer and very shortly I saw a native boy hail me from the opposite shore. He and several adults immediately jumped into their boat and paddled across to me.

They could speak a little English and lost no time in getting me into their boat and across to their village on the other side of the river. The men assisted me up the hill to their village, and by the time I arrived there they had two boxes arranged in chair and table fashion with a steaming hot cup of tea on the larger box for me. Nothing else at this time could have been any better. I thoroughly enjoyed it. Once I had got them to understand that I was an American flyer, just about the whole village turned out to see me. My first request was for a banana, for I thought that is what would be convenient and I was very hungry.

Everyone wanted to shake his hand. The men folk gathered around close and swamped him with questions, while the women and girls stood back and gazed at this strange specimen. Rehrer was taken to a hut and hosted by the Headman, or chief, who had been taught by missionaries to speak English. They tried to feed him but his throat was so swollen he couldn't get anything down.

No sooner had I sat down than everybody in the village began to bring some food of some kind for me. Yet I was so hungry that I couldn't eat – only the tea tasted good, and I had two large cups. They produced clean and dry clothes for me which they insisted I wear, especially since my clothes were in tatters, torn and wet. I was glad to do this and felt fine when it was completed. They then got a basin of hot water with an antiseptic in it and bathed my sore and now blistered feet. This operation included my scratched and bitten legs and knees and truly rendered no end of comfort.

After my legs and feet were bathed they brought out a clean woven mat, a clean sheet and a clean mosquito net and prepared to make me comfortable for the night. I emphasise how clean everything was because one would hardly expect this in an out of the way village. The phones were out of order or they could have notified my squadron just as soon as I arrived.

While the villagers were caring for Rehrer, they threw question after question at him, and one of them seemed to have very good English. Rehrer did not know at the time, but he had fortunately been taken in by the people of Brown River village, who had been recruited by his squadron as part of an air raid early warning system.

As soon as it became dark an oil lamp was supplied for me in case I did not want to sleep. I was very anxious to do so and turned in promptly. My shoulder hurt quite a bit so I did not have a real good night. In the morning water was brought for me to wash and shave, and breakfast soon followed.

Very soon I was taken down to the river where we once again got into the boat that first picked me up. After crossing the river again, I was placed on a donkey and a young native took the reins and we set off through the jungle with five other natives, two of whom were searching for a break in the telephone line which connected their village and Port Moresby.

Two other donkeys were used; one was really just a colt. The journey was not too bad for the path was rather well defined, and the leading native slashed back jungle growth and overhanging trees that would have brushed me. He also cleared spider webs and as a whole the trip was not a bad one, but each time the donkey stepped up or down a terrible jar went through my body to my right shoulder.

About 3:30pm that Sunday Rehrer and his guides came to a European settlement.

A lad from the settlement took me in a GI truck to the airfield from which I had originally taken off. Here I walked up to our operations tent and was heartily, and I mean heartily, greeted by the officers of our squadron and flight who were on duty that day. They were certainly glad to see me, for they had given me up for lost. The feeling one gets to walk in upon friends like that is quite emotional. Soon after this welcome, I returned to our camp area and went through the whole unexpected arrival thing again.

Rehrer had indeed come back from the dead. He had been extremely fortunate not only to have been thrown involuntarily from a fighter aircraft descending in an accelerating death spin, but also to have been able to pull his ripcord to open his parachute, and make a safe landing in the hilly ravines of the New Guinea jungle. Blessed with a spirit to never give in, after five days wandering on foot and by raft without food, clean water or shelter, he was lucky to encounter friendly villagers, when he was close to exhaustion. Another day, perhaps two at the most without help, and he would have died. In seven days he had lost forty pounds in weight.

It had been the policy at 39th Pursuit Squadron to leave a person's equipment alone for several days if they disappeared on an operation, so Rehrer's personal possessions were just exactly as he had left them.

The squadron commander gave me permission to return to Townsville for a few days and obtain an x-ray of my shoulder. When I arrived in Townsville I was very anxious to see Miss Norma Cox. First of all I had to get a haircut and then walked into the shop at which Norma worked. She was very surprised to see me and I of course was very glad to see her.

Since I had already gone seven days with my shoulder in the condition it was, I felt that another day could not possibly hurt, especially since the Doctor diagnosed it as only a pulled arm muscle. So that night I went home to Norma's place. All her family were quite surprised and glad to see me. The following day I turned up for admission at the hospital.

*   *   *

On Rehrer's return to the Lalokie airstrip and base camp, the Brown River natives were rewarded with whatever they asked for, which included Epsom salts, tobacco and flour. The entire camp gave up their cigarette rations for his rescuers. Everything the natives asked for, and more, was loaded onto three donkeys. As they left, the Brown River Headman went to Rehrer, hugged him, and handed him a small orange.

> This orange got into my pocket and was really the only thing in my possession, when I got back to Townsville. My girlfriend's mother, Mrs Daisy Cox, treasured this orange, which she put in a small jar with a lid. Even more strange, that jar went with me to every military change of station, back to the Philippines, Japan, all over the USA, to Alaska and, to this day, is still in the original jar. This jar, with the now almost powdery orange inside, is always a conversation piece for Norma and I with visitors, as it sits on a bookshelf in our family room.[3]

Lieutenant Colonel H.E. 'Gene' Rehrer passed away peacefully surrounded by his family and friends on 28 October 2010 in Sacramento.[4]

Chapter 9

Wounded badly in both legs, drowning in the North Sea – or swim for your life!

Flight Lieutenant Eric Maher[1]

On the night of 8/9 June 1942 on a homeward return flight following a raid on Essen, the Wellington of wireless operator Eric Maher is crossing the Dutch coast south of Rotterdam, when it is attacked by an enemy night fighter. A cannon shell explodes at Maher's feet where he stands in the aircraft's astro-hatch, and hits the main spar of the aircraft. Red hot splinters shower him and he falls on the floor, near unconscious. The bomber's navigator assists him to get to the escape hatch. Critically injured in both legs, Maher drops into the North Sea. His parachute wraps around his head, dragging him deeper and deeper under the water – yet swimming to the Dutch coast is the only option!

*   *   *

A taut strand of red cotton on a map display, like a thin vein of blood, traced the course to be flown to the night's target, Essen. In the early afternoon of 8 June 1942 Flight Lieutenant Eric Maher,[2] a wireless operator, sat in the briefing room of No. 460 Squadron RAF. It was a room full of bomber aircrew at RAF Breighton, East Yorkshire. To Maher the red cotton thread led yet again to the 'terror target' of Germany's Ruhr industrial area, known as 'Happy Valley'. What Maher learned in the briefing seemed to him to be worse news, and it left him with sense of foreboding.

In the absence of our normal skipper who had just been commissioned, our crew was taken over by Sergeant Doug Hurditch. We were told our own aircraft, a Wellington bomber was unserviceable, and we were instructed to flight-test a new Wellington aircraft, No. E.1412. After completion of the flight test, Sergeant Hurditch was satisfied with the new aircraft, and gained permission from the squadron leader to fly the new aircraft in the raid on Essen. This permission was much to my displeasure because it meant a lot of hard work, rush, and hurry, getting the W/T equipment into shape, and placing the large number of odds and ends into their places in the new aircraft. [3]

Flight Lieutenant Eric Maher, 1942. (*Private collection, Kate Schafer*)

It was during this time between 16.00 to 19.00 hours that Maher learned that their new Wellington had been intended as a replacement for another aircraft, which had been put out of action a few nights previously, and which had been captained by their new pilot, Sergeant Hurditch. Maher had something of a premonition: that things on the night's operation were not going to turn out for the best.

The usual feeling of fear before an operational flight has itself to be experienced to be understood. This was something more, and I believe was made more pronounced by the general hustle in getting everything settled for the late take-off before midnight. It was a feeling the like of which I do not want to experience again, and it regularly haunts me when I turn my memory to the events of this night.

Shortly before take-off Maher paced up and down besides the new Wellington, willing himself to get on board. It was to be his thirty-fifth operation, his last mission, after which he was due a break. Eric Francis 'Bluey' Maher was twenty-two, a stocky five feet eight inches in height, fit and strong, with red curly hair, a fair complexion and blue eyes. From Sandgate in south-east Queensland, Australia, Maher enrolled in the RAAF and trained in Banff, Canada, before shipping across to Britain to join the RAF. He had an engaging personality, but perhaps his most valuable trait was an energetic positive approach to life.

Wellington E1412 duly took off as scheduled at 23.14 hours.[4] The aircraft was so new it had no squadron letters painted on its fuselage. On the route across Holland to Germany the flight went as planned, despite Maher's premonition.

The outward flight was normal, the equipment was functioning satisfactorily, and to all appearances it looked like being just another trip. As we began to approach the target area, a few light bursts of anti-aircraft fire, and a few waving searchlights, seemed harmless. However, as the first few aircraft of the force began to bomb the target area ahead, we could see the highly concentrated searchlights and flak of Essen.

At the same time our starboard motor began losing revs and backfiring. This spell quickly passed, however, and everything was once more in good order as we made our bombing run. Receiving more than our fair share of attention by the ground defences, we released our bombs, dodged and weaved through the flak, took a photograph, and headed away from the target.

The return course home had been planned so as to take the bombers south beyond the Ruhr area, on a route between Dussseldorf and Cologne, then west over France, before crossing the coast between Dunkirk and Ostend. It was longer, although expected to be safer. However, Hurditch was worried whether the misfiring engine would last. Maher agreed with him and the rest of the crew, that the longer return route was now too risky. 'We decided to turn back because of the shaky motor, and head out on the same track as we used coming in.'

Apart from occasional splutters from the engine, as they approached the Dutch coast at around 8,000 feet the return flight was proving to be quiet and peaceful. Maher was standing in the astro-hatch searching the sky for enemy fighters. Then, just south of Rotterdam, his pre-flight premonition was fulfilled.

I had just taken the speaking-tube plug from the intercom system, in order to return to the wireless position, when an unidentified enemy aircraft fired its first burst at us from the starboard bow. I heard a sort of muffled rattle of machine guns, and saw long streaks of red tracer cutting the aircraft longitudinally just to the right of where I was standing.

In the next instant a cannon shell explodes at my feet, when it hits the main spar of the aircraft. Red-hot splinters of shrapnel shower all over me. I feel dazed and giddy from the blast.

Shrapnel from the exploding flak hit Maher in the legs, upper body and his head, before he fell to the floor unconscious.

My next recorded memory is of hearing a second rattle of machine guns, probably from a second enemy fighter, and I feel the lurch of our aircraft as Sergeant Hurditch attempts to take evasive action. At this moment I am shaken by the navigator, who with some difficulty helps me to my seat at the wireless table. Blood flows from the top of my head, and I throw off my flying helmet. I am thinking, 'How much of my head is missing?'

Discarding his helmet isolated Maher from the intercom system. When a German night-fighter made a third attack, the Wellington's starboard engine was hit and burst into flames, of which a semi-conscious Maher was unaware.

My first knowledge of the skipper's orders to bale out came when the navigator pointed to the escape hatch, handed me my parachute, and helped me to reach the opening to make the jump. I was overcome by temporary blackouts lasting a few seconds at a time. However, I was fully alert when the night-fighter made its fourth attack, which shattered most of the pilot's instruments, but miraculously missed Hurditch himself.

After receiving strict instructions, repeated three times by the navigator – 'Be sure and pull the silver handle', I dropped through the hatch. The swirling slipstream picked me up like a feather, and I tossed and lashed through space, legs apart, arms flailing, rolling and tumbling. I felt I was almost suffocating from the rush of wind in my nostrils and down my throat, until I pulled that handle.

A mighty jerk shook the living daylights out of me, totally sweeping away any tendency towards unconsciousness. My chute flowed open and I swung pendulum fashion to and fro in the darkness. I little realised where I was or how I got there, and was caring less, until my waving feet crashed against the surface of something or other, and I doubled up to meet the impact. But it was not to be. I was still sinking, and then my chute crumbled down all over my head. 'Water! I am in the sea!'

Madly struggling like a crazy man with his jumbled thoughts, and despite wounds to his legs, Maher kicked off his flying boots and endeavoured to undo his parachute harness. The wind, however, decreed otherwise.

A breeze filled my chute and off I went being dragged by the neck like a baby kitten being rescued by its mother, with my legs just breaking the surface of the water. My right leg sent agonising shooting pains right up to my brain, every time it thudded against a wave or swell. Still struggling, I turned the knob on my parachute harness, and the shoulder straps flew off, but the leg straps caught and would not release.

Then upside down he went, his head hitting the water first, then his feet, then his head again.

I swear to myself, 'Let go, you ....!' Mercifully the strap slips, gives way, and the parachute, still filled with air, careers away as I drop down gently into the water. In a flash I urge myself, 'Quickly, get your clothes off!' if I am not to drown. I struggle free of my Mae West jacket, and my flying suit. My legs are stinging, and my mind full with racing, maddening thoughts.

'You fool, you …. fool, you've thrown away your Mae West!' It would have kept me afloat for nine hours. Too late now though. 'Swim! Swim!' fills my mind. But where to? Which way? 'There! Look, there's something on the horizon,' I tell myself. 'If it's not land, then you've had it. Get going, it's your only chance.'

In terrible pain Maher began to swim in the rolling sea, swallowing mouthfuls of water, and quickly becoming bitterly cold. Yet constantly a voice within him repeated and repeated, 'Keep going, keep going!'

My legs are stinging. Then suddenly I touch bottom. 'I've touched bottom! My hand touched the bottom! Try with your feet. I've made it. I'm safe! Wade to shore. Get going.' Another despairing voice in my head says, 'I'm falling. But I mustn't fall now. Keep on. Keep on going. It's not deep here, I'll rest for a minute, and then I'll be all right.'

Exhausted, Maher passed out. He awoke to find himself lying at the water's edge with the waves breaking gently over the lower half of his body, as if they were trying to push him ashore, like some flotsam.

But I couldn't get up. I had no strength. I just had to lie there until my strength returned. My legs were in such pain! I turned my head and then I saw it. There was blood mixing with the water around my legs. I couldn't attempt to stop the bleeding because I couldn't move. My every muscle seemed paralysed. That other doom-laden voice told me, 'I must go to sleep. I'm so tired.'

No! I must stop the bleeding. So, clutching the sand with my fingers and digging in my knees, I began to move, snail-like, out of the water, resting every few yards to regain my breath. I looked at my watch in the dark, and made out that the time was eighteen minutes past two. I put it to my ear. It had stopped.

The wind blowing against his wet clothes was bitterly cold, and the pain from his legs and throughout his body was increasingly agonising.

I crawled forward in the darkness until I was clear of the water, and eventually reached a sloping bank of loose, fine, sand. Every time I clutched at the sand it just ran maddeningly through my fingers. And then a dreadful thought struck me, 'Perhaps this beach is mined! Don't move, stay where you are.'

The wind was far too cold to just lie there; I was shivering and had to get some shelter. So by crawling forward, after what seemed hours of pain and frustration I scrambled over the bank, scooped out sand by way of digging a trench, climbed in and pressed the sand over my body still wearing my wet clothes. Then, completely exhausted, I fell asleep.

The gently soothing rays of early morning sunshine awakened Maher, and he opened his eyes. He looked at the position of the sun, and guessed it to be about 9.00am.

When I became fully awake my whole body was aching. Agonising darts of fire were burning through my head, and I felt a continual throbbing from the waist down. I pushed back the covering of sand and felt my head. It seemed to be all there, though fresh blood came away on my hand. I pulled back the legs of my battle trousers and was horrified to see the flesh of both legs lying open and still bleeding, luckily not profusely, and two bone ends appearing through the gash in my right ankle.

I suddenly felt sick. The sight of the coagulated blood and bloodstained sand turned my stomach and I began to retch. I covered my legs with the tattered trousers and, because of a sudden twinge of pain, felt my right hip. It had been torn in a furrow several inches long, presumably by a stray bullet. My fingers were torn in several places and both shoulders were bleeding slightly. 'What a mess I thought, and what a place to be, when in such a mess!'

Maher gazed about him. There appeared to be nothing for miles around. The land immediately inshore gave the appearance of being swampy, with a few isolated, barren trees leaning like farmers' scarecrows in all directions. On the far horizon the sky line was interrupted by a rising ridge. He guessed that there was a village or perhaps a town in that direction.

The pain was now becoming almost unbearable and I decided to make my way as best I could in that general direction. My first movement, however, sent such stabs of pain through my body that I decided to just lie there and hope for the best; and if there was no best, to fade away as gently and as peacefully as possible. Lying there I discovered that there was also a broken bone in my left leg. As I began to examine it, I raised my eyes to see a party of armed soldiers. They were about 150 yards away spread out in a half circle, and making their way through the long grass with their rifles at the ready.

It was obvious that they were searching for any members of the Wellington's crew who had baled out, such as Maher, and who might be in the vicinity. His first thought was that they might not see him and that they might pass him by some way off.

On the Dutch coast, the crashed Wellington of Flight Lieutenant Eric Maher, shot down on 8 June 1942 during a raid on Essen. (*Private collection, Kate Schafer*)

Despite them appearing to not see me, I decided it was useless to lie and just die there, and so I gave a long shout. They turned quickly and confronted me 'en masse'. I had a ringside view of about fourteen rifle barrels pointed at me!

At around this time at RAF Breighton, it was noted in the Operations Record Book of No. 460 Squadron that Wellington E1412 and its crew 'Failed to return to base'. It was the typical understated wartime entry, as if an outdated stock item was being written off.

*   *   *

The German troops approached Maher cautiously, gesticulating and shouting. He took their exhortations to mean 'put your hands up' and he did so without delay. One soldier detached himself from the party and gave him a thorough search. As he had no revolver, hand grenade or similar weapon, they all lowered their rifles to Maher's very great relief.

If they had put a bullet or two in me, I would not have resented it, I was in such a bad way. I was extremely thirsty and weak and decided to ask for water. I said the word 'water' in what I thought to be every conceivable way. But did they understand? Finally one of the soldiers, who must have been slightly less dim than the rest, said 'Ja, Ja! Wasser.' But I still did not get any water.

The party of soldiers then broke up, four staying with Maher, while the other troops pressed on with their search.

Two of my guards I took to be officers, since the other two were clicking their heels and saluting them with monotonous regularity. The two officers took off their greatcoats – beautifully long ones that trailed almost on the ground, and they placed one on the sand. Then, by taking me by the legs and under the arms, placed me upon it. The other greatcoat they spread over me. As I was almost blue with cold by this time I can't remember anything in my life for which I was more grateful, and I must say that I began to have quite a regard for the thoughtfulness of these two men even though they were Germans.

When the two soldiers then disappeared in the direction of the town, the two officers sat down by Maher to keep vigil.

They offered me cigarettes and tried to find out the whereabouts of the other members of my crew by employing an elaborate sign language. My brain was fairly clear by now and I thought of the other members of the crew possibly making their escape. I pointed to the water and made a gesture of hopeless despair with my hands, shoulders and face. They appeared to understand that my 'Kameraden' (comrades) had gone into the sea with the plane, and they returned my gesture of resignation.

After about an hour, the two soldiers reappeared with a horse and dray, onto which they lifted Maher. They also brought flasks of water and black coffee, both of which he drank straight off.

We set off over a bumpy, winding trail. After travelling for some time, I discovered that I still had my escape equipment and emergency food rations in a small tin in my pocket, and a copy of the wireless frequencies for the previous night also. I extracted these articles cautiously and, awaiting the opportunity, flung them far out into the marshes. My action, thank God, went unnoticed.

Eventually we arrived in a small village and drove up to a dilapidated two-storey building outside of which was flying the largest flag that I have ever seen in my life. It was my first sight of a Nazi war flag, with the big hooked cross. That cross was indeed an ominous sign. I was carried by two men into a small room where I was searched thoroughly by an officer in a black uniform with a swastika armband and given another drink of water. His first words to me, spoken in perfect English, were 'For you the war is over'.

Maher was transferred about an hour later to another Gestapo police station, on a stretcher into a fairly large room where he met the pilot Hurditch and three other members of his crew. Colin Campbell, the rear gunner, was also on a stretcher with a very bad leg wound. Maher learned that, after he left the aircraft at a height of somewhere between 700 and 1,000 feet, Sergeant Hurditch noticed the water glinting below and decided that he was too low for the rest of the crew to bale out, and so took the only alternative, to crash land on the beach.

By remarkable skill, despite the fact that the starboard engine was on fire, the tail unit damaged, wheels and flaps down, and all instruments damaged, Hurditch somehow managed to crash land on the beach after hitting the top of a ridge, and settled the aircraft onto the sand without further injury to the remaining members of the crew. Hurditch and the front gunner were uninjured, and were sent off to Stalag Luft III PoW camp.

The navigator, rear gunner and Maher were taken by ambulance to the German Military Hospital in Amsterdam. Even compared to his excruciating ordeal so far, what followed was to be far worse. He was stripped naked, and wheeled into an operating theatre, where German and Dutch surgeons and nurses, in long white gowns, placed Maher on a table and strapped him down.

> After a few minutes I noticed a doctor and a couple of nurses preparing instruments and laying them out on a wheeled table near my feet. The next instant the surgeon put his hand on my right leg and I felt a searing pain burn right through my body. I let out such a scream of agony as could have been heard throughout Holland. Despite my restraining straps I was rolling around the operating table until it was on the verge of tipping over. The surgeon had made an incision in my leg without giving me any anaesthetic!

A Dutch Red Cross nurse who could speak English came over to Maher, and said, 'I am your friend.'

> I blurted out, 'It bloody well looks like it, when you let those bloody bastards do that!' She appeared to not understand, but eventually by using sign language I was able to convey my meaning. In my opinion the anaesthetic had not been accidently overlooked but disregarded deliberately. It was well known that the Germans were short of medical supplies, and I shall always believe that it was their policy at the time not to waste their scanty reserves on PoWs. I then received an injection in my back, which paralysed my body from the hips down.

Shrapnel was removed from Maher's legs and his broken bones set, after which he was taken to a room where there were four other patients. Two of these were the navigator and rear gunner from Maher's aircraft, and two other RAF aircrew who had been shot down on a previous night.

I had only just been placed on a bed when they returned with the stretcher, and took me down to the operating theatre once more. They had forgotten about the small splinters of shrapnel in my hands, arms and head and, after shaving off all my hair, they set to work to dig these pieces out, without further anaesthetic. I shall never forget the awful crunching noises as pieces of shrapnel were recovered from my head. I would relive that time in the operating theatre repeatedly, in dreams, nightmares, and recollections.

Over the next seven days Maher was in a hazy stupor most of the time. Later he could only recall one or two incidents which happened in that week, even though he was taken out of the room every morning to be washed and redressed.

When I eventually became sufficiently sensible, I found that I had been placed in the care of a German Luftwaffe hospital orderly who, I must say, treated me with every sympathy and, despite the language difficulty, with every understanding. It was he who took me every day to the surgery's bathroom and changed my dressings – all paper bandages were used – and washed me.

At this stage, I had my right leg in plaster to the knee, my left leg in removable splints, my head bandaged so as to only leave uncovered my eyes, nose and mouth, and both hands swathed in paper bandages. I was in a pretty hopeless state in so far as helping myself. I remained at the Amsterdam hospital approximately three weeks, then taken with our navigator and several other PoWs to Dulug-Luft, which was an interrogation centre for Allied airmen on the outskirts of Frankfurt.

After five days of interrogation at Dulug-Luft, during which Maher only divulged his name, rank, number and address of his next of kin, he was transferred to a hospital ward, where there were other RAF aircrew with wounds and injuries.

It was here that the spirit of comradeship prevalent in PoW camps was revealed to me. Those few who were able to move around played the game magnificently and waited hand and foot on the less fortunate ones who were confined to bed. I was later to admire this quality in many more fine fellows that I met, all of whom had gone through their own terrifying experiences. I determined to do my best to emulate their spirit and example. I grew to learn how very fortunate I was compared with many others.

Overall, however, medical treatment of PoW patients at Dulug-Luft was abysmal. A German doctor visited just twice a week, and patients' dressings were renewed only once a week. Maher was in danger of gangrene in his legs and losing them. Only the intervention by a senior British officer prevented the German medical staff from amputating both his legs. Many patients did suffer amputations. At the end of July Maher and other patients were transferred to Obermassfeld, a PoW hospital staffed by British PoW doctors and clinicians.

> At Obermassfeld I had several operations for the removal of further pieces of shrapnel and bone splinters, before moving to another PoW hospital at Wasungen. By this time I was able to hobble about with the aid of crutches and walking stick, and felt infinitely less miserable than the time when I was confined to bed.

Compared with the patient care Maher had received previously since his capture, the medical treatment at Obermassfield and Wasungen, although constrained by PoW conditions and restrictions, was excellent, and no doubt saved his life. Later he was transferred in October 1942 to another PoW hospital with British medical staff, Stalag IX AH (Kloster Haina). Subsequently, Maher survived as a PoW until the end of the war.

An indomitable spirit was at the core of Maher's will to live. It was a remarkable recovery from horrific injuries, which in most cases of this severity would have proved fatal. Yet that recovery had begun with the unexpected consideration and care given to Maher by the two German officers, who had found him washed up on the beach and close to death. It had been just in time to give Maher a chance to live.

* * *

Maher's ordeal, his resilience and sacrifice typified the selfless service of so many. By the end of the war aircrew of No. 460 Squadron had flown over 6,000 operational sorties, one of the foremost records of Bomber Command. The price paid was appalling: 1,018 airmen killed, 201 taken prisoner, and countless more wounded and maimed. While a tour of operations was thirty missions, the average life expectancy of aircrew was only six operations.[5]

Towards the end of the war, in an exchange of wounded prisoners, Eric Maher was repatriated to Britain, where he spent many more months in hospital. On his return to Australia, he married Veronica Harloe on 26 February 1946 and they raised a remarkable nine children: Robert, Kathleen, Philip, Bernard, Geoffrey, Carmel, Paul, Christopher and David. Eric Maher had a successful career in sales with the multi-national oil company Caltex, until his early death in 1973, aged only fifty-four.

While Maher's horrific injuries failed to prevent him from leading a meaningful and productive life, yet the ordeal of his survival left a legacy. One of his ankles was set in a permanent position and he often lost the feeling in one leg. For many years after the war little pieces of shrapnel worked their way out of his head and face. It is no surprise that he suffered what used to be referred to as War Neuroses, now more commonly known ass PTSD. He was never able to get on a plane again.

Chapter 10

Training flight collision – 'Don't crash into the town!'

Lieutenant Colonel Malcolm C. Sponenbergh[1]

In south-east Queensland in Australia on the morning of 2 July 1942 Charles Rossiter worked in his market garden in the coastal town of Redcliffe, less than 100 yards from the sea front at Queen's Beach. The market garden sat between Silvester and Josephine Streets, and close to where children were attending Scarborough School.

Rossiter was kneeling on the ground, carefully pulling up weeds that had grown between the cultivated rows of vegetables. The drone and whine of American fighter aircraft overhead did not bother him. He was used to their regular training flights, and practice

Lieutenant (later Lieutenant Colonel) Malcolm C. Sponenburgh, No. 80 Squadron, USAAF, 1942. (*Hart, Duane, Redcliffe Pictorial History, Vol. 2 1824–1949*)

firing at a gunnery range across the nearby Moreton Bay.

Suddenly Rossiter became aware of a roaring aircraft engine that was growing into a crescendo. He looked up in horror as a plane crashed into the ground about 100 feet from him. Instinctively he staggered away in terror, as behind him the aircraft exploded into flames in a deep crater. A great cloud of black smoke burst into the sky and bullets tore through the air in all directions from the aircraft's exploding ammunition.[2]

In a classroom at Scarborough School at the time of the crash Bette Bray was told by her teacher that they were being attacked.

> She told us to run to the air raid shelter and its trenches, which would have been disastrous because of all the bullets flying around. Next thing she was yelling for us to get under our desks. One of the plane's doors

landed right outside the headmaster's office. The school was littered with plane parts and exploded ammunition.[3]

*   *   *

While Rossiter tended to his plants, Lieutenant George L. Austin and Lieutenant Malcolm Sponenbergh of No. 80 Squadron USAAF were on a training and gunnery practice flight over the Redcliffe peninsula on the south-east coast of Queensland. The Redcliffe peninsula juts into Moreton Bay, a little to the north of Brisbane. In March 1942 Nos 35, 36 and 80 Squadrons of the 8th Fighter Group USAAF had arrived in Brisbane for training and the defence of Australia, and subsequent postings to the north for operations against the Japanese in the Philippines and New Guinea. In this exercise, Lieutenant Sponenbergh was flying behind Austin as his wingman.

> Lieutenant George L. Austin was the flight leader and we were returning from gunnery practice, flying at about 1,000 feet. He gave me the standard signal to move up to him a little more, below his aircraft, and closer in.[4]

Austin and Sponenbergh were flying P–39 Airacobra fighters, based with No. 80 Squadron at a USAAF airfield at nearby Petrie. Sponenbergh closed up on Austin's aircraft, still below but nearly abreast, watching Austin's cockpit for any further signal.

> We flew along for a couple of minutes, but he never looked back in my direction, nor could I detect any movement either by his head or hand. Suddenly he slumped over the stick, and his airplane turned into me and started diving. I closed the throttle and tried to turn, and dive with him.
>
>   Seeing that we would soon be in a vertical dive with little altitude, I tried to break off. But it was too late. I wasn't quite clear of him and his wing collided with my aircraft's propeller. All three of its blades were bent backwards.[5]

Such damage to the propeller meant that Sponenbergh's aircraft was uncontrollable, and it continued to dive. Time seemed to slow down as his limited options raced through his mind.

> I tried adding power, but the aircraft vibrated so badly that I knew that it could not continue to fly. I released the Airacobra's door lock in order to bale out, then I noticed I was directly over Redcliffe town.[6]

Perhaps in a few micro seconds, he recalled subconsciously a flight instructor saying that if you are going down 'Don't crash into the town!' 'I did not want

Sponenburgh's rescue by rowing boat, 2 July 1942. (*Hart, Duane,* Redcliffe Pictorial History, *Vol 2 1824–1949*)

the plane to crash in the town, so I headed out to sea, and as soon as I crossed the shoreline I jumped.'[7]

By this time Sponenbergh's fighter was down to 500 feet or even lower. It was fortunate that the side-door access of the Bell P-39 Airacobra allowed entry and exit to the cockpit, which enabled Sponenbergh to bale out quickly. It all happened so fast that, when he hit the water, he was not sure whether his parachute had fully opened. 'I was so low I had little time to prepare for landing in the sea. I went straight down and came back up to the surface entangled in the parachute's shroud lines.'[8]

He began pulling at the lines, to try to inflate his Mae West life vest. Nothing happened. He was in danger of being pulled under by the drag of the waterlogged parachute. Luckily the sea was reasonably calm, with only a light swell. Desperately treading water, Sponenbergh struggled to find the release cord for the life vest.

> Finally I pulled the right line, and the life vest inflated. Using my survival knife I cut my way out of the other shroud lines. Just as I came free of the lines, some fishermen in a row boat reached me. I certainly was glad to see them.[9]

He was rescued by a local fisherman, Thomas Larkin, and his two sons, Thomas and Ted, who by sheer chance were fishing close by in the bay at the time of the accident. They hauled Sponenbergh into their rowing boat, and headed back to the beach.

> On reaching the shore some kind soul brought me a mug of scalding hot tea.
>
> Luckily I had no injuries except a scrape on my cheek, because I had not disconnected my throat mike.[10]

A local nurse, Jean Houghton, was quickly on the scene to treat the pilots.

They said that Austin tried to miss the Scarborough School, which he did by landing in Rossiter's market garden, but he was killed on impact. The other pilot, Sponenbergh, was brought in by some young teenagers into a house near Queen's Beach. Gertie and I went in and we attended to him.

Not long afterwards three American officers arrived and told him, 'Come on, you've gotta get up and fly again.' I said to them, 'He's not capable.' You can imagine the distressed state he was in, but they got him up very roughly and took him away. One officer stayed behind and said to me, 'I'm sorry that you had to witness that, but we had to do it because otherwise he'd never fly again, if we didn't get him up straight away.'[11]

*   *   *

Flight Surgeon Captain Patrick reported that Lieutenant Austin had been asphyxiated, and was no doubt unconscious when his aircraft hit the ground. Sponenbergh's Airacobra was never recovered, and still lies about 300–500 yards offshore of Queen's Beach.[12]

In 1993 Lieutenant Colonel Sponenbergh returned to the site of the collision, and his ditching in the sea, and met some of his rescuers. 'After nearly fifty years as a pilot with over 4,500 hours flying, I remain convinced that in the circumstances the collision was absolutely unavoidable.'[13]

Yet both Austin and Sponenbergh avoided crashing into the town, and causing civilian casualties.

Chapter 11

Surviving flying training in Bomber Command – and that first operation to join a select brotherhood

Squadron Leader W.W. 'Bill' McRae DFC AFC[1]

I n the Second World War flying training at every stage was fraught with accidents, injuries and deaths. During aircrew training in RAF Bomber Command the overall casualty rate was a shocking 15 per cent.[2] There were also many lucky escapes, some quite freakish. Then, if an air crew made it through, they faced that acid test, a first operation into enemy skies. For some that first operation was to fly out to North Africa.

In mid-1942 the challenge of flying new air crew and aircraft to RAF squadrons in Malta and Egypt was fraught with risk, and subject to heavy losses from interception by Axis fighters, as well as attrition from mishap en route. Enemy fighters shore-based in Sicily, southern Italy and islands such as Pantelleria

Squadron Leader W.W. 'Bill' McRae DFC AFC, 1913–2019. (*Private collection, Col Frize*)

were taking a heavy toll on any Allied aircraft that ventured across the Mediterranean skies.

Rather than being sent via the only alternative flight route, trans-Africa from Takoradi on the African west coast over to Sudan, then north to Cairo, some priority aircraft were flown through the Mediterranean to Cairo. One such flight was to deliver the latest Wellington Mark VIII torpedo-bomber to Cairo and bolster the interdiction campaign which was seeking to blockade supplies to Rommel's command, *Panzerarmee Afrika*.

In the UK in July 1942 Flight Lieutenant Bill McRae had recently completed his final training as a pilot of a Wellington. He and his crew were awaiting a posting to an operational squadron. Without any prior notification, and with him and his crew lacking any operational experience, McRae was given an unexpected and critically important mission.

> We were handed a brand new Wellington Mark VIII and ordered to fly to Cairo via Gibraltar and Malta. This Wellington was rather a special one – festooned with radar aerials, associated instruments and equipment, and modified to carry torpedoes. It was to be used to locate and attack enemy vessels at night. At the time the equipment was highly secret and we were briefed on how to destroy the aircraft should we be forced down in enemy territory.
>
> I must say the thought occurred to me that my RAF superiors were taking a bit of a risk in entrusting this aircraft to me. A ferry flight they called it! The later part of the flight would be at night into Malta to hopefully avoid enemy fighters, and I confess I was none too confident of my ability to fly in the dark. My night flying training in England had been very limited.[3]

Bill McRae was twenty-nine-years old, originally from Sydney, Australia and, at the outbreak of war, was working in London. He joined the Royal Artillery and, in November 1940, was temporarily attached to the RAF with whom he learned to fly light aircraft for directing artillery. A year later McRae sought and gained a permanent transfer to the RAF and in April 1942 commenced training as a Wellington pilot.

He was being perfectly honest in July 1942 when he said that he was not very confident about flying at night. During training on a night exercise flight in a Wellington he had found himself over Liverpool by mistake, and in the middle of a Luftwaffe bombing raid. Pinpointed by searchlights and anti-aircraft fire as an assumed enemy aircraft, McRae took immediate evasive action and sharply changed course. Luckily, he avoided being shot down by 'friendly fire', and headed back towards home base at Harwell. It was an early taste of what to expect on active operations to come.

> We were diverted with a lot of other aircraft, to another aerodrome in the West of England. After landing safely as I thought, the ground crew told me they found a tree branch stuck in the under-carriage. I must have clipped the top of a tree coming in to land. A few more inches and it would have been a disaster. I did not report this, or even tell my own air crew!'

McRae's lucky escape in the German air raid and on landing was typical of near disasters during training. While at RAF Morton-in-Marsh he saw another pilot of a Wellington come in for landing too low, and clip a haystack which ripped away an engine. 'Despite this he touched down safely, and we stared in astonishment at the gaping hole in the wing, and the hanging cables where the engine had been.'

In another training flight incident while stationed at RAF Lossiemouth another pilot in McRae's section reported engine problems with his aircraft after a night training flight.

> Inspection by ground crew found that about four inches had been torn off the engines' propeller blades. He had been slow taking off, and not gained enough height to safely clear some hills close to the runway. The propeller blades touched ground, shearing away part of the blades. An inch or so more and it would have been a fatal crash.

At 0800 hours on 29 July 1942, McRae had to put all those hazardous training experiences behind him and lifted the RAF's latest radar-equipped Wellington into the air at Portreath in Cornwall. For McRae and his crew, on their first operational flight with a new specially-equipped aircraft, it truly was a flight into the unknown.

> On the flight out to Gibraltar there were no problems until I asked my navigator to come up front into the cockpit to see the Rock. Suddenly the airspeed fell away and we began to lose altitude. I opened the throttles fully to try and maintain height.

McRae tried to keep calm. Visions swirled in his head of having to ditch in the sea. It could be the end of him and his crew on their first operation. Strong cross winds around the Rock and across the Bay of Algeciras made landings extremely dangerous. After a couple of minutes on full power, struggling to maintain height, McRae realised that the flaps were fully down. His navigator had accidentally put his hand on the flap lever when he was leaning over to get a better view.

At 1600 hours McRae put down in Gibraltar and, after England, it was another world – sun, clear blue sky, hot weather, plenty of food and drink. However, McRae and his crew got little sleep that night bunked in a hut next to the runway, roused constantly by continuous aircraft landings and take offs.

> Late afternoon the next day we took off on the 1,000-mile hop to Malta. At the briefing we were told to keep radio silence and call up Malta about half an hour before reaching the island. They would respond to us with a course to steer. We were warned that Malta lay only about eighty miles south of Sicily, and its Axis air bases.

An error in navigation could bring them close to Sicily's southern coast and marauding Axis night-fighters. The flight was uneventful until they believed that they were nearing Malta. Although given a course by radio from control in Malta, almost immediately they were enveloped in low cloud and unable to see the ocean or the horizon.

> We were at 3,000 feet and although there was a half moon, heavy cloud was blotting out any lights of Valletta town and its airfield. After circling around for ten minutes, we thought we spotted it through the cloud. Keeping in mind we might be over Sicily, and also aware there were hills reaching up to 700 feet in Malta, we descended carefully. Suddenly there was break in the cloud, and we caught sight of the aerodrome flare path. We touched down at 01.00 on 31 July, and my night landing was reasonable.
>
> When we reported to the aerodrome control officer, the first thing he said was, 'You seemed to be wandering around a long time. We were beginning to get a bit worried.' I felt like replying, 'So was I'. He told us to taxi the aircraft away into a blast shelter and be back at daybreak. We then went into the mess for a cup of tea and ran into a party.
>
> The chaps in the mess were a mixed bunch of British, Australians, Canadians and New Zealanders. One of the Canadians was Flight Sergeant Beurling, who was something of a local hero, a Spitfire fighter ace with some twenty victories. They were a happy crowd and morale was high. I could sense the special bond that exists between those who go to battle in the sky. Sometime in the early hours we went back to the aircraft in the blast shelter at the airfield, and tried to sleep.

Next morning McRae and his crew took a trip into the main town of Valletta, took a ride in a horse-drawn 'taxi', saw the bomb damage, air raid shelters in the cliffs, the lean and hungry look of the locals, and endured a couple of air raids accompanied by bursts of fighter gunfire.

> Later in the day we reported back to the aerodrome and had a briefing at 1700 for the flight to Egypt. The main thing was to keep an eye out for the Italian Navy. We were told to taxi out half an hour before darkness and to leave at last light. However, if an air raid began, to get off the ground immediately and fly south at low altitude.
>
> We duly taxied to the take-off runway, switched off, disembarked and waited outside in the warm air. About ten minutes before darkness the air raid sirens sounded and the aerodrome controller started flashing a green light – 'Get going fast!'

We scrambled aboard, I hurried the Wellington onto the runway and pushed the throttles fully open. Unhappily, there was a cross wind blowing, and after a couple of hundred yards the aircraft swung off the runway. Fortunately we stopped without bogging down in loose sand. I turned around, taxied back and began again.

By the time we took off on a second attempt, searchlights were sweeping around, and guns beginning to flash. Looking back from a couple of miles out to sea the view was spectacular – flares, flashes, heavy flak and searchlights, like a large fireworks display. We were glad that we were not on the receiving end. When we made landfall over the Nile delta, the Pyramids stood out in the now clear morning light. I flew around them and landed at a nearby aerodrome.

I think the most lasting impression of the flight was the meeting with those pilots in the mess in Malta. Being my first flight out of training, it was the first time I had mixed with, and been accepted by, operational types. It gave me the feeling of being a member of a select brotherhood. As a crew I think we realised that the long haul of training was behind us, and ahead lay the excitement, as well as the unknown and unavoidable risks of injury and death.

McRae and his crew knew that, in the operations to come, exhilaration would always be mixed with fear. They had come of age, but the brutal cruelties of war lay in the missions to come.

* * *

Squadron Leader W.W. 'Bill' McRae DFC AFC LdH CdG passed away on 31 May 2019 in Sydney, aged 106. From Koraki, NSW, Bill served in the Royal Air Force from 1939 to 1945, flying Wellingtons in the Western Desert in actions such as Tobruk and El Alamein as well as Crete and Italy.

Chapter 12

First operation as Second Pilot, ditched in the sea … can there be a second chance?

Wing Commander J.L.V. 'Jim' Comans DFC and Bar[1]

Before a bomber pilot's first operation it was the practice to send him as a second pilot on a raid with an experienced crew, who usually viewed the carrying of a 'Second Dickey' as an unlucky omen. In August 1942 Flying Officer Jim Comans, on his first day at No 9 Squadron RAF, finds himself in this position on a bombing raid to Dusseldorf. On its approach to the target in Dusseldorf his Wellington is hit by flak and catches fire. The pilot nurses the struggling aircraft back across Holland and over the North Sea, before eventually shouting to the crew 'Prepare to ditch!'

* * *

On 31 July 1942, coming directly from completion of operational training, Flying Officer J.L.V. 'Jim' Comans arrived by train with his crew in the late afternoon at No. 9 Squadron, RAF Honington in Lincolnshire. Comans was immediately confronted with the pressure of an operational squadron of Bomber Command.

> As captain of my crew I was taken to see a Wing Commander who said to me very casually, 'You can fly to Dusseldorf tonight as a second pilot. Your crew can have the night off. It will be good experience for you.'[2]

The operation was scheduled for a late departure, so even on a light summer evening by the time Comans boarded the aircrew bus night had descended fully.

> My aircraft was a Wellington bomber L-for-Love. I introduced myself to the captain and climbed up next to him. The crew chatted among themselves on the inter-com – usual procedure. But no-one spoke to me. Not even the captain, Sergeant Hall.

James Leopold Vincent 'Jim' Comans was born on 2 March 1917 in Sydney, New South Wales, Australia. After leaving school, Comans gained a law degree at the University of Sydney. He became a solicitor with a law firm in Sydney and married Gwendoline before enlisting for service as a pilot officer in the RAAF in August 1941. Having played rugby for Sydney University and being a strong swimmer, Jim Comans had an athletic build with fair hair and blue eyes. It was said that he was tough, fair and a 'good bloke'.[3]

Flight Lieutenant J.V. 'Jim' Comans DFC*. (*Private collection, Chris Whiteman*)

After initial training in NSW in Australia, Comans was transferred in early 1942 under the Empire Training Scheme to Britain. There he did further advanced training at an Operational Training Unit flying heavy bombers, before being posted on 31 July 1942 to No. 9 Squadron RAF at Honington, as the pilot and captain of a Wellington bomber.[4]

The bombing raid on Dusseldorf on the night of 31 July/1 August 1942 would be Jim Comans' first operation. Because no amount of rigorous training could prepare bomber pilots and their crews for the real thing, before a first operation it was the practice to send the pilot as a 'second pilot' on a raid with a seasoned crew to gain experience. In the circumstances the lack of communication between Comans and the crew of L-Love was not out of the ordinary. He had been ordered to join them at the last minute without any prior introductions. In addition the crew would have thought of the common superstition in Bomber Command, that taking on board a second pilot, a 'Second Dickey', provoked a jinx on L-Love and their flight.

With a delay to departure it was not until between 00.53 and 01.25 hours on 1 August 1942 that thirteen Wellington bombers of No. 9 Squadron took off from Honington. Wellington L-Love with Comans as 'second pilot' took to the air at 01.16 hours. The flight across to Germany was uneventful until they neared Dusseldorf when Comans was jolted suddenly out of his involuntary solitude.[5]

> As we approached the target we were hit. Suddenly we were on fire. Being on my first operation I, least of anyone, understood ... what was happening. But I knew enough to realise that the captain, Sergeant Hall, was all the time losing considerable height. We must have struggled

back to the coast, because the next thing I heard was when he shouted, 'Prepare to ditch!'

In thick cloud and the black night, Hall was fighting a damaged aircraft that was continually losing altitude. It is quite likely that the altimeter was faulty because, suddenly, the Wellington plunged into the North Sea waves, water cascading into the plane. There was no time for the wireless operator to transmit an SOS signal. 'The plane was under water within seconds. I managed to get out, tearing the skin off the top of my hand, but that's beside the point.'

Without knowing how he got out of the sinking aircraft, Comans found himself swimming in freezing water, desperately trying to keep his head above the surface, as his flying suit and boots were dragging him down. Had the second pilot jinx struck again?

I swam around for a while, and my flying boots were giving me a lot of trouble. So I took them off. That later proved to be very stupid. Suddenly the self-inflating dinghy surfaced and a few of us climbed in. Then we came across the rear gunner, face down in the water. We got him aboard with a lot of difficulty. What a strange position for me to be in. I knew no one in the dinghy. I had never met them before, hadn't spoken to them before, didn't have a clue as to who or what role they had been in the crew.

And in the dark I couldn't even see them clearly until daylight. The rear gunner was very ill. He had a broken leg, his pelvis was smashed and his skull was fractured. His nose was broken too, he was a mess. He moaned and groaned, and rolled from one side of the dinghy to the other, making us take in a lot of water to be bailed out. Some of the crew talked of throwing him overboard, as he didn't appear to have much chance.

But they held onto him, stopping him from lapsing into unconsciousness. Comans and the others bailed out the dinghy continuously and kept the rear gunner and themselves alive for three days and nights. Incessantly tossed around by the seas, they were nearing the time when hypothermia, hunger, thirst and dehydration would kill them. They clung to vain hopes that a search by air–sea rescue might find them. But they had seen no ships or planes at all, nothing but sea and sky. It was as if they were in the middle of a desert. Then fate intervened. 'Suddenly from seemingly nowhere a fishing trawler appeared, saw us, picked us up, and took us into Grimsby.'

Being found by the fishing trawler was fortunate indeed for Comans and the others, but particularly for the rear gunner who could not have lasted much longer. 'Some years later I saw the rear gunner with a girl walking along a seaside pier. I nearly told him how close he'd been to death … but stopped myself.'

When Comans returned to RAF Honington, he learned that he had been listed as 'missing in action', and the Wellington aircraft L-Love had been officially recorded as 'Nothing heard of this aircraft after take off'.[6] His own crew had been sent away to train with a new captain, while his personal belongings were on their way to the Air Ministry. Having come so close to drowning, and then nearly dying of exposure in the dinghy, he was not the least dismayed: 'The spirit moves quickly in wartime. Within two days I had my crew back, and we were flying again.'

After completing a tour with No. 9 Squadron, in December 1943 Comans joined No. 97 (Straits Settlement) Squadron in the elite No. 8 (Pathfinder) Group flying Lancasters. Between 1 January and 15 June 1944 he completed thirty-six operations with No. 97 Squadron.[7] This included completion of the disastrous Nuremberg raid, and fourteen of the major bombing operations on Berlin. Overall, during the war he completed over 100 separate bombing missions over Germany and Nazi-occupied Europe.

So, as well as his miraculous rescue in the North Sea, to complete and survive so many active operations is equally remarkable. It is an understatement to say that fate was kind to Jim Comans.

In June 1944 it was for his 'coolness and courage in times of stress' that he received the Distinguished Flying Cross. The award citation was glowing in its praise for Comans, who was hailed as 'an outstanding Captain … whose excellent leadership and skill as a pilot have been largely responsible for the many successes gained by his crew.'

He was further decorated for his devotion to duty when he was awarded a Bar to his DFC in October 1944, and subsequently promoted to squadron leader, and finally wing commander. After the war Comans left the RAF in October 1945 and returned to Australia. He resumed his career and became a very successful solicitor, as well as attaining prominent national roles in Australian sports administration and associated judicial functions.[8]

When he left the air force he threw away his uniform. 'I didn't want another war, I'd had it. I never flew myself again, and I never will.' The words and sentiment reveal perhaps the hidden stress and disillusion with the trauma of war. Yet it is clear that, without that lucky survival, straight out of training on his first operation with No. 9 Squadron, he would not have gone on to be an outstanding pilot and leader in the elite Pathfinders of Bomber Command, and after the war fulfil a distinguished civilian career.[9] Despite the second pilot jinx, Comans did not waste his second chance.

Part IV

1943

Chapter 13

Baling out on the Bengal coast – mangrove swamps, wild jungle, crocodiles, snakes, Japanese troops – the wildlife of Burma is awaiting!

Flying Officer D.J. 'Barney' Barnett[1]

Floating down towards the murky water and mangrove swamps of the Mayu river estuary, Flying Officer 'Barney' Barnett fully expected to hear at any moment the high pitch of a Japanese fighter's radial engine bearing down on him. It was the custom of Japanese fighter pilots to machine-gun Allied airmen as they dangled from a parachute. Even if Barnett reached the ground safely, he dreaded what he faced – drowning, crocodiles, snakes, a slow death from hunger and thirst, or capture and a brutal execution by Japanese troops. He was a long way south of Allied forces' lines, and the odds were heavily against his survival.

* * *

On the Bay of Bengal, east coast rivers such as the Naf, Kaladan and Mayu run north to south through some of the thickest jungle in the world and in their river deltas close to the sea sit extensive mangrove swamps. Beginning in December 1942 in north-east India, the British Eastern Army under Lieutenant General Irwin moved out from Cox's Bazar and pushed south along the Bengal coast. Over the next few months, Eastern Army advanced southwards into Burma until, just north of the Mayu river delta and Akyab island, strengthened Japanese forces blocked any further progress. In support, Allied air forces carried out low-level ground attacks, bombing and strafing of enemy targets.[2]

In one of those bombing raids on 28 February 1943, by Blenheims on Akyab Island, Flying Officer D.J. 'Barney' Barnett was one of the pilots of No. 136 Squadron RAF (The Woodpecker) flying Hurricanes as top cover escorts. In order to keep visual contact with the well camouflaged Blenheim bombers

Flying Officer D.J. 'Barney' Barnett (extreme left), No. 136 Squadron RAF, January 1944, Burma. (*Private collection, Geoff Constantine*)

below, the Hurricanes were flying at around 8,000 feet. They risked being jumped by fighters of the Imperial Japanese Army Air Force (IJAAF) from a higher altitude. To make it worse, Barnett's radio was refusing to come to life.

'Barney' Barnett was born in 1918 in Richmond, Queensland, Australia, and joined the RAAF in March 1941. After preliminary training in Australia and Canada, he transferred to Annan in Scotland for further training with the RAF. In November 1942 Barnett was posted to No. 136 Squadron RAF, then based at Dum Dum airfield near Calcutta. In the operation of February 1943, escorting the Blenheim bombers, he was still a relatively inexperienced fighter pilot.

As they approached the mouth of the Mayu river near to Akyab Island, Barnett felt the isolation of having no radio contact with the other Hurricane pilots. If there was any radio warning of 'bandits' – enemy aircraft approaching – he would, of course, not hear anything. Suddenly his cockpit seemed to blow up. 'It filled with smoke. A huge hole had been blasted in the panel on my right. The aircraft plunged down into a vicious spin, and I thought I was done for.'[3]

Instinctively Barnett unstrapped himself, and clambered out of the spiralling Hurricane and somehow remembered the advice to get himself out on the inside of the spin. Floating down towards the murky water and mangrove swamps of the Mayu estuary, he could see the burning wreck of his Hurricane well offshore. There was also the fading drone of the other Hurricanes heading away to the north, making for the safety of their base. Barnett's mind raced at the thought of what he faced – drowning, crocodiles, snakes, and the Japanese troops watching his conspicuous parachute floating down.

Once he hit the water his training snapped in and he immediately released his parachute harness before pulling out the pin from his bottle of compressed CO_2. Barnett's Mae West life-jacket and dinghy sprang to life, inflating in a garish yellow. Now feeling even more noticeable to searching eyes, he began to paddle towards the nearest shore, fearing that the Japanese were bound to see him. Luckily some natives in a canoe spotted him and helped him to land but then left him alone. Barnett wondered where their loyalties lay, and whether they might inform the Japanese of his whereabouts. If the Japanese found any local people helping the Allies, they would execute them and burn their village.

It was very likely that his presence would be reported to the Japanese. He had to get away from the area. Barnett began to wade laboriously through the mangrove swamps. Each step sank into cloying mud and very soon both of his shoes had been sucked off his feet. 'It was one chaung – a tidal inlet – after another, the banks and mud flats covered with mangroves ....'[4]

Barnett knew that Allied forces were trying to push south down the Mayu peninsula, so his only very slim hope was to head northwards. He hobbled on, and his exposed feet were quickly ripped bare and ragged from stepping onto mangrove roots. One night, only a few yards away from the bank where he hid, as he peered through the leaves of a mangrove tree he glimpsed a boat of Japanese troops glide past. With no food and water he was in some kind of daze, in and out of snatches of sleep and near total exhaustion.

When the next dawn came, Barnett trudged on again. He had long since given up hope of rescue; his only instinctive thought was to keep going. Each day he waded through a morass of mangrove mudflats and tidal waterways. On one day the current flowed against him so strongly that the waves were surging into his face. The tide pushed him back almost to where he had begun and he was forced to wait for the ebb before making another start.

Another night came, and he dozed a little as his Mae West kept his head above water. He came awake with a start. Again, only a few yards from him in the dark, a number of boats paddled past with cargo that looked like supplies for the Japanese. It made him move again, wading from one clump of mangroves to another, and at each one stopping to rest for a while until he found a place to lie down.

At first light Barnett thought that the Mayu river seemed narrower, so he decided to attempt to cross to the north bank. Once ashore, he found that he was on an island with a further stretch of water on the other side. He was extremely weak from no food or water for three or four days and nights. It might have been more: he had lost count, and knew he was close to collapse.

Sometime after this he was spotted by some locals who were foraging in flooded rice *padi* fields. Barnett somehow made them understand that he was British, which they welcomed, giving him water, and bathing him. Then they took turns to carry him across another river, to the other side of the Mayu peninsula. There he was handed over to some forward units of 14th Indian Division which had fought its way south as a spearhead operation, but which was about to begin a withdrawal back to the north. A day later and they would have been gone.

At first the Punjabi troops were suspicious of him. They tied his hands and took him by boat across yet another river before presenting him to a British officer. Through his dazed stupor Barnett heard an English voice, and knew that he was in safe hands. After a few days being cared for by the troops' medical staff, he then had to make a twenty-mile walk before embarking on a ship back to Chittagong in India.

For four days and nights he had survived in Burma's jungle and swamps without any food or water. Then, when death from the heat, hunger, thirst, dehydration and sheer exhaustion was surely only hours away, a miraculous rescue had saved him. Barnett did not know it at the time, but he had just survived to become one of a select few to qualify for membership of each of three iconic associations of airmen: 'Caterpillar Club' (baling out of an aircraft), 'Late Arrival Club' (late return from an operation) and 'Goldfish Club' (ditching in water). [5]

Barnett's spirit and determination to survive was rewarded by fortuitous rescue, first by local people finding him, and then by an unlikely meeting with Allied troops. He would return to No. 136 Squadron, which became the highest-scoring fighter squadron in Burma, and play a prominent part as a Spitfire pilot in wresting air superiority in 1944 from the IJAAF. Barnett would appear in a famous photograph with Squadron Leader Noel Constantine and three other Spitfire pilots on a day when the media reported 'RAF 15 – Japan 0'.

At the end of the war 'Barney' Barnett returned to Australia and, with his wife Peg, lived in Brisbane, Queensland, then later in Tweed Heads in northern NSW until he passed away in 2017.

Chapter 14

Flying through the Alps,
while running on empty!

Wing Commander Albert Hollings DFC[1]

On a bombing raid over Milan, Italy, on 12 August 1943 at the controls of a Lancaster bomber, Flying Officer Albert Hollings is on only his second operation, and with his crew on their first. The Lancaster is hit by flak, putting the starboard inner engine out of action. The damaged aircraft is losing height and fuel, and for the return flight to Britain they no longer have the range to take the planned longer route to the north-west. Their only slim chance is a more direct course to southern England over the towering Swiss Alps. The stricken bomber on its three engines loses height down to around 10,000 feet, and is unable to climb over the Alpine mountains. Is it to be a crash landing or baling out? Or is there a way back before the fuel runs out?

Flying Officer Albert Hollings, No. 207 Squadron RAF, 1943. (*Private collection Geoff Hollings*)

* * *

At 21.46 hours on the evening of 12 August 1943, at RAF Spilsby in Lincolnshire, Flying Officer Albert 'Bert' Hollings took the controls of Lancaster ED 586 F-Freddy of No. 207 Squadron RAF, and lifted the heavy bomber into the air.[2] For Hollings and his crew it was their first operation, a long-range raid to Milan in northern Italy, in that initial mission which so many crews failed to survive. At that time of the war the ground anti-aircraft defences and night-fighters around Milan were light, and such an operation was viewed by experienced aircrew as 'a piece of cake'. Two nights earlier, Lancaster F-Freddy had successfully completed a raid on Hamburg with another crew. The aircraft itself was no newcomer to the trials of the air war at night.

Albert Hollings, known as Bert, was born in 1919 in Leeds, Yorkshire, and as a child emigrated with his parents to Adelaide, South Australia. He joined the RAAF in Australia in 1941 and trained in Adelaide, Temora in New South Wales and Point Cook in Victoria, where he gained his wings and commission. He had a strong character, an enthusiasm for work but with an infectious sense of humour.[3] During training in England, his crew, some of whom had also aspired unsuccessfully to become pilots, gained a full confidence in Hollings' leadership and flying skills. They were not to know that his skill and their trust would immediately be tested to the extreme, in a way no one could have foreseen.

In the late summer evening of 12 August 1943, the crew of Lancaster F-Freddy,[4] who were harbouring their first-night nerves, were as follows:

Crew member	Role
Flying Officer Albert Hollings	Pilot
Flying Officer Albert Hallam	Flight Engineer
Flying Officer Rex Y. Kenyon	Navigator
Flying Officer George Lapham	Bomb Aimer
Flying Officer Cyril T. Harper	Rear-Gunner
Pilot Officer John Denton	Mid-Upper Gunner
Pilot Officer Joe Blake	Wireless Operator

Although Milan was seen as being lightly defended compared to cities in Germany, the long distance haul across the whole of France and the Alps was a formidable challenge on a crew's first operation over occupied Europe. The navigator, Flying Officer Rex Kenyon, was under enormous stress to keep them exactly on the plotted course. In some ways navigators were under more pressure than pilots, since a small error in reckoning could draw the aircraft off course and result in disaster. On this raid to Milan the long distance would exacerbate the consequences of any mistake on the part of a navigator.

The outward flight by Lancaster F-Freddy across France and over the Alps proved to be uneventful. Yet the unsaid question was: would their course bring them onto the target in Milan accurately? As they approached the city at 17,000 feet, Kenyon was tense but confident they were on course and on time and, over the intercom, said to Hollings: 'The target indicators should go down dead ahead any moment now, skipper.'[5]

Hollings looked down on the supposed target area, which was quite clear except for some smoke. It was 01.31 hours. Almost at once the target indicators dropped by the leading Pathfinder bombers exploded directly ahead in a cascade of green flares. Kenyon could breathe more easily.

The night sky lit up from an estimated forty searchlights. Hollings thought the accompanying flak from Milan's air defences to be light and ineffective. His and the crew's senses on their first operation and in their first air battle were not attuned to the sounds and impacts on a plane of anti-aircraft fire. None of them heard any noise when a fragment of a bursting shell hit the starboard inner engine. They did not know it but Freddy had been maimed.

On the first run at the target, the bomb load hung up. Hollings took Freddy around and, on a second run, bomb-aimer Flying Officer George Lapham found that the bomb release mechanisms were hung up again. Hollings decided to jettison all the bombs into the target area where fires appeared to be well concentrated. Down went a 4,000lb bomb and fifteen small bomb containers (SBCs) of incendiaries. Five minutes later, as they headed back west to commence the return leg, the damaged starboard inner engine caught fire. Not far ahead of them lay the Alps.

Hollings cut off the engine's fuel and feathered the propeller. Freddy was at least a four-hour flight from their home base at Spilsby. A Lancaster was well able to fly long distances on only three engines, if there was no other damage or malfunction, but it would gradually lose height. Imperceptibly, Freddy's nose began to decline from 17,000 feet. Hollings asked his flight engineer, Flying Officer Albert Hallam, to give the three engines more power to counteract the aircraft's downward trajectory.

Once they had lost the starboard inner engine, Hallam had quickly done some calculations. He told Hollings that if he increased the power on the remaining three engines there would be insufficient fuel to reach Spilsby. Yet Freddy needed height to fly back over the Alps. To go around the Alpine mountains would have required even more fuel. Were they destined to crash-land or bale out in Italy?

Around a hundred Alpine mountains are above 13,000 feet with some, like Mont Blanc, above 15,000 feet. The Lancaster had gradually lost height to about 12,500 feet and Hollings was unable to lift Freddy any higher. It seemed he had run out of options. The thought of a crash-landing, or baling out somewhere in enemy territory and being taken prisoner was anathema, especially so to Hollings and his crew on their first operation. There was, however, one alternative and unsaid option, which was the most dangerous of all to their lives.

Hollings was faced with making an immediate choice. Any indecision in course direction would just waste more fuel. He decided to put all his faith in his flying ability, and held Freddy's nose pointed directly towards the towering mass of the Alps. He meant to thread his way through unknown Alpine valleys. Although it was the middle of the night, Hollings had one crucial factor on his side. The Alpine mountains looming ever larger in front of him were bathed in moonlight.

Very soon they were cut off from the sky, as Hollings held the Lancaster steady, probing through a narrow valley with steep rocky slopes. They were entering a dark and unknown labyrinth of Alpine valleys and the crew glanced nervously at the higher peaks of mountains on either side. Some peaks above the Lancaster rose like dark monoliths and some were tipped with snow. Unable to see any way out, Hollings pressed Freddy forward. Gradually the valley opened out into another, then another, and another, sometimes with a glistening moonlit lake or river below. There was no turning back now.

Now and again they caught sight of a light from a house or car, but there was no possibility of putting down or even making a crash-landing. Their survival depended upon Hollings' flying skill, the Lancaster's three remaining Rolls Royce Merlin engines, and their fuel. If another engine failed it would bring them down. Freddy was like a trapped flying insect, desperately seeking clear air.

Yet the three engines purred on relentlessly, and Flight Engineer Hallam juggled the fuel tanks, eking out the dwindling supply. After what seemed like an eternity the hills dropped away below them. They were out of the Alpine region. As the sky behind them began to lighten with glimmers of dawn, Freddy flew on, a Lancaster alone and insistent over the still dark French countryside. Was there enough fuel to get them home? Could they reach the English Channel under the cloak of night?

By the time Hollings looked down onto the waves breaking on the French coast, they were in daylight. The danger then for Freddy was that a lone British bomber would be easy prey for an early morning patrol of Luftwaffe fighters. Their luck held. As they crossed the Channel no other aircraft were seen and in no time at all they were flying over England's green fields. The fuel was holding out, and they were heading for Lincolnshire. Finally, some five hours after leaving the skies over Milan, Hollings began his approach to Spilsby.

At RAF Spilsby it was thought that Freddy was not going to return and the Control Officer had the runway lights switched off. When Hollings came through on the radio, Spilsby ground staff were overjoyed. The dreadful but frequent task of posting another new crew as lost on their first operation was avoided. A remaining uncertainty was whether the Lancaster's undercarriage had been damaged by the flak, which had hit the starboard inner engine. Luck stayed with them. Hollings touched Freddy down safely, to bring his crew home unscathed, and that first mission accomplished. He noted routinely in his diary with typical air force understatement: 'Returned all the way home on 3 motors and crossed the French coast in daylight. Journey 9 hours 10 minutes. Landed OK but tired.'[6]

In the opinion of Section Intelligence Officer Joyce Brotherton MBE MiD, Hollings and his crew would become 'one of the best all-round crews we ever had'.[7]

Yet in their first operation, despite a unique and miraculous return flight back to Spilsby, they had only made a start, a single step in their quest to complete thirty operations. To get through those first half dozen or so missions, and learn some of the ropes, was still ahead of them.

Chapter 15

The Battle of Berlin –
Escape from the 'Big City'.

Wing Commander Albert Hollings DFC[1]

It was less than two weeks since Flying Officer Albert Hollings and his crew
had survived their first operation with No. 207 Squadron. On 12 August
1943 Hollings had piloted their damaged Lancaster on a nerve-racking
return flight from a night raid on Milan by threading the bomber on three
engines through Swiss Alpine valleys. Only two days later, on 14 August, they
had completed a second operation, once more a bombing attack on Milan,
while on the 17th they were forced to abort an operation to Leverkusen in
Germany because of mechanical problems.

Now, on 23 August, they waited to hear what would be the destination later
that evening for what they hoped would be their third completed operation.
Shortly after lunch, prior to a pre-operation briefing at RAF Spilsby in
Lincolnshire, Hollings' navigator, Flying Officer Rex Kenyon, was sitting
in conversation with the squadron's Intelligence Officer, Joyce Brotherton.[2]
Kenyon wondered aloud where they would be sent that night. Brotherton
knew the target destination but did not respond. Kenyon indicated that he did
not care too much, except if it were to be Berlin. At the subsequent briefing

Flight Lieutenant
Albert Hollings
(kneeling right)
with his crew at
RAF Spilsby, 1943.
(*Private collection
Geoff Hollings*)

later that afternoon it was announced that the operation was indeed Berlin, or as it was generally known to aircrew – the 'Big City'.

Between August 1943 and March 1944 Bomber Command launched nineteen major raids on Berlin, in which more than 10,000 aircraft sorties dropped over 30,000 tons of bombs on the Big City. The Battle for Berlin was the longest and most sustained RAF bomber offensive against one target in the Second World War.[3]

At a meeting held from 09.00 to 10.00 on 23 August at Bomber Command HQ at High Wycombe, Air Chief Marshal Sir Arthur Harris took the decision to attack Berlin that evening. In the opening raid of the Battle of Berlin, a force of 719 bombers would target the south of the city. Planning for the operation commenced at once, although a final decision on 'Go or no go' depended upon an assessment of weather conditions over continental Europe and Berlin.

At 12.40 hours a Mosquito took off to evaluate the weather over Germany, and what would be the likely conditions over Berlin during the night. Shortly before 16.00 hours the Mosquito returned. The resulting forecast was for good visibility, with only intermittent cloud at low altitudes. Harris gave the go-ahead and the plans went out by tele-printer just before 16.30 to the Bomber Command groups. From there orders were sent out to squadrons, which left little time for final preparations by air and ground crew. Bombers would begin taking off at 19.30 hours.

Bomber Command was despatching a total force of 719 aircraft to attack Berlin, with another sixty-nine in support roles, e.g. route marking, mine-laying etc. Most briefings of aircrew did not mention that this operation would be the opening of a lengthy battle to try and bring the Big City to its knees. It was generally recognised that Berlin had the strongest air defences of all German cities. Flak batteries and searchlights stretched in belts across an area up to sixty miles wide. Three huge flak towers held twenty-four 128mm guns, eight in each tower, which could fire up to a height of 45,000 feet. Eight shells from one flak tower fired in a pattern would explode in a zone of 240 metres across.[4]

For Hollings and his inexperienced crew, this was only their fourth operation, including the aborted operation on 17 August. Hollings was about five feet nine inches tall, of average build, excelled in sports, particularly football and sailing, and was an accomplished ballroom dancer. With a tanned complexion, blue eyes, black wavy hair, always smartly dressed whether in a tailored uniform or not, he socialised easily. He may have been young and inexperienced but his crew and other colleagues found him to be energetic, enthusiastic and diligent in everything. Those qualities were soon to be put to the ultimate test in the raid on the 'Big City'.[5]

As Hollings and his crew made their way out to dispersal and Lancaster DV186 J-Johnny to head off into the night to bomb Berlin, there was surely no truer meaning of the term 'baptism of fire'. It is extremely difficult to prepare yourself mentally and physically to go somewhere you have never been before. All aircrew were about to fly into a cauldron of dazzling light, explosions, and flak surging up in incessant waves from Berlin's anti-aircraft guns. The crew of J-Johnny (see below) could have no real understanding of what would confront them.

Crew member	Role
Flying Officer Albert Hollings	Pilot
Sergeant F.G. 'Ernie' Scott	Flight Engineer
Flying Officer Rex Y. Kenyon	Navigator
Flying Officer George Lapham	Bomb Aimer
Flying Officer Cyril T. Harper	Rear Gunner
Pilot Officer John Denton	Mid-Upper Gunner
Pilot Officer Joe Blake	Wireless Operator

At 20.31 hours Hollings took J-Johnny into the air, one of twelve Lancasters from No. 207 Squadron to join up with the main bomber stream.[6] The outward route was direct, flying due east after crossing the Dutch coast, then over Germany slightly south-east, so as to avoid the strong air defences of Bremen, Hanover, Brunswick and Magdeburg, before, some thirty miles south-east of Berlin, turning north-west to first bomb, then leave Berlin on the same heading.

Aircrew have described the approach run into Berlin as if you were flying towards and into a wall of searchlights – hundreds of them, some in cones and some in clusters. Beyond the wall of searchlights could be seen even brighter lights, but those were red, green and blue – exploding flak. Those who had been to the Big City before knew it would be hell over the target.

With the mistaken complacency of the uninitiated, and an outward flight without incident, Hollings was thinking it a good trip as they began their run in, and were nearly over the target.

> We were suddenly attacked by a Fw190 night-fighter from the starboard bow. I knew nothing about it until it opened fire at about 400 yards. I saw shells exploding in the cockpit, and George Lapham, the bomb aimer, yelled that he was hit, and also Ernie the flight engineer.[7]

Harper and Denton, the two gunners, opened fire, hitting the Fw190, which they claimed as damaged. J-Johnny was also damaged, and Hollings was not sure how much punishment the aircraft had taken, nor the state of Lapham's injuries. 'We got George up from his bomb aimer compartment, and laid him on the floor behind Rex to keep him warm.'

Lapham had been shot badly in the top of a thigh, and was in excruciating pain. Scott, Kenyon and Blake were all suffering from shrapnel wounds to feet, arms and legs, but were able to carry on, and at the same time try and patch up Lapham. Meanwhile Hollings was throwing J-Johnny around in corkscrew manoeuvres to avoid another attack. First aid for Lapham was delayed since Hollings' evasion tactics had sent the medical kit tumbling away somewhere. A search for the kit was not helped by a loss of internal lighting in the aircraft.

Although J-Johnny was holed by flak in numerous places, Hollings found that, as far as he could tell, there was no serious malfunction and took the Lancaster into a bombing run. With Lapham unable to fulfil his bomb-aiming role, Hollings planned to jettison the bombs: 'I found that the jettison toggle did not operate, so I sent the flight engineer, Scott, down to the bomb-bay to manually push the jettison bars across.'

Despite his injuries, Scott was able to get the bombs jettisoned. Shortly after, they were coned by thirty to forty searchlights and held in a blinding glare for the anti-aircraft guns to pinpoint their range. Instantly Hollings reacted just as he had been trained.

> I pushed the nose down a long way, and threw J-Johnny into a spiralling dive. The engines really began to scream, and this went on for six to seven minutes before we freed ourselves from those searchlights. As luck would have it we were not hit by any more flak.

About ten minutes later as they continued to traverse north-west away from central Berlin but still in the Big City's area, Hollings saw a twin-engine Bf110 night-fighter attacking another Lancaster.

> It was on our starboard quarter, about 800 yards away, and somewhat below us. As he broke away he headed towards us, so I told Cyril, our rear gunner, to give him a burst if he could line him up.

Despite the damage they themselves had sustained, and rather than take evasive action, Hollings instinctively wanted to draw the German fighter away from their fellow bomber crew. Rear gunner Cyril Harper opened fire on the enemy aircraft which had an unusual white light shining from its nose. Hollings watched it close on them from some 700 yards down to 300 yards and saw Harper aim long steady bursts at the Bf110: 'What a burst, about 1,000 rounds, but it did the job properly.'

Smoke began to stream from underneath the German fighter's fuselage, and the light in its nose went out. Then flames flickered from the aircraft's underbelly and a few seconds later the Bf110 broke apart. The two sections of the plane fell like stones before exploding on the ground. It was a sobering sight. With heightened motivation to get them out of the Big City's killing zone, Hollings turned J-Johnny's four Merlin engines onto full power: 'We made all haste we could – and said a prayer or two.'

The return route of the bomber stream was to continue north-westerly from Berlin, as far as the Baltic coast, before turning more westerly across the Danish peninsula. Once over the North Sea the course changed to south-easterly towards the airfields of eastern England. It was a longer route home, designed to avoid flak and German fighters. Hollings remembered that, at the pre-operation briefing, they had been warned that the Germans would be holding back some fighters in coastal waters to catch the bombers on their return flights. 'When we finally crossed the English coast, it was with great relief.'

Hollings radioed Spilsby to arrange for an ambulance to be ready on landing for Lapham and Scott to be dashed to hospital. He brought J-Johnny down towards the runway – it was the acid test. What unknown damage to the landing gear might still bring disaster?

> As I was landing the port tyre burst, but I managed to keep her straight and the right way up. It had apparently been hit when we were attacked. We had a hell of a job getting Lapham out and, together with Scott, into the ambulance. Only then did I learn that both Kenyon the navigator, and Blake the wireless operator had also been hit, but had not said anything to save worrying me anymore. Good lads, all of them. Then to the debriefing by which time I was myself really buggered. But we made it, thank God. Our guardian angels watched over us tonight.[8]

Subsequently Hollings and his crew received a letter of commendation from 5 Group HQ, for shooting down an enemy fighter that was attacking another Lancaster. Their action not only saved the other bomber, but almost certainly themselves.

* * *

For Bomber Command 23/24 August 1943 was the worst night of the war thus far. In the heaviest loss by Bomber Command on a single night of the war up to this date, sixty-two bombers were lost, 8.7 per cent of the 719 despatched. A loss rate of anything above 5 per cent was seen as unacceptable, and unsustainable.

In respect of aircrew, 298 were killed and 117 taken prisoner. In contrast, the Luftwaffe lost only nine fighters, four airmen killed, and two injured.

On the ground in Berlin the bombing killed 854 people and destroyed 2,611 properties. However, analysis of the bombing found it to be very scattered. The section of Berlin which had been intended in the planning as the target was largely undamaged.[9]

Although Hollings, his crew and aircraft Lancaster J-Johnny were damaged they had survived and made it back to Spilsby. As an inexperienced crew on only their third completed operation, their first to Germany and its most fiercely defended city, Berlin, they had defied the odds. And, in a very different way, fate had not finished with Hollings.

While on some leave his flair on the dance-floor made an impression when he met Kathleen Else in Nottingham where they later wed on 25 November 1944. Hollings completed his first tour of thirty operations in June 1944, after which he was transferred to be an instructor at Stirling and Lancaster conversion units until, in March 1945, he was promoted to wing commander at No. 466 Squadron where, in April 1945, he was appointed commanding officer.

In November 1945, after the end of the war, Albert and Kathleen Hollings moved to Australia where they lived in Adelaide and Sydney, raising six children, Tony, Geoff, Brian, Steve, Tina and Rob. Hollings joined the Amphol Petroleum Company and progressed to senior management roles before, at only fifty-three, he passed away in 1972. His children remember him as an understanding and encouraging father, but insistent that they do any job properly.

Chapter 16

Evading the Gestapo, climbing the Pyrenees in winter – to reach Gibraltar is the only hope

Group Captain Herbert A. Penny OBE[1]

Flying Officer Penny decided to knock on the back door of a small house. He did so as quietly as he could, so that only someone inside the house could hear the knocks. Eventually a man opened the door. Penny flapped his arms like a bird and whispered as quietly as he could, 'R-A-F, R-A-F'. In that instant Penny did not know whether he was confronted by a Nazi supporter or not.

* * *

On the night of 31 August 1943 No. 35 Squadron RAF, part of No. 8 Group, the Pathfinder Force, took part in a raid on Berlin. Flying Officer Herbert A. Penny,[2] accompanied by Squadron Leader W. 'Butch' Surtees, was the pilot of Halifax II HR878 'TL-J-Johnny'. It was Penny and his crew's eleventh Pathfinder operation after converting from Main Force operations. Their target for the night was the city of Berlin. It was another in the series of mass bomber raids on the German capital, the 'Big City', known as the 'Battle of Berlin'.[3]

For Flying Officer Herbert Penny himself it would be his forty-second operation. He was from Bow in London, over six feet tall, with blue eyes, dark hair, and just twenty-one

Flying Officer Herbert A. Penny, No. 35 Squadron RAF, 1943. (*Private collection, Nick Penny*)

years old. He had joined the RAF in 1940 and, after flying training, served with No. 77 Squadron before being posted to No. 35 Squadron. At 20.10 hours on

31 August at RAF Gravely near Huntingdon, Penny lifted Halifax J-Johnny into the air. 'The route to and from Berlin took us over the Ijssee Meer – a landlocked bay formerly known as the Zuidersee – and then across the Dutch/German border. It was a route we had flown before.'[4]

In another maximum effort operation in the Battle for Berlin, Bomber Command was despatching 613 bombers, which included 331 Lancasters, 176 Halifaxes, and 106 Stirlings. Many crews were tired from the previous night's raid on Mönchengladbach and Rheydt. The outward flight path was to be south-easterly over northern Holland, skirting to the south of Hanover, before approaching Berlin from the city's south. However, the German air defences were tracking the bomber force as it traversed Holland. Helped also by good weather and visibility, Luftwaffe night-fighters found the bomber stream and attacked them in strength before and during the approach to Berlin.[5]

At around 16,000 feet over Berlin on its bombing run towards the target J-Johnny was badly hit by flak, crippling the aircraft. Penny attempted to take J-Johnny back on the return flight over Holland and the North Sea, but was unable to prevent the Halifax bomber from losing height.

> Somewhere around the Dutch border our aircraft was picked up by searchlights, and flak anti-aircraft batteries, so that inevitably we became an isolated target for a Messerschmitt 110 night-fighter. With our starboard wing and fuselage ablaze, we suddenly became uncontrollable, and began spiralling down.

With the aircraft certain to crash Penny shouted the order for the crew to bale out immediately.

> In what seemed just seconds available to get out, I managed to clip my parachute pack on to my harness. There was little time for an emergency evacuation drill, and the closest exits – front, mid and rear – had to be used.
>
> Struggling against the centrifugal force and buffeting of a large aircraft spinning out of the sky, I sidled crab-like along the floor to the front exit. It had been left gaping open by those crew who had already evacuated.

Penny and Squadron Leader 'Butch' Surtees clawed their way towards the rush of cold air from the open hatch, as the stricken bomber corkscrewed into its death dive. In the rush to get out, Surtees inadvertently left his radio intercom cable connected. Penny unplugged it to avoid being tangled up by the long cable, which could easily trip one up.[6]

> 'Butch' and I left the aircraft almost together in a rather undignified scramble, but we were separated in an instant when the gale-like air

outside hit us. I can only describe my exit as being like a champagne cork leaving its bottle! Fortunately my parachute opened satisfactorily, after I had reacted to the fact that, in my haste I had clipped it on my harness with the release handle on the left rather than the required right-hand for right-handed people. The aircraft crashed and began exploding and blazing furiously, while I was still in the air drifting away in the wind from the crash-site.

Penny landed clumsily in the dark onto unknown terrain, and stumbled into a muddy bank overhanging a dyke. He took some time to collect his thoughts, gave thanks to the Almighty for his survival, and hoped for a similar outcome for his crew.

I also thought of the reactions of my new wife and parents when they received official notification from the Air Ministry that I was 'Missing in Action'. Automatically I got out of my parachute and harness, used a knife to cut off the top portions of my flying boots, and with my badges of rank and aircrew insignia, disposed of everything by pushing it all into the mud of the dyke bank.

He was uncertain whether he might be on the German side of the border. By rough estimation and using as best as he could the uniform button compass issued for just this dilemma Penny moved off in a westerly direction,

It was necessary that I get away from the crash-site as far as possible, but I had to rest from time to time to gather my wits. I moved from cover to cover stumbling into unforeseen obstacles, until it became obvious to me that I was travelling in a wide meandering circle. I began to feel very much lost, alone and desperate!

In that frame of mind I eventually came across what looked to be a small wooden bridge. All was silent, the bridge seemed unguarded, and I decided to try my luck! If I was in Holland, and very fortunate, I might find somebody not antagonistic to the British, and sympathetic to my situation, or at least be picked up by local police rather than a German patrol – not an attractive prospect for Bomber Command aircrew at that time of the war.

After crossing over the bridge Penny found that he had arrived in what looked to him at the time, and in the dark, to be a small farming village. Still not sure whether he was in Germany or Holland, and hoping that it was unlikely that there were any German troops in such a small place, Penny thought that he would take a chance and look for a place to shelter in the village.

First concealing myself by the bridge and surveying the lie of the land, I then crept along the darkened streets, ducking from one building to another. In the end, finding nowhere to hide, I decided to knock on the back door of a small house. I did so as quietly as I could so that only any occupant could hear my knocks. Eventually the door was opened by a man. I flapped my arms like a bird and whispered hoarsely, 'R-A-F, R-A-F'.

In that instant Penny did not know whether he was confronted by a Nazi supporter or not.

Instinctively, a startled man in the doorway ushered him quickly into his back room. It turned out that he was in the small Dutch town of Ossenzijl, and the house-owner was Jan de Boer, who seemed welcoming. It could have been so different.

Once Jan had apparently satisfied himself that my scruffy appearance and distressed state of mind was authentic, he put me at ease, gave me some food, and did his best to make me comfortable. I wondered what would happen next, but in a while I drifted off to sleep.

Fear of arrest by the Gestapo was pervasive amongst the civilian population. Even a sympathiser with the Allied cause might have slammed the door in Penny's face. A Gestapo ploy at the time was for one of them to pose in a discarded blue battledress of a captured or dead RAF airman in order to infiltrate the resistance and escape organisations in occupied countries. Penny had been lucky.

He slept for some time, albeit fitfully, but deep enough not to notice when Jan de Boer removed what was left of his RAF battledress and took it away to be destroyed. 'Soon after I awoke things began to happen. Some visitors came in to inspect who had arrived in their midst.'

Later a police officer came in. Penny thought that this was the forerunner of being taken into custody, and then a subsequent handover to German authorities.

After close questioning I found that the police officer was putting me at ease, and he then began talking of my repatriation back home to England. In my conversations with him, and any of those I met while in the de Boer household, I had to be very careful not to disclose any information of a sensitive military nature. Our training in that regard was that we should disclose little beyond 'number, rank and name'. However, the police officer and the others who visited me impressed me with their obvious friendliness, vigorous hand-shaking, and surprisingly their singing of 'It's a long way to Tipperary' and other songs in the English language.

At the same time this openness worried Penny a great deal since he was well aware that, if word got to the German authorities that they were keeping a British airman hidden, all concerned would be in grave danger of imprisonment, torture and death.

> By this time a complete set of civilian clothing had been produced to replace my RAF battledress, and I had handed over my European money pack. The clothing was second-hand but quite presentable, and I had no further use of money. A few days had passed when a young Dutchman, Peter, arrived, and talked to me about plans for my return to England. He was impressive, assured and competent, and only about three to four years older than myself I thought, yet he was instrumental in helping people through Holland and on to Belgium. Peter and his girlfriend, Mimi, got to know me pretty well, but for obvious reasons I wasn't allowed into their confidence.

In the next few weeks Peter arranged Dutch identity papers, photographs and ration books for Penny in a false name. He never divulged his own full name, nor did he mention the deadly risks being taken to obtain these forged documents. When it was considered time for Penny to move on, Peter and others, one of whom was known as 'Pop' Zietima, arrived with bicycles on which they rode to the town of Meppel.

> There I made the acquaintance of the Pastor van Nooten and his wife, with whom I was to stay for a time. They had four children, who all attended school while I was there. I would bet that there are very few children of their age who could keep the secret of harbouring an RAF airman, especially when it was 'news' one could boast about to friends!
>
> The van Nootens shared their meagre food rations with me without hesitation. At times, probably because of being a young man, I was served with more than my fair share, leaving me feeling very guilty. They treated me as one of their family and readily risked their lives, and those of their children, to look after me. The penalty in most cases at that time was torture by the Gestapo to identify accomplices, then execution.

For most of the time Penny was confined to a small attic room unless there was a warning of a possible raid by the police, German troops or the Gestapo. Then in a matter of seconds he would race downstairs, out to the back garden and into a tiny 'bolt-hole'. The building opposite the van Nootens' house was a police post frequented by Germans. Although this close proximity meant it unlikely that the German authorities would suspect Pastor van Nooten of anything, the need for secrecy was of no less paramount importance.

On one occasion I was made aware that I could be compromised quite innocently. A school teacher warned the van Nootens that their RAF 'visitor' should refrain from teaching the children English songs such as 'Old McDonald's farm'!

As Penny's stay with the van Nootens stretched out to three weeks, he was increasingly anxious to leave. While being worried about his presence in their house and the risks it brought, at the same time he was also somewhat reluctant to say farewell to such a fine family. 'On occasions plans for my departure were either cancelled or postponed, due no doubt to breakdowns in escape routes. However, eventually Peter came to me with a plan.'

Arrangements had been put in place with resistance organisations in Belgium, France and Spain, who supported the Allies, to escort Penny overland to the Spanish border, then through the Pyrenees and Spain to Gibraltar. In a journey south through Holland to the Belgian border, at times on foot, by bicycle, bus or other vehicular transport, Penny was to be always accompanied by a Dutch person. In each country Penny was provided with a different fictitious identity, supported by fake documentation.

After passing through towns such as Zwolle and Tilburg they reached the Belgian border where immigration officials demanded identification papers from Penny. They were false of course – would they be accepted? Penny played dumb, relying on his Dutch companion to speak for him. Fortunately, he was not forced to speak, his papers were accepted, and he was able to ride his bicycle into Belgium.

After travelling in various ways and being housed at various locations I reached Brussels, where I was taken to stay with M. and Mme Pirart who cared for me. I encountered many other Belgian 'helpers', whose names understandably were not made known to me. In the larger cities there was far more of the German military in evidence, and in Belgium I had some tricky moments.

My travel on foot was usually a process of following a previously identified person at a safe distance whereas, in trains or motor transport by necessity, we travelled closer or together. Through Belgium and France travel was at times spasmodic, and interrupted by gaps in the 'Comet Line' escape organisation, which was processing my passage. I felt like a parcel in a way, but I accepted the problems involved with such unrehearsed undercover travel as it was beset with danger and security considerations at every step. This was a lethal business for everyone concerned.

Once in France Penny was handed over to people in the French Resistance. Within the resistance movement in occupied France, there were groups such as the 'Comet Line' whose chief mission was to rescue downed Allied aircrew and guide them to the south by devious undercover means so as to reach political safety in neutral Spain.[7] On reaching Paris, Penny was housed by a Mme Lucienne Dugarde, who hosted a regular Paris radio programme with tacit German approval. Penny heard it rumoured that Mme Dugarde was said to even have a personal liaison with a German officer as a deception to hide her true sympathies.

> If true this would have been a most advantageous arrangement, as a cover for her role of assisting evaders. After a day or so with her I was taken by a 'Comet Line' operative to the Paris Gare du Nord station where we made contact with a young attractive girl who had purchased train tickets for the two of us to Bordeaux.
>
> I think her name was Anne Brunelleman but, as with many others, I was unable to confirm it. She was another 'Comet Line' heroine who sat by my side in a carriage all the way to Bordeaux and we sought to give the impression of being two young lovers. It was a little fraught when a ticket inspector confronted us. Fortunately he checked our tickets without a word being exchanged.

On reaching Bordeaux, Penny was taken by another escort to a small village at the foot of the Pyrenees. A local 'helper' housed him until Basque guides could be arranged to lead Penny over the mountains to Spain.

> I hoped that my age and fitness level would stand me in good stead, since now in November the journey over the Pyrenees would be very cold and strenuous. Although we wore the cork-soled Spanish footwear that we had been given, we were flimsily dressed for what I was told would be arduous non-stop hiking and climbing. One early evening, accompanied by two Basque mountain guides and four other French 'evaders', we left the village under cover of darkness. We had to reach the first hideaway before dawn of the next day.

So as to avoid detection the practice employed for crossing the Pyrenees was to walk at night and rest at pre-arranged hidden locations during daylight. Local Basque guides were well prepared for the mountains, with sheepskin coats, mountain boots and survival gear in knapsacks. Because of the danger of being seen and caught, the guides preferred to choose moonless nights for crossing the Pyrenees, being able to rely on their ingrained knowledge of the terrain.[8]

> Our guides were obviously very knowledgeable and experienced. On one occasion they amazed us by producing from a bush, which appeared

no different from any others, a bottle of particularly fiery drink. This was most acceptable, since clambering through uneven rocky paths, and wading hand-in-hand through very cold mountain streams, was an exhausting ordeal. But there was no quarter given in the pace set by our guides, who were of course conscious of the dire consequences of being apprehended.

Even under the best of conditions the walking and climbing routes over the Pyrenees held many risks of a fall, with no recourse to any rescue service, that could result in serious injury or death. To cross the Pyrenees on foot was an arduous, harrowing and dangerous trek, and even more so at night to evade capture. Patrols by the German Gestapo, Vichy French police and German Alpine troops on one side, and Spanish authorities on the other, each on the lookout to catch Allied airmen or French Resistance escapers, made the mountainous route to Spain a fearsome challenge. To take it on in winter was doubly so.[9]

For four nights or maybe more (Penny did not remember exactly) they trekked over little-used tracks, often on terrain where one slip would send a man crashing over a precipice to his death. Each day they hunkered down, huddling to keep warm and out of the wind, hardly daring to move, and praying that a distant drone was not a German patrol aircraft searching for them. Even the gradual descent into Spain required similar precautions, so as to avoid being caught by patrols of the Spanish border police.

Naturally Penny and the other evaders were very relieved to find themselves in Spain undetected, although they knew that the Allies were not much in favour with the Spanish authorities at that time. They were then housed in several locations en route as they were taken by various means of transport to San Sebastian on the Bay of Biscay.

There while still undercover we were contacted by an Englishman, who turned out to be an Under-Secretary of the British Embassy. He drove us in his Diplomatic Corps car to Madrid, where we were accommodated with a number of other evaders in a hut built for that purpose in the British Embassy grounds. Although it was not uncommon for the Embassy to be assaulted and stoned by the local population, I began to feel reasonably safe for the first time, seemingly on protected British soil.

Penny's next move was by British Embassy transport to the UK's military base at Gibraltar, where he arrived on 30 November. It was three months since he had taken off in the Pathfinder Force to bomb Berlin.

I was able to send a telegram to my wife and parents, so at last they heard from me, and would know that I was alive. And I was provided with an RAF uniform, so that I could change out of my civilian clothes. From Gibraltar I flew to England in a Dakota aircraft.

In June 1943 Herbert Penny had married Gladys Major at Chingford in Essex. After three months of only knowing that her new husband was missing and probably dead, Gladys received his telegram from Gibraltar, telling her that he was alive and safe on her twenty-first birthday.

Of the rest of Penny's crew that night of 31 August/1 September 1943, Squadron Leader Surtees and Pilot Officer Wooley were taken prisoner by the Germans. Four others were killed when the bomber crashed: Flight Lieutenant Newsham DFC (navigator), Flight Sergeant Griffin (air gunner), Pilot Officer Brown (flight engineer), and Sergeant Sutton (air gunner) were buried at Kuinre General Cemetery, south-east of Lemmer, Holland. Penny's aircraft J-Johnny was one of twenty Halifax bombers that did not return. In a bad night for Bomber Command, forty-seven aircraft in all were lost, 7.7 per cent of the total force despatched.[10]

* * *

At the end of the war Penny progressed in the RAF to become a group captain, and served in Japan, Jordan, Iraq and Singapore, before becoming CO at RAF Uxbridge. He and Gladys had three sons, Andrew, Nicholas and David. In 1970 Penny left the RAF, and took up a management appointment in Tasmania, Australia. Following that, he held a number of senior management positions in various government organisations until retirement. In 2016 Herbert Penny passed away at age ninety-four.[11]

Penny became a supporter of the RAF Escaping Society and its Charitable Fund. On 20 June 1944 he had attended a memorial service at the Church of St Martin-in-the-Fields, London, for the RAF and Allied air forces officers, who were shot by the Germans after escaping from Stalag Luft III. Two of those victims had been comrades of Penny when he served in No. 77 Squadron.

The RAF Escaping Society's Charitable Fund was established to provide financial assistance to the thousands of people, known as 'Helpers', who secretly helped Allied airmen escape back to Britain.[12] In the post-war years Penny made a number of visits to Steenwijk, near to Ossenzijk where he first sought help, to thank some of his Helpers such as Jan de Boer, Peter and Memie van den Kurk, and Pastor van Nooten. He was instrumental in the bestowing of British awards on many Helpers.

Penny was profoundly moved and grateful to the Dutch and other Helpers 'who risked their lives in helping myself and many others to escape to freedom'. Penny's wartime experiences were always in his heart and mind, and he and his wife felt 'a part of Ossenzijk, Meppel, Kuinre, and Steenwijk communities'. To them, and so many other Helpers on his nerve-racking journey to Gibraltar, Penney owed his life.[13]

Chapter 17

Salerno survival – in the air, on the beachhead, and behind German lines

Pilot Officer Alan Peart AM DFC[1]

A t around 10,000 feet above the Salerno beaches on 13 September 1943 Pilot Officer Alan Peart, a New Zealander of No. 81 Squadron RAF, in a flight of six Spitfire fighters was on the lookout for Luftwaffe aircraft. After only four days ashore, the Allies' main amphibious landings by Fifth Army on the Italian mainland were in danger of being thrown back into the sea by powerful German counter-attacks. A crisis point had been reached for a bloody and strategic retreat from Salerno was too horrendous for the Allies to contemplate.

Naval staff plainly stated that the troops could not be re-embarked. Any attempt to do so would result in a killing

Pilot Officer Alan Peart, No. 81 Squadron RAF, 1943. (*Private collection, Alan Peart*)

ground. Such a defeat would undermine the early planning for Operations NEPTUNE and OVERLORD, the landings and battles in Normandy to occur in the summer of 1944, and put those operations at risk of being postponed. A bombardment by every Allied ship, and waves of attacks by USAAF strategic bombers, carrier-borne aircraft and Spitfire fighters of the Desert Air Force from bases in Sicily, were thrown at the German counter-attacks to avert a disaster. [2]

Peart, with five other Spitfires, all equipped with long-range fuel tanks, had flown from Milazzo in Sicily to undertake a thirty-minute defensive patrol over the Salerno beachhead. Because of Allied air superiority Peart was thinking it would be a quiet operation.

We entered Salerno's congested airspace at Angels 10 well under the umbrella of American P-38 twin-engine Lightning fighters, which were higher at about Angels 20. The place buzzed with British and American C-47 'Dakota' transports bringing in supplies. Every now and again one or more of the P-38s would dive down to a lower altitude before climbing back above us.

We were assuming that they would have picked up any German bombers that might be daring enough to enter the area above our height unescorted in broad daylight. When HMS *Warspite* in the bay suddenly erupted in flames, I immediately assumed that a submarine must have torpedoed it. However, the sea was calm with no sign of the tell-tale foam trails of torpedoes, so I scanned the space around us more closely. I was astounded to see three Dornier bombers racing away to the north.[3]

The Luftwaffe's three Dornier Do217 bombers had launched radio-guided bombs, identified later as Fritz-X and Hs293, which, in their first recorded use in the war, had sunk the USS *Savannah* and damaged HMS *Warspite*. Although the air was thick with Allied fighters, those three aircraft had crept in unobserved, by everyone as well as Peart's flight of Spitfires.

How on earth had we missed them? It was very hazy, and while we always kept a good lookout for enemy aircraft within our three-mile visual range, those we encountered were nearly always fighters above us. Bombers we hardly ever saw. Why hadn't the Americans seen them?

With no hesitation we opened our throttles wide and took off after them. The three bombers had split up to make things difficult. Flight Lieutenant Bill Goby with his number two chased one bomber, whilst I with my number two, Bryan Young, and Pilot Officer Bill Fell with his number two, all found ourselves chasing one other Dornier. The third escaped our attention.

Whereas Fell and his number two were fast closing on the bomber's tail, Peart and Young were soon in an attacking position on the port side of the Dornier at a slightly higher altitude.

The Dornier's pilot showed all the signs of hardened experience by weaving around as we approached, and suddenly changing position as we came within firing range. Bill Fell precipitately made the first attack from directly astern, aiming to get in a telling burst. The enemy gunner promptly hit him hard in reply. Fortunately for Bill the big Rolls Royce Merlin engine in front took the brunt of the fire.

With Fell's condition unknown and his aircraft damaged, his number two pulled away and joined up with Peart and Young. From an angle on the Dornier's port side Peart was the next to attack.

> I approached the Dornier deliberately applying slipping and skidding. As I came within range I straightened up, applied deflection in front of the target, and opened fire with both cannon and machine guns. For about a second nothing happened, and then flashes of bursting cannon shells appeared on the bomber's port wing.
>
> I broke off to one side making sure that I was slipping in one direction, while appearing to be flying in another. This made it difficult for the opposing gunner to shoot accurately. My colleagues also made attacks but without any apparent result. I then made my second attack adopting the same approach tactics while the bomber pilot did his best to dodge.
>
> I opened fire again with both cannon and machine guns, and this time my fire hit the bomber solidly. A large piece flew off and there was a big bang as my aeroplane flew into it. I broke off my attack and checked all instruments to see if anything was badly amiss.

The Dornier lost height, and eventually crash landed on the side of a scrub-covered hill. While obviously badly damaged, it was not on fire and Peart thought that at least some of the crew might have survived. Any such interest in the German crew's fate was quickly cut short when Peart heard Bill Fell calling for their assistance. His Spitfire, which had been badly hit in his first attack, was on fire.

> We quickly caught sight of Fell by his smoke trail some distance away and flew to his aid. His aeroplane was trailing smoke and flames, and in his cockpit it must have been blistering hot – decidedly uncomfortable. Obviously, he had to leave his aircraft at the earliest moment. In his favour he had sufficient height to use his parachute, but was having difficulty in controlling his Spitfire.

The 'abandon aircraft' procedure required the pilot to trim his aeroplane heavily nose down, in preparation for rolling it upside down. Having done this, he had to hold the aircraft level against a strong tendency to dive. He had next to undo the electrical connections to his helmet, unclip an oxygen tube, jettison his plastic canopy, release his Sutton harness which normally held him tightly to his seat, roll the aircraft upside down, and eject himself downwards so that he would miss the tail.

When entirely clear of the aeroplane, Fell must pull the D-ring near his waist and release the parachute. This procedure sounds logical and sequential but when the cockpit is searing hot and the aircraft on fire, essential steps can be overlooked. The imminent probability of an almighty explosion could also spur a too rapid execution of the exit procedures, and Fell had all of those problems to face. Peart watched in trepidation.

Fell rolled his Spitfire onto its back and left the cockpit but, as so often happens, things did not go to plan. The aircraft immediately started to dive before he was clear, and his parachute deployed at the same time. His parachute hooked over the tail-plane and the Spitfire, with Fell trailing behind, dived vertically towards the ground. We watched in horror at the certain death of a well-liked and experienced colleague.

However, just before reaching the ground he broke free and to our surprise his parachute opened. The Spitfire went into a wooded area with an explosion and a great gout of flame and smoke while Bill did one swing in his harness before his body disappeared through trees and I assumed he hit the ground close by. My wish and hopeful thought was that in the circumstances he may just have escaped with his life, but possibly with broken limbs. My colleagues didn't see the parachute open, and thought he must certainly have died.

Peart had no time to dwell on Fell's fate. He and the other two Spitfire pilots faced their own crisis. They had instinctively chased and attacked the Dornier bombers, using up fuel with the result that they had insufficient fuel remaining to return to Sicily. With little fuel left to make an urgent landing anywhere, they must find the single beachhead landing strip quickly. The strip was only about a mile from the beaches, less from the front lines of the battle, and there was no air traffic control whatsoever to give Peart any navigational guidance.

We headed in the direction of a great mushroom of dust, which I guessed may indicate the location of the heavily-used strip. As we neared it I told my two colleagues that each was on his own, and to land as quickly as possible. Landing was quite a tall order as there was a queue of Dakotas in the circuit, all trying to put down into a thick pall of dust, which completely obscured the strip itself.

As well as trying to find a descent path through the murk, the three Spitfire pilots had also to hope that they were not hit by a few Allied light anti-aircraft batteries, which were located around the perimeter and firing at barely discernible targets. It was not only atrocious visibility and dwindling fuel that was making Peart desperate to land.

My aircraft might not last much longer as it had been damaged in the engagement and my instruments told me that something was seriously wrong. I made one attempt to get into the circuit but was cut off by a Dakota forcing its way just in front of me. In desperation I flew over the top of another one that was following, and gave him my slipstream. He wobbled badly and gave way so I entered the dust pall. There was no alternative, I had to land down there.

Visibility was minimal, at times it seemed only a few yards, but I managed to put my Spitfire down somewhere at the start of the strip, with the hope that everything was clear in front. To my horror, while still at speed, another Spitfire loomed up sitting on the strip right in front of me. To avoid crashing into it, I had no recourse but to veer off the strip into the rough on the left-hand side.

There my aircraft hit some obstacle, and tipped onto its nose into a vertical position. My first reaction was one of anger at the stupid fool who had forced me to lose the first aircraft in my flying career. Then I became alarmed at the thought that my aircraft may go right over onto its back, possibly trapping me in the cockpit.

But I was lucky because my Spitfire chose to fall back onto its undercarriage. I felt furious and quit the cockpit in a hurry, to go to the stalled aircraft on the strip. I have no idea how he got there, but it was Goby's number two.

Peart helped move the aircraft a little way so its pilot was able to taxi it to a safer position. Other aircraft were rushing past unseen in the murky dust, which also cloaked constant explosions, anti-aircraft fire and the plucking sounds of passing machine-gun bullets. In fact an Allied artillery battery was firing at the enemy from the cover of some olive trees on one side of the landing strip, and their shells were traversing the landing paths of aircraft. It may have been the only time in the war that Allied fighters operated from a landing strip in front of their own artillery. Despite the chaotic situation, Peart went back to his own Spitfire, but at once realised that it had to be abandoned.[4] 'I decided that I had better find some cover. Before doing so I had to destroy a secret device we had at that time called IFF.'

The IFF (Identification, Friend of Foe) communication device, was an airborne radio identification system that consisted of a small box in the cockpit. It had a red button, which the pilot should press if there was any danger of the aircraft falling into the hands of the enemy. Pilots were informed that an explosive device would destroy the IFF box completely. As Peart looked at the red button he had a moment of hesitation.

We were not told how big the explosion would be, and whether there was any delay to allow the button pusher to escape. I didn't want to be crippled, or lose my fingers, or even my hand, so I felt just a little bit cautious. Nobody to my knowledge had ever had to press the button. It seemed obvious though, that the enemy weren't far away because of the disturbing bangs and phuts which were going on, so I had to do the deed. In the event all that happened was a fizzing sound and some smoke, but it sounded very destructive.

Peart was increasingly aware of the precariousness of his situation, so decided not to assess the damage to his crashed Spitfire, and leave it to the army to destroy the aircraft if necessary. His next problem was to trudge through the smokey murk and enemy fire, to locate where the transport aircraft were unloading and turning around to take off again.

I found an RAF Dakota pilot who was returning to Milazzo in Sicily and persuaded him to take a passenger. He was another New Zealander as it turned out. His take off was right over the German lines, where I could just about see the whites of their eyes. At any moment I expected to see holes sprouting in the floor of the aircraft, as their gunners homed in on us.

I was the first of our flight to get back to Milazzo and made my report, claiming a bomber destroyed, to be shared between the three of us. Darkness came and there was no word from the others, and we began to have grave doubts as to their safety. The next day I was amazed to find that only one other pilot from our flight of six had returned to Milazzo. Three aeroplanes had collided on take off at Salerno, and one pilot had been killed.

In a tragic multi-aircraft accident at the Salerno beachhead strip, Flight Lieutenant Goby and Sergeant Ryan were injured. Goby subsequently died of his injuries, and three aircraft were lost. This was in addition to the loss of Pilot Officer Fell, shot down by the Dornier's gunner, and whose fate was unknown. Peart had been extremely lucky to survive his crash landing on the chaotic Salerno landing strip, and get away unscathed from the front lines of the battle. It had been one of the most unfortunate days in the history of No. 81 Squadron, and a very gloomy spirit pervaded the mess.

Astonishingly, a few days later Pilot Officer Fell arrived back at the squadron uninjured. He had been listed as missing, and increasingly presumed dead. In reality he had survived his disastrous last second parachute landing, been taken prisoner by the enemy, and then incredibly escaped back through Allied lines.

As so often happened, what had seemed to be an uneventful patrol suddenly turned into a lethal encounter, resulting in disastrous consequences.

The recently gained Allied air superiority did not prevent the enemy from mounting destructive air raids. The intrusion by the Dornier bombers and their successful attack on British and US warships showed the even more severe impact they may have had without the Allies' protective air umbrella, and the role played by pilots such as Alan Peart and his colleagues. Peart's victory claim of the Dornier bomber[5] was his final victory in the Mediterranean theatre, before he and No. 81 Squadron transferred to Burma.[6]

Chapter 18

Flying blind in the blackout – catastrophe beckons.

Flight Lieutenant Verner Leslie 'Vern' Scantleton DFC[1]

When darkness descended on a Bomber Command airfield and a blackout was imposed so as to hide from Luftwaffe intruder aircraft, a bomber squadron's home base could be a dangerous place. A typical airfield which comprised two runways, one of 2,000 yards, criss-crossed by another of 1,200 yards, was a large flat featureless expanse.

Bomber Command operated predominantly at night, and all aerodromes had strict blackout conditions. In these conditions, taking off or landing meant taxiing a large heavy bomber with perhaps an all-up weight of approximately 75,000 pounds, around a perimeter to or from various dispersal points spread around the airfield. On a black, moonless, windy, wet winter's night with only a few pinpoint lights as a guide, taxiing in itself could be very demanding.

Even so, moving a heavy bomber around a blacked-out airfield, relative to other perilous challenges, was one of the lesser risks. To fly a crippled bomber back to its base airfield at night in blackout conditions, on only three of its four engines, with much of its instrumentation out of action, was one of the severest tests of a pilot's nerve and flying skills. Yet such an ordeal was faced on many occasions by pilots as they attempted to nurse a damaged aircraft, often with badly wounded or injured crew onboard, back from an operation to the safety of their home base.

*   *   *

On a winter's night above Cambridge on 6 November 1943, Flight Lieutenant Vern Scantleton held the Stirling bomber steadily climbing at approximately 7,000 feet. Vern Scantleton was twenty-two years old from Kerang in Victoria in Australia, five feet ten inches in height, medium build, and seen as having a calm personality. He had enlisted in the RAAF at age twenty, and after initial pilot training at Benalla in Victoria, he transferred to Britain, more training and eventually to No. 214 Squadron.[2]

Scantleton and his crew had taken off at 21.30 hours from Stradishall airfield which had full blackout conditions in force.[3] From his cockpit Scantleton peered into a dark moonless night.

> Suddenly out of the corner of my left eye, I saw a dark object looming up on the port side. Instinctively, I wrenched back on the control column, pulling the aircraft into a steeper upward trajectory.[4]

It was too late. Almost immediately something smashed into the port side nose of the Stirling. The tail plane of a Wellington bomber below them had collided with the nose of Scantleton's aircraft, although at the time he did not know what aircraft had hit them.

> At the moment of impact, I pressed the intercom button on the control column and called out, 'Christ!' Beyond any doubt, pulling back on the control column saved us, otherwise our two aircraft would have collided at exactly the same height, with almost certain death for both crews.

The Wellington bomber's tail ripped a massive jagged cavity, approximately ten feet in diameter at its widest, in the Stirling's nose. To Scantleton, it felt as if it was a direct hit in the bomb-aimer's position, but in those first few seconds

Flight Lieutenant Vern Scantleton's Stirling with collision 'cavity', November 1943. (*Private collection, John Scantleton*)

he did not know the extent of the damage. Was the aircraft still airworthy or was the damage fatal?

> Immediately following the collision, I was able to ascertain that we still had the aircraft under some control, but the starboard outer motor was running roughly, so I feathered it. I consulted with the navigator and we agreed that we should fly back to Base on a reciprocal course. Due to the impact of the collision, however, we assumed that the gyroscopic compass would have probably toppled and be useless, and we should rely on the P15 magnetic compass.
>
> Little were we to know that the gyroscopic compass had not toppled, and in fact the P15 compass had been knocked out by at least 45 degrees. So we were in fact not flying a reciprocal course! An urgent assessment of damage to the aircraft, which we could determine internally, showed that the airspeed indicator recorded zero which meant that the pitot head, which is located externally under the nose had been ripped off.

Compared with the Wellington which they had hit, Scantleton and his crew still had a chance to avoid a crash whereas the pilot of the Wellington, because the impact with the Stirling bomber had demolished its tail, would have lost control of his aircraft immediately. The bomber would have gone into a corkscrew spin, and centrifugal forces would have made it impossible for the crew to bale out.

The advantage for Scantleton and his crew was that the Stirling was the 'Rolls Royce' of aircraft, made by Short Brothers, the makers of the famous Sunderland flying boats. The Wellington was only a two-engine aircraft and about a third of the weight of the Stirling, which was a close adaptation of the four-engine Sunderland. Nevertheless, after around thirty minutes of effectively flying blind on the Stirling's three engines, their disastrous predicament became clear. Scantleton realised that, besides the calamitous state of their aircraft and its wrecked instruments, they were lost.

> To add to our woes we had other problems to contend with. At the time of the impact, which gouged open the port side of the Stirling's nose, the bomb-aimer was lying on his stomach in that area, map reading through the perspex viewer. The poor fellow copped the full blast of the impact, but miraculously did not suffer any broken bones. Unfortunately, his parachute was ripped open, and he was found enveloped in some seventy square yards of silk, which he was manfully trying to repack without any success.

For any pilot, knowing the air speed at all times is a vital and essential piece of information needed to fly any aircraft, particularly a large and heavy bomber.

It must be kept above stalling speed at all times in the air, except at the point of landing, and this thought was uppermost in Scantleton's mind.

> The thought of bringing an aircraft in to land with an all up weight of 75,000 pounds, at night, without knowing my air speed, was I thought, hair raising to say the least. Whilst a Stirling bomber had dual controls, I was the only pilot. The bomb-aimer was trained to act as second dickie to assist the pilot in take offs and landings. One of his functions on preparing to land was, on my instructions, to call the air speed every three or four seconds, from when the aircraft was at a height of about five hundred feet, and on the descent in the approach funnel.
>
> Without a known air speed, the only way to attempt to bring the aircraft in safely, was under high power and going like a 'bat out of hell'. Our attempts to call Base on R/T proved useless as the set was damaged during the impact. We called, 'Mayday', 'Mayday', which was the international distress call, a number of times but obviously we were only talking to ourselves. The trailing aerial must have been ripped off in the collision, and this meant that the wireless operator was unable to transmit or receive messages.
>
> Having decided we were lost, Roy Forbes, our New Zealand navigator, took some Astro shots and determined our position. By some outstanding calculations under extreme pressure, he worked out a course to set for our Base, this time using the gyroscopic compass.

By reverting to the operable gyroscopic compass, Forbes got them back on a home course and approaching their Stradishall base airfield.

> On arriving over our Base, we fired a number of red Very Lights to indicate our distress situation and hoped that they would clear the runway for our sole use.
>
> At one stage I gave the opportunity to some of the crew to bale out, but all refused to do so. This was surprising as they must have thought our chances of survival in a crash landing to be fairly grim. It was unsaid but as one of the parachutes was useless, it meant that in the event of a forced bale out one of us faced certain death going down with the plane.

The option of leaving someone in a doomed aircraft was not broached. Fortunately, the overwhelming trust of the crew in Scantleton's flying skill and judgement meant that such a terrible decision did not have to be made. But he could not know whether the collision damage had extended to the aircraft's undercarriage.

Since we had decided to land, I selected the undercarriage to be lowered. Bad luck again, nothing happened. The huge wheels and the 16-foot oleo legs of the undercarriage are operated independently by electric motors on either side. As these were obviously unserviceable, we were left with no alternative but to get the wheels down manually. This was a slow, laborious job as it takes six hundred turns for each wheel to be lowered. All this time we were stooging around above the airfield at a fairly low altitude in an aircraft with unknown external damage.

Eventually, once the wheels were locked down, the time had come for Scantleton to land the aircraft. Without the airspeed indicator and other instrumentation, he faced a moment of truth.

I brought the aircraft in under high power and in hindsight at an excessive speed. Over the start of the runway, I pulled the throttles off and hopefully expected the aircraft to settle. Instead, our excessive speed would not let the aircraft stall into a landing, and we went tearing down the runway using its length up at an alarming rate. Finally, the aircraft settled onto the runway and it was a great relief to find that the undercarriage did not collapse on impact. Our relief, however, was short lived. On applying the air brakes they failed completely.

The braking system had been damaged, we had total loss of air pressure and therefore no braking power whatsoever. As it had become apparent that we would overshoot, the only remaining option was to ground loop the aircraft, hope that the oleo legs would not collapse, and that, in the wide arc required, we would not collide with some stationary object, which of course we would have no way of avoiding. Fortunately the oleo legs withstood the stress of a complete ground loop, and in time we ground to a halt. We were all pleased to be back on terra firma, and were met by a welcoming party who were all keen to learn what had happened.

Ground staff at Stradishall were aware that a collision had taken place. With no R/T or W/T response from Scantleton's aircraft they had assumed that his was one of the planes involved and were hoping that it might have survived and arrive back. The gaping hole in the nose of the Stirling drew many onlookers, astounded that the bomber had been able to land safely. Photographs were taken, some with Scantleton and crew posing beside the huge cavity.

I noticed over the next few days that the Senior Medical Officer on the station sought me out in the mess on several occasions to pass the time of day. Was it that he was looking for some twitching in my eyes, or the shaking of my hand which was holding a pint of beer? Next day the aircraft was assessed as a total write-off, and was towed to a remote part of the airfield. No doubt it supplied valuable spares over the next few months.

Because the collision occurred between two RAF aircraft over Britain, and seven crew of the Wellington bomber had lost their lives, it was deemed necessary to hold a court of inquiry. The interrogators' prime target was of course Scantleton.

Two Investigating officers interviewed me and also took statements from three senior members of the crew. A date was set for the forthcoming Inquiry about a month after the collision. A dour Legal Wing Commander was President when the Court was convened. After the preliminary waffle, the Clerk began reading the statements made by the three crew members. The first stated that the first knowledge of the impending collision was when the Skipper pushed the intercom button and called out 'Christ'.

The second statement followed similar lines and again quoted that the first he knew of the impending collision was when the skipper called out 'Christ' on the intercom. The third statement was being read and as it also reached the part concerning my exclamation of 'Christ!', the dour President held up his hand to stop proceedings, turned to me and said 'Mr Scantleton, tell the Court, was that blasphemy or were you just appealing for help?'

Scantleton did not record his answer, but the court of inquiry cleared him of any charge. He continued to fly with No. 214 Squadron and, after completing thirty operations, transferred to a training role. Subsequently he volunteered to undertake a second tour with No. 214 Squadron flying B.17 Flying Fortresses. Clearly the Medical Officer had also not seen any tremors as Scantleton held his glass of beer in a firm hand.

Part V

1944: January to June

Chapter 19

The jungle is the only refuge

In late December 1943 Catalina flying boats of three RAAF squadrons, Nos 11, 20 and 64, began bombing the Japanese-held port of Kavieng, as US forces prepared to invade the south-west of New Britain at Arawe. Kavieng sits on the north-west promontory of New Ireland, which is an island to the east of Papua New Guinea. New Ireland, and the island of New Britain to its south, form part of the Bismarck Archipelago, lying between the south-east coast of Papua New Guinea and the Solomon Islands. Those bombing operations by Catalinas were designed to destroy and disrupt Japanese shipping, port facilities, oil and other supplies, and continued throughout January and February 1944.[1]

*　　*　　*

E & E Report No 44/408 – Secret, HQ Allied Air Forces, South West Pacific Area, 15 April 1944 Secret (Interrogation by MIS-X Section)

The following account relates to an operation by a Catalina (PBY-5) flying boat No. A24–34 of No. 11 Squadron RAAF on 7 February 1944, based upon E & E Report No 44/408 (see above). It includes the edited testimony as stated by the four following crew members, who were joint narrators at the briefing:

Flying Officer Ian D.V. Ralfe
Flying Officer Allan B. Liedl
Sergeant Murray R. Howard
Sergeant Harry F. Jones

On 7 February 1944 at 10.40 hours from an RAAF coastal base near Darwin in the Northern Territory of Australia, Catalina flying boat No A24–34 took off on a night bombing raid on the Japanese-held port of Kavieng in New Ireland. Carrying 4,300lb of bombs the Catalina was the sole aircraft in a nuisance raid.[2]

For an outward flight of around twelve hours the Catalina's crew of ten comprised:

Crew Member	Role
Squadron Leader John F. Todd	Captain, First Pilot
Flying Officer Ian D.W. Ralfe	Second Pilot
Flight Lieutenant Brian Stacey	Extra Second Pilot
Flying Officer Frank Pocknee	Navigator/Observer
Flying Officer Allan B. Liedl	First Wireless Operator/Air Gunner
Flight Sergeant Murphy	Second Wireless Operator/Air Gunner
Sergeant Frederick Woolley	First Engineer
Sergeant Earnest Kraehe	Second Engineer
Sergeant Murray Howard	Fitter
Sergeant Harry F. Jones	Armourer

In undertaking a nuisance raid the captain and his crew were ordered to inflict as much damage as they could to airfields and shore installations at Panapai and Kavieng. After some twelve hours flying, at approximately 23.00 hours, the Catalina's crew looked down in bright moonlight on the Kavieng target area.

> Before we made our first run over the Panapai strip, we were flying at an altitude of 9,000 feet. No bombs were dropped on our first run, and the A/A fire was light. On our second run over Panapai, two 250lb bombs and numerous incendiaries were tossed out, and photographs were taken. A/A fire this time was heavy and intense, but not accurate, aimed at us from ships in the harbour. Our third run was made over the Kavieng strip, and this time intense and accurate A/A fire caused us to take violent evasive action. We dropped two 500lb bombs and took photographs. Large fires were observed on the south-east corner of the Panapai strip.
>
> We made a fourth run over the Kavieng strip, dropping the remaining bombs. Heavy A/A fire could be seen in the moonlight, and because of a little difficulty that we experienced in trimming the aircraft, it appeared that the tail plane and fin had been hit. Despite this we did a fifth run over the Kavieng strip with the object of taking photographs. However very intense A/A fire forced us to abandon the run.

By 24.00 hours the Catalina was out of the target area and proceeding south towards the north coast of New Britain. No serious damage to the flying boat from Japanese anti-aircraft fire was apparent, and their raid on Kavieng seemed to have been carried out successfully.

> As we were flying over the coast of New Britain, the Captain, Squadron Leader Todd instructed Sergeant Jones to bring the three 4.5 reconnaissance flares from the aircraft's blister section of the fuselage

Flying Officer Allan Liedl (front right) with Catalina crew, No. 11 Squadron RAAF, February 1944. (*Private collection, Allan Liedl*)

forward to the bunk compartment. These flares had been set for 5,000 feet. Squadron Leader Todd instructed Sergeant Jones to change the setting on one flare to 4,000 feet. As Jones in the bunk compartment turned the setting ring on one flare, a stream of sparks flowed out of the flare in the manner of a Roman candle firework.

The blister compartment towards the rear of the fuselage contained two 0.5in lateral-firing machine guns, one either side in each beam position of the blister.[3] Flying Officer Liedl was in the blister section when the flare ignited in the bunk compartment.

Just after the stream of sparks ceased, Liedl saw a thin trickle of smoke coming out of the flare, and jumped into the bunkroom. He grabbed the flare with the idea of throwing it out of the ship. Sergeant Howard, seeing what was going on, had already opened the blister to make it possible for Liedl to throw the flare out of the aircraft. Just as Liedl picked it up, the flare exploded, burning his eyes, face and hands.

The two remaining flares also exploded and everything in the bunk compartment caught fire. Flying Officer Liedl, Sergeant Jones and Flight

Lieutenant Stacey, who had been lying in the top bunk, scrambled into the blister section. With Sergeant Howard the four men were trapped there.

Squadron Leader Todd was immediately informed of the fire by First Engineer Woolley, as all crew members positioned forward of the fire took all possible measures to extinguish the flames. Sergeant Jones used the fire extinguisher in the blister, and it seemed to increase rather than diminish the blaze.

To add to our predicament, we were almost suffocated by the black smoke from the burning rubber of a dinghy, which had been stowed underneath the lower bunk in the bunk compartment. The black smoke passed through into the cockpit, where, despite opening all the windows, the First and Second Pilots were almost unable to continue operations.

When the fire first started Sergeant Howard closed the No. 6 bulkhead between the blister and the bunk compartments. The fire was so intense that it burned holes through the metal bulkhead, and the flames were being forced out as if from an acetylene torch. The situation of the four men in the blister was becoming increasingly serious. The fire was clearly out of control.

Squadron Leader Todd instructed Flight Sergeant Murphy, the Second Wireless Operator, to send out an emergency report to Fifth Bomber Command on the reconnaissance frequency. Murphy heard Fifth Bomber Command pass a message on to our base to the effect that we were going down in flames, and giving our approximate emergency position at that time. After hearing that the message had been received, Murphy was forced to evacuate his position because of the suffocating fumes that were sweeping into the compartment. Thus we were unable to give any later reports about our position.

On being notified that the fire could not be extinguished, Squadron Leader Todd immediately dropped off height rapidly from 8,500 feet, and turned about fifteen degrees to port. We reached the south coast of New Britain at an altitude almost at sea level. It was the Captain's intention to try to follow the south coast of New Britain west as far as possible, in the hope of reaching the Allied forces' bridgehead at Arawe.

By this time the fire had spread to the engineer's department, and the First Engineer, Sergeant Woolley, advised Squadron Leader Todd that the aircraft was in danger of breaking in half. From the cockpit Woolley could see flames coming through the side of the fuselage and the engineer's window.

Squadron Leader Todd immediately crash-landed the Catalina into the sea about fifty yards from the shore. The landing was made very difficult by the fact that a portion of the hull had been burned through, and the floats could not be lowered because of the fire in the engineer's compartment. On touching the water, the aircraft swung to the right and rose fifty feet into the air. Striking the water a second time the Catalina once more swung violently to the right, and it took both pilots to keep the aircraft's nose from diving in.

Todd cut the engines and the Catalina drifted into a reef still some fifty yards from the shoreline.

Sergeant Jones was the first to leave the aircraft, jumping into the water from the blister before the Catalina came to a stop. As soon as the aircraft struck the reef Flying Officer Liedl jumped into the water and swam around to the nose under the bow. By this time the fire was raging intensely inside the engineer's compartment, and .38 calibre ammunition and sea markers were exploding. Since the petrol tanks were also now in danger of exploding, the Captain ordered all crew members to abandon the aircraft. As the water was not very deep, we all waded onto the beach safely, with nothing more serious than a few burns and scratches.

As we came ashore the .50 calibre ammunition began to explode in the Catalina, and the pounding of the waves broke the aircraft in two.

Flying Officer Allan Liedl
(standing at back) with Catalina
No. A24-34 'Some Chicken'.
(*Private collection, Allan Liedl*)

Having come to the beach, we were forced to drop behind rocks because the .50 calibre ammunition was flying everywhere. We could do nothing but watch the Catalina burn. At approximately 02.15 hours Squadron Leader Todd and Flying Officer Ralfe made a reconnaissance to find a more convenient spot to spend the rest of the night. They found a place about a quarter of a mile from where we came ashore, and some fifty yards inland.

Some crew members then returned to the aircraft to attempt to destroy the classified codes, and special equipment. They found that the bow and stern were high in the air, the aircraft's fuselage having broken in the middle. Also, because the main plane was broken, the floats were swinging forward and back with the surf.

Sergeants Jones and Woolley tried to board the aircraft and were able to do so, but were unable to get inside. As they crawled along the fuselage, flames continued to shoot out of the engineer's compartment, although the petrol tanks did not explode contrary to our expectations.

The fire had been partially subdued by the breaking of the waves over the aircraft. However, the metal was so intensely hot that, as soon as the waves abated, flames would break out again.

Sergeant Jones was only able to reach inside the engineer's compartment, and drag out some small water tanks, and the thermos flask containing cold tea. Sergeant Woolley recovered a pair of binoculars from the cockpit. By now it appeared to Squadron Leader Todd that any further attempt at that time to recover anything further from the ship would probably be fatal to those trying to do so. He decided to leave any such further attempts until the morning when the fire would probably have gone out, and he ordered all members of the crew back to shore. We all returned to the place previously chosen, we posted guards, and the burns of crew members were attended to with applications of the cold tea.

Various other items and equipment, which the crew recovered from the stricken Catalina, included such as: one rubber dinghy complete with a medical kit and a marine distress signal flare, one parachute, four revolvers, five jungle knives, and four of the regular RAAF-type emergency jungle kits.

During the night the guards were changed at regular intervals. At the first sign of dawn, Flying Officer Ralfe and Sergeant Jones made more reconnaissance to the west to find out whether there were any Japs in the area. They proceeded about a half mile to a point where they could see all about the bay with the binoculars. No sign of any Japs were seen.

Shortly after Ralfe and Jones had returned, our guards saw three natives approaching from the east of the beach. Squadron Leader Todd was at once advised, and although two of the natives upon seeing the guards ran back in the direction from which they had come, one approached us and Squadron Leader Todd questioned him.

He spoke quite good English, and told us that the Japs had seen our aircraft crash in flames and sent him to look for us. He advised us to get away from the beach, back to an abandoned plantation and hide there. Among the things he said were words to the effect, 'Why the hell didn't you get out of here last night?' He seemed very frightened of the Japs, and appeared anxious to leave us.

He told us that had there been just four of us instead of ten, he might have been able to hide us himself. He told us that the Japs had made slaves of the local Kanakas people in this area, and had them working on a big road a few miles to the east. After he left us, Sergeant Woolley and Flight Sergeant Murphy were posted as guards along the beach and Squadron Leader Todd set about organising our retreat into the interior.

Todd proposed that the crew of ten should be split up into three groups, each to seek refuge separately in the jungle. The first group would consist of Todd, Pocknee, and Kraehe, the second of Ralfe, Liedl, Howard, and Jones, and the third Stacey, Woolley and Murphy. They then began separating equipment to be divided among the three groups.

Suddenly we heard sounds of Jap commands from the direction of the beach. Some of us were certain that the commands were in English, and were shouts of 'Halt … one … two'. Hearing this, although we heard no shots fired, we gathered that our two guards, Woolley and Murphy, had been jumped by the Japs and taken prisoner.

The rest of us immediately gathered some of the equipment, which was lying on the ground, and dashed into the bush in an approximately north-westerly direction, with the exception of Flight Lieutenant Stacey, who ran off roughly to the north-east.

In the panic of the moment Stacey fled without any equipment whatsoever, and the others did not know why he went in the opposite direction. The remaining seven crew members came together about a hundred yards further into the bush, where they held a short council of war.

Squadron Leader Todd decided that we should split into two parties as previously agreed, and go in different directions. Thus if the Japanese should pick up the trail of one party, it might be possible for the other party to escape capture. Squadron Leader Todd took his party to the west, and the four of us, Ralfe, Liedl, Howard and Jones, went in a north-westerly direction.

The equipment taken by the four members of our party, consisted of: two .38-calibre revolvers and sixty rounds of ammunition, three knives, one parachute, one first aid kit from the dinghy, one complete RAAF-type emergency jungle kit, and a second such kit lacking the compass and the cloth map.

Flying Officer Ralfe took the compass and map out of the kit, and planned for us to follow a course due north. We set out on this course for approximately a quarter of an hour, when two small calibre shots were heard from the direction of the beach.

Although they had a cloth map from the intact emergency jungle kit, it was soon lost. Ralfe had placed it in a pocket of his flying suit. On hearing those two shots from the direction of the beach, the four men ran on as fast as they could. In the rush the cloth map must have fallen from Ralfe's pocket. The sounds of the two shots were ominous for the fate of the two crew left behind, posted as guards on the beach, Woolley and Murphy.

It was our plan at this point to go into the interior, because of being told that the Nips occupied the coast. We thought that we would go as far into the mountains as possible and see if we could live off the land. On that first day when we travelled away from the beach, we were for the most part in swamps. We then came through some low mountainous country, where sufficient palms and water vines to sustain us could be found.

For two and a half days they proceeded into the mountains living entirely off palm trees and one pawpaw taken from a deserted and overgrown cultivated area. Their jungle knife enabled them to cut down the limpong palms for food. At one point they had to cross a fairly wide crocodile-infested river, by tying several logs together with shroud lines from the parachute.

After crossing the river we found a little bay where a fresh-water stream ran into a brackish river. At the head of the bay there was a small clearing in which we saw an empty Jap rice tin, and a trail leading away from the clearing. The Jap rice tin made us feel that the spot was insecure, and that it would be unwise to follow the native trail. So we continued beyond the clearing and made our camp that night on a ridge. During the night we heard two shots and a burst of machine-gun fire, which bore out our thought that Japs were in the vicinity, making us go on further inland.

Around mid-day the group ran into extremely rocky country, full of dry gullies and lacking any possible food from wild vegetation or water.

At this point we decided to turn back, and make for the coast in a south-westerly direction toward the Allied beach-head. Very soon we came upon a native trail that led in a south-easterly direction. Despite our intention to walk south-westerly, we thought it advisable to follow this trail. In three hours we found that we had returned to the clearing where we had seen the Jap rice tin, a distance which we had covered in one and a half days of wandering around the bush. We decided to make our camp in a clearing on the opposite side of the bay, and built a fire.

The jungle cover was so dense that even on high ground it was impossible for them to get their bearings.

While we were at this camp Jones shot a pig and Liedl shot a scrub fowl. We ate the pig with relish, it being the first real food since the crash, and kept the scrub fowl for next day. Ralf made several attempts to increase our food supply by shooting fish, but his attempts proved the lack of utility of the .38 calibre revolver. Even when the revolver was shot directly into a school of fish from a stationary rest at about five feet range, it only caused the fish to scatter. And that attracted a crocodile to come down to examine the cause of the disturbance in the water.

They made other efforts to catch fish with homemade fish hooks constructed from safety-pins, and a three-pronged spear fashioned out of wood. Despite baiting the safety-pins with prawns and shellfish, the fish were not attracted. The wooden spear was also ineffective.

On our third day at this camp, while sitting around the fire, we saw a Jap river patrol coming up the river. First we sighted a small canoe with two natives and two Nips coming from the river into the bay. The two Japs and one native jumped out onto the beach, while the other native paddled the canoe away back up the river.

Within five or six minutes a large canoe with eight Nips and two natives came around the river bend and into the bay, followed by the other native in the small canoe. The Japs had obviously seen our fire, and as we saw them begin to head our way, we dived into the swamps at the back of the clearing, without attempting to recover any of our equipment.

In a panicky flight they left behind a parachute, the medical kit, one knife, and much of their clothing. Avoiding capture and staying alive were their only thoughts.

We waded through swamps, and then, to throw the Japs off our trail, we forded the river to its opposite bank. Then we struck a south-westerly course back towards the coast. We avoided all native trails, and saw no natives whatsoever. For four days we had no food other than from the palms, and one malted milk tablet every other day for each of us. We had saved our atabrine tablets, and took one also every other day.

After four days we reached a Jap road near the coast, and spent the night in a deserted village. Plenty of coconuts and water were available at this place. The next morning we set off along the Jap road going south-west. Eventually we reached a river, where the road came to an end.

Despite the evidence of Jap troops being not far away, the four airmen decided to spend the night where they had come to a halt. They were in no condition to go on anywhere in the dark.

Next morning we found a large native canoe on the beach. It was in a dilapidated state, the outrigger having rotted through, and the canoe itself was holed in its hull by borers. We decided to try and repair it. We could then fill it with coconuts, and once we had paddled it to the sea, we would sneak down the coast at night, and hide close to the beach at night. The necessity of using a canoe for the journey along the shoreline had become apparent to us in crossing streams and rivers infested with salt-water crocodiles.

Their intention was still to keep going, to try to reach Allied lines. Jones and Howard worked all day plugging the holes in the canoe hull. But when the four of them tried it out on the river they found that the canoe was so heavy in the water that, in their weakened condition, they did not have the strength to paddle and control it.

We also lacked equipment and material to make it fully watertight and sound. We therefore opted to abandon the canoe, stop for one more night back in the deserted village, and continue on foot. It was a group decision in spite of Flying Officer Liedl's and Sergeant Jones' boots being almost torn through. Mosquitoes and sandflies were biting us continuously. Those bites and scratches on our exposed skin from the swamp undergrowth were becoming increasingly infected. Flying Officers Ralfe and Liedl, who were wearing shorts, short-sleeved shirts and short socks, were suffering from big sores that were developing on their bodies.

During the afternoon, as we rested in this deserted village, four natives appeared. They didn't say much to us but offered us food, taro, kau kau and sugar cane, which we gladly accepted, and gave them safety pins in exchange. The natives told us that they were from a new village, which they had built back in the mountains, when they had evacuated the village where we were camped.

Since their abandoned gardens were in this neighbourhood, they had come down to get some food. These four natives left us, but at about 20.00 hours two other natives from the same mountain village came to us, and told us in Pidgin English that the Japs were coming back to this deserted village tomorrow. They had been sent by their *Luluai*, their headman, to tell us to come with them to their new village.

Although the natives told them that the Japs were only about four miles away, the four airmen did not want to move until first light. They were in no condition to contemplate stumbling through the jungle in the dark and so spent the rest of a tense night in the deserted village.

The next day we walked with the two natives north-east into the mountains to their new village. It took us about four hours, sometime walking on native trails, and part of the way in a native canoe. Shortly after we arrived at the mountain village, they told us about a white man settlement on the north side of the island. We asked if they could take us there, and they agreed to do so, but told us that it was a seven-day journey.

They suggested that we stay with them for three more days, eating their food until we had enough strength to do the journey. During these three days the sores on our bodies became worse, and extremely ugly tropical ulcers appeared on Flying Officer's Liedl's right leg. Despite the fact that his entire leg was inflamed as high as his thigh, after the three days' respite we set off for the north coast.

In response to their enquiries of the natives as to whether they had seen, or had any knowledge of the other crew members, they said they knew nothing of them.

We started off across the island with eighteen native carriers and walked for a full day. Our progress was slowed considerably due to the deteriorating condition of Flying Officer Liedl's leg. On seeing Liedl's leg the natives suggested that we rest for a day at our first night's stopping place, and we should write a note for help, with which they would send one of their men ahead to the white settlement.

After a day's rest we continued on and, by easy stages but through extremely difficult country, we climbed over to the north side of the mountain range. Our native messenger made the journey to the white settlement in just two days and after four days the natives despatched by the white settlement reached us. They brought with them European food, clothing, medical supplies, and equipment, as well as a cook boy and a doctor boy.

By this time the number of natives had grown from eighteen to around eighty. All of the natives appeared to know of the white settlement.

> The natives seemed anxious to join us in our efforts to reach them. After six days one of the men from the white settlement came out and met us. We were forced to remain at the spot where we met him for some time, due to him developing a fever, and also on account of Flying Officer Liedl's condition. Eventually on or about the 4 or 5 March, the three of us, excepting Flying Officer Liedl, walked into the white settlement.

Approximately one week later Flying Officer Liedl arrived on foot. The four airmen remained there until 8 April 1945 when they were evacuated from New Britain and flown back to Australia. It was two months to the day since the disastrous fire in the Catalina and the crash landing into the sea. The jungle had indeed been their refuge, but it was only the help and care of the local people that saved their lives.

The six other aircrew of the Catalina had been captured by the Japanese and only Stacey survived until liberation at the end of the war.[4]

Chapter 20

A baptism of fire in the 'Big Week' for B-Beer

Flying Officer Bryan Good DFC[1]

For one crew of a Lancaster bomber fresh from training and flying their first operation over enemy territory it would truly be a baptism of fire. It was 19 February 1944, the day when Allied air forces began Operation ARGUMENT, the 'Big Week' onslaught against Germany in the largest air battle of the war. The objective of 'Big Week' was to destroy Germany's factories for Luftwaffe fighter aircraft, so as to enable Allied air forces to gain air superiority before D Day without which the liberation of Europe could not go ahead.

Over 6,000 aircraft of the US Eighth Air Force and RAF Bomber Command commenced a week of round-the-clock raids on German cities and targets. It would be the most intense air bombardment ever, and see the USAAF lose 254 aircraft and the RAF 157. For any new inexperienced crew, to fly a first operation on this day, and in the subsequent operations of 'Big Week', the odds on coming through unscathed were long.[2]

*　　*　　*

Survival in disastrous circumstances against all the odds in an air operation in the Second World War, e.g. being shot down, baling out, crash landing, ditching into water, escaping enemy troops on the ground etc., was both extraordinary and fortunate, yet was experienced by many airmen. However, to complete thirty operations or more in RAF Bomber Command and still be alive was, in a different way, even more remarkable.

In almost every case such an achievement included narrow escapes from serious injury, wounding or death, which included almost always much good fortune. Invariably a number of operations were aborted or categorised as a 'partial operation', making the actual target a higher figure than thirty. Long before the thirtieth operation could be attempted, aircrew became fatalistic about their survival chances, and often resigned themselves to 'cashing in their chips' unwillingly along the way. Bomb aimer Flying Officer Bryan Good would be fortunate in two ways to survive his first operational flight.

Visit of the Queen and Princess Elizabeth to No. 622 Squadron RAF on 5 July 1944 – Flying Officer Bryan Good (behind Princess Elizabeth in an officer's peaked cap, partially obscured). (*Private collection, Suellyn Everett*)

On completion of final training on Lancaster bombers, Flying Officer Good, Pilot Officer Ray Trenouth and the rest of their crew, had been posted on 13 January to No. 622 Squadron in Bomber Command at Mildenhall, Suffolk. There, during four weeks of familiarisation, air firing and bombing practice, even before flying on an operation himself, Good was confronted with the brutal reality of an operational squadron.

> It was noticeably very different than anything we had known previously. As operations against the enemy went on nightly whenever weather permitted, crews continued to fail to return. Our pilot Ray Trenouth did two trips as a second pilot to gain 'know-how' with an experienced crew, before we as a crew attempted our first operation on 19 February 1944.[3]

The target was Leipzig in eastern Germany. Close to midnight, at 23.50 hours, Lancaster ED 631 B-Beer took off.[4]

> Our pilot, Ray Trenouth, who was thirty and some eighteen months younger than me at thirty-two, was the only married man in our crew. We began to confide closely on tactics just before take off. The target of our first operation was Leipzig in eastern Germany. We were about three hours into our flight when an engine caught fire, and our rear gun turret

became unusable, forcing us to abort. We jettisoned our bombs in the North Sea and returned to base, an unfulfilled operation.

Trenouth, Good and their crew not only survived losing an engine a long way out over the North Sea, they also inadvertently avoided a devastating night for Bomber Command. The raid on Leipzig on 19 February commenced with a total of 823 bombers, of which 561 were Lancasters, 255 Halifaxes, and seven Mosquitoes. Of the 823 which set out, seventy-eight aircraft were lost, 9.5 per cent of the starting force, and over 550 airmen did not return. It was one of Bomber Command's most disastrous operations.

B-Beer and its crew were lucky to limp home on three engines. As an inexperienced first time crew, they had also been fortunate to not go all the way to Leipzig. The bomber stream was subjected to continual attack by night-fighters from the Dutch coast all the way to Leipzig and on the return, as well as receiving heavy flak over the target. It was improbable that an inexperienced first-time crew would have come through the ordeal.

Flying Officer Bryan Good was born on 8 April 1912 in the small town of Battleford in Saskatchewan, Canada. He was tall, slim with brown hair and eyes. He worked as a printer in Calgary, Alberta, before his optimistic, outgoing personality and work opportunity took him to Sydney, Australia. When war broke out Good joined the RAAF and, in 1942 under the Empire Training Scheme, transferred to the RAF in the UK.

Following training at West Freugh in Scotland, and Westcott Operational Training Unit (OTU) in Buckinghamshire, in November 1943 he was posted to RAF Woolfax Lodge in Rutland. Woolfax Lodge was a conversion unit where new crews were trained and converted from twin- to four-engine aircraft, first on the giant Stirling bomber, then the Lancaster. It was also at Woolfax Lodge that Good found that all aircrew trainees were for the first time assembled together for the purpose of 'crewing up'.

The pilots, flight engineers, navigators, bomb aimers, wireless operators, air gunners, had all been training in their respective disciplines for many months. We assembled together in one large gathering with the explicit instruction to 'sort ourselves out' into crews. The crew of a Lancaster numbered seven and most comprised men from all parts of the British Empire, and other freedom loving countries.

One can imagine the difficulty for each as we mingled, talked and made acquaintances. At Westcott OTU I had met Pilot Officer Ray Trenouth from South Australia, and it was a lucky day for me when he asked me if I would be his bomb aimer.

The rest of the crew in Lancaster ED631 B–Beer who came together that day consisted of four Englishmen and another Australian:

– Sergeant Dave West, RAF, navigator
  Sergeant Bill Atkins, RAF, wireless operator, from Abingdon in Wiltshire
– Sergeant Ray Francis, RAF, flight engineer, from Warwick, our youngest crew member at nineteen
– Sergeant Charles Pulman, RAF, mid–upper gunner, from Cambridgeshire
– Sergeant Don Harvey, RAAF, rear gunner, from Brisbane, Queensland

On 21 February Good and his fellow crew members were briefed on the next operation of No. 622 Squadron, to Stuttgart. It would be a six-and-a-half-hour round trip for their second attempt at completing their first mission.[5]

> It was our initiation into enemy territory. The searchlights, flak and enemy fighters, the sight of comrades going down in flames was distressing. Yet we were ever conscious of our daunting duty to press on regardless till our target had been reached, and our task satisfactorily performed.
>
> During training of course we were never confronted by enemy fighters, nor did we stay airborne for several hours, and nor were we troubled by flak or searchlights!

On 24 February they completed their second operation, once again in B–Beer, bombing a huge ball-bearing factory in Schweinfurt in Bavaria.

> Again we witnessed the German air force in full fury as many bombers were shot down in flames. Hundreds of searchlights groped the dark skies, blindly reaching out their tentacles. Enemy fighters and ground flak necessitated constant vigilance. How glad we were to leave hostile territory, and welcome again the sight of England.

In just a single week Good and his crew in their first three operations had been thrown into the Allies' 'Big Week'. Only with hindsight can it be seen as bordering on miraculous that Trenouth, Good and their crew, in their first experiences of air combat, came through one aborted operation, and two completed in the space of just six days of 'Big Week'.

On 18 March a lack of engine power soon after take off prevented their Lancaster B–Beer from climbing above 1,000 feet, which caused Trenouth to abandon their flight. In a six–hour return flight to Frankfurt on 22 March in the same B–Beer aircraft they completed their third operation. Good reported that they came up against similar air defences to those experienced in 'Big Week'.

Eight days later Good and the crew of B-Beer would take off on an operation that would surpass the horrors of all previous raids on Germany. 'On the 30 March our fourth operation took us to what has now been referred to as the 'Nuremberg Catastrophe'.'

For the raid on Nuremberg on the night of 30/31 March 1944, Bomber Command despatched 781 aircraft. Once over German territory the bomber stream's planned route took them between the Ruhr and Coblenz areas, which were heavily defended by flak and searchlight batteries. The Ruhr and Coblenz air defences flanked a twenty-mile-wide airspace known as the 'Cologne Gap'.

Knowing that Bomber Command sometimes used this route, the Germans had placed the fighter beacon *Ida* only a few miles from the gap, which, with a flashing light and a radio signal, provided a crucial navigation aid for their night-fighters. On this night about fifty fighters on their way to rendezvous at *Ida*, by chance came across the bombers. Already at or in the vicinity of *Ida* were some additional 100 night-fighters, most of which were twin-engined and experienced in radar-guided combat within a bomber stream.

With a half moon's rays illuminating the night's clear skies, the Luftwaffe's night-fighters began their attacks. Having spent little time searching for the bomber stream, some fighters had fuel for up to two hours flying. In an inexplicable occurrence the unusually clear weather also made it even easier for the German pilots to find their bomber prey. Vapour or condensation trails, known as contrails, were stretching out behind each bomber. These contrails were normally only found above 25,000 feet, and although the bomber stream was at around 19,000 to 20,000 feet, the ribbons of vapour marked out every bomber as a potential victim.[6]

Bomber crews were shaken to be attacked by so many German night-fighters before they had even reached the Nuremberg target area. Some of the more experienced pilots did leave the bomber stream to seek an altitude and airspace of their own, and avoid leaving a tell-tale contrail. Bombers were being blasted out of the sky in countless numbers and sent plunging to fiery destruction on a scale and in an intensity never before experienced. Good was stunned by the swarms of attacking fighters, and the carnage they were inflicting. His thoughts like so many others turned to a silent plea for divine help.

Bomber Command lost a total of ninety-five aircraft, due mainly to the prowess of the ubiquitous German night-fighters. A tragic loss of more than 500 gallant airmen. It was a night of terror for all participating crews, and one which I will never forget. Someone's prayers must have been with us to bring our crew safely back from such a hazardous mission.

In only an hour and a half between the German border and Nuremberg, as the near 800 bombers streamed towards the city, eighty aircraft were lost to night-fighters and air defences. Overall Bomber Command lost ninety-five aircraft out of 781 despatched, a rate of 13.1 per cent. The total number of airmen killed, wounded or taken prisoner was 723, of whom 545 were dead. It was a disaster far in excess of the supposedly sustainable casualty rate of 5 per cent.[7]

Like so many other new crews in their early experiences of operations over Germany, Good was shocked by the brutal air war and its horrendous casualties.

> After Nuremberg I was resigned to what I sincerely believed to be the inevitable. How could I possibly expect that we might be spared to survive thirty trips such as on our first four? It was impossible. I was determined, therefore, that I would do my duty to the utmost while I could.

Operations by No. 622 Squadron continued through April and May over both occupied France and Germany, and so did the arrival of new crews to replace those lost. Some missions were during the day, and the longest of seven more operations by Good and the crew of B-Beer was an eight-hour round trip to Angers in southern France.

> This was a low-level attack, first at tree-top height across England to Land's End, then south across the Bay of Biscay low down over the sea to avoid German radar. At Angers we attacked a concentration of enemy rolling-stock in marshalling yards, and then came back to England still at tree-top height. These daylight attacks were a new and exciting experience after bombing at night.
>
> Nevertheless losses still persisted, and when friends failed to return I found myself accepting a more philosophical attitude than previously. Such was the conduct of life on an operational squadron. One had to be pragmatic and accept reality, thankful that you had not suffered the same fate, while silently hopeful that lost friends may still be alive and one day return safely.

In June 1944 the first operation by Good and B-Beer was on D Day, 6 June, when they were among thousands of Allied aircraft supporting the invasion of occupied Europe.

> We bombed a heavy concentration of German tank units to assist and open the way for our ground forces. More than 1,300 medium and heavy bombers dropped 5,316 tons of bombs to precede Allied troops. During the rest of June we continued more bombing operations over a wide range of enemy targets in both Germany and France.

The Queen and Princess Elizabeth speak with airmen of No. 622 Squadron RAF on 5 July 1944 – Flying Officer Bryan Good (behind Princess Elizabeth in an officer's peaked cap, partially obscured). (*Private collection, Suellyn Everett*)

Our tenth operation in June, like our first was a concentration of enemy armoured units, which we totally obliterated. On this occasion we took with us a war correspondent from the *News Chronicle*, whose report appeared under the headline – 'RAF heavies pin-pointed German gun positions' – with a photograph of our crew and our names with Lancaster ED631 B-Beer.

They made three more trips in July with a final elusive thirtieth on 1 August; that saw their tour completed without any casualties.

We were all elated and thankful to be spared and felt extremely lucky. At the briefing congratulations came thick and fast from all quarters including the intelligence officers, the squadron commander and many crews, both new and old. I could hardly bring myself to believe that we had actually completed our required thirty trips. My mind went back to Nuremberg on 30 March when ninety-five crews failed to return. I was then of the firm opinion that to complete thirty trips was quite beyond the bounds of reason, but now we had done it.

In those final days and operations of June and July 1944, Good and his comrades in B-Beer found that thoughts of leave at the end of their tour were uppermost in their minds. It helped them counter the accumulating stress, and keep at bay the intensifying feelings of impending tragedy, as they got closer to the magical figure of thirty completed operations.

> We were all looking forward to getting away from operations for two glorious weeks to do with as we pleased. Little did I realise at the time just how traumatic the splitting up of the crew was to be on my return. We had been together for a full year, seeing each other daily, training together, flying together and, more importantly, putting our lives on the line and fighting the enemy together.
>
> Now we were to be separated and sent to different instructional training stations for a six months' rest from operations to train new crews. For a crew who had once been so close, so deeply involved with each other's welfare, like blood brothers, we now as a crew no longer existed.
>
> So many emotions come into play, the relief of finishing one's tour of operations, two weeks' leave, then losing your crew was a climatic event. I realised a sudden deep hurt inside, an emptiness, and of being very much alone, after all those months of sharing life, and the possibility of death together.

Crew of Lancaster B-Beer, No. 622 Squadron RAF – left to right: Don Harvey, rear gunner; Charles Pulman, mid-upper gunner; Ray 'Vic' Francis, flight engineer; Bill Atkins, wireless operator, Bryan Good, bomb aimer/front gunner; Dave West, navigator; Ray Trenouth, pilot.

They had fought for so long to survive, and created their own world to do so, and now in a different way their life together had come to an end, in a way they had not anticipated.

*   *   *

In 1945, after the end of the war, Bryan Good returned to Australia, via Canada where he visited his sister in Calgary, and his parents in Vancouver. Back in Sydney he reunited with Elwyn Ruth Coterill and on 17 November 1945 they married. He pursued a successful career in sales and management, and he and Elwyn brought up six children.

Like so many veterans Good was left with a legacy from those brutal war experiences. For many years he suffered from insomnia, and those suppressed memories of the battles in the sky over Germany visited him in nightmares. He had paid a price for the freedom and prosperity we have enjoyed to this day.[8]

Chapter 21

Ferry pilot for a B-17 Flying Fortress – or would it be a flying death-trap?

Flight Lieutenant Vern Scantleton, DFC, Legion of Honour.[1]

Some airmen, who came close to death multiple times, seemed to make their own luck, and sometimes it was as if they were determined to defy the risks, only for fortune to fly along with them. After a miraculous escape from a mid-air collision flying a Stirling bomber of No 214 Squadron in early November 1943, Flight Lieutenant Scantleton was back in the air within a few days, and undertaking more operations. 'It was my good fortune to survive thirty operations with No. 214 Squadron flying Stirling bombers. My second tour began flying B-17 Flying Fortresses.'[2]

After Scantleton had filled a training role for a period, he requested a transfer back to No. 214 Squadron to fly the B-17 Flying Fortress bomber. His second tour would be a goal of twenty completed operations.

*   *   *

After Bomber Command had discontinued the use of the B-17 Flying Fortress as a bomber in 1940 they did not use those aircraft again for bombing operations. However, by 1943, the invention of radar and other highly sophisticated electronic devices were being used by both sides. The RAF and Bomber Command decided that they needed a bomber support squadron in which the aircraft carried only specialised radar and other equipment which was to be operated by two German-speaking crewmen. The only aircraft available that could generate the power required for such equipment at the time was the American B-17 Flying Fortress series G & H. Bomber Command selected Scantleton's No. 214 squadron to be the chosen squadron for this role.

So we converted from Stirling bombers to B-17s and the whole squadron and station at RAF Stradishall were classified top secret. On bombing raids, our squadron's B-17 aircraft were placed throughout the bomber stream, that is at the head, tail and middle. Our problem was that we had

Flight Lieutenant Vern Scantleton, No. 214 Squadron RAF, 1944. (*Private collection, John Scantleton*)

to carry home with us the same pay load that we went out with, unlike the Lancasters and Halifaxes that dropped their bomb load over the target, then put their noses down and clocked about 270 miles per hour, whilst they got to hell out of the target area.

To enable operation of the radar and associated special equipment, the B-17 bristled with antennae and possessed a large perspex blister under the nose. These external protuberances and the extra weight of the special equipment reduced the aircraft's speed.

Within twenty minutes of leaving the target, the B-17s were at the tail end of the stream heading for home. That was not a good place to be when the night-fighters came up. Statistically, one had to have a lot of luck to survive two tours as it had been worked out that over a period the chances of survival were about one in thirteen on each raid. This, therefore, was somewhat akin to playing the poker machines. If you play long enough, you will lose eventually in the end.

I was very fortunate in having two very good crews which I must admit I was very severe on regarding training and discipline. With a total crew of ten on a Flying Fortress this was essential. Of course I was well aware that, at times, some of the younger crew members hated my guts, especially as I myself was only about twenty-three at the time.

Actually, I only completed nineteen operations on the second tour with B-17s, as the Station Commander, Group Captain Dickens refused to let me do the twentieth by saying 'you've done your share, you have completed your second tour'. And it is rather difficult for a flight lieutenant to argue with a group captain.

Soon after being stood down from his twentieth operation, on 11 March 1944, Scantleton was called to the Wing Commander's office.

I was told that I was to take another pilot, Flight Lieutenant Cam Lye, and Roy Forbes, my navigator and a skeleton crew and go to Langford Lodge RAF station in Northern Ireland and fly back another B-17 Flying Fortress aircraft. Pilot Officer George Mackie and crew were to fly us over and wait until we had taken off on our return which was to be the following morning. This on the surface looked to be a simple and routine exercise.

At this stage it is worth giving a few comments on George Mackie. George was one of the great characters of the Royal Air Force. In 1940 he was studying architecture at Edinburgh University when he joined the RAF and gained his wings as a pilot. George was well read, witty, highly intelligent and one of the few to have had his log book endorsed as an exceptional pilot.

I well remember the trip across the Irish Sea as it was a beautiful day and, as we approached the Isle of Man, George took the aircraft down to zero feet and skimmed across the waves. This is a very dangerous stunt as water is very deceptive and a moment's inattention can put the aircraft into the drink. As we approached the Isle of Man, George raised the nose of the aircraft and we slid across the Island at tree-top height, no doubt frightening the hell out of animals and humans alike.

On landing at Langford Lodge, we sought out the Station Engineering Officer, and were stunned to learn that the aircraft we were to pick up had been grounded on the station for about four years. It had been flown over the Atlantic and dumped at Langford Lodge and forgotten. He was unable to give us any details and obviously was only interested in getting it off his hands.

He was able to confirm that no maintenance had been carried out and that the motors had not been run, nor had the compasses been 'swung' in that time. Finally, we were taken to the aircraft and were somewhat staggered to see that it was an early B-17 Flying Fortress Mk I, which didn't even have the fairing on the tail plane.

Why had a B-17 Flying Fortress Mk I aircraft been left at Langford Lodge and forgotten? Before the Americans entered the war, twenty B-17 Flying

Fortress bombers were purchased from the USA in 1940 for use by RAF Bomber Command. These aircraft were found unsuitable, and this particular aircraft was probably the last to be flown over the Atlantic and left forgotten and neglected at Langford Lodge. Some years earlier Scantleton had seen something of this first version of a B-17 Flying Fortress.

Whilst most boys of the 1930s had dreams of becoming pilots, my doom was sealed when in about 1939 I saw the pre-war film *I Wanted Wings* which, amongst others, starred the gorgeous but absolutely dumb blonde, Veronica Lake. The film must have made quite an impact as I can still recall most of it today. Needless to say, at the tender age of about eighteen it was not only the dumb blonde who mesmerised me.

The B-17 Mk I Flying Fortress at that time was a remarkable four-engine bomber. This aircraft was featured throughout the film and would have been one of the first four-engine bombers to be in service anywhere in the world. Little was I to know as I watched the film in the cinema one Saturday night that I would be flying the latest version of this aircraft on my second tour of operations over Europe in 1944.

Our interior inspection of the B-17 showed that various spiders and other insects had taken up residence for the duration. The aircraft had no radio telephone or wireless capability and, as the RAF flying equipment and the American were totally different, we would have no intercom communications throughout the flight.

On the squadron we were flying the latest B-17 Flying Fortress Series H aircraft with twin-row Wright Cyclone radial motors. The motors in this B-17 Mk 1 aircraft were a single row of unknown power and capabilities. This all added up to the fact that the aircraft was totally unairworthy and under no circumstances should it have been flown, especially as the return flight was over water and with no means of communication.

I have always prided myself that during my flying career I always paid particular attention to detail and did not take unnecessary risks. Why then should I decide to take off in an aircraft which was certainly not airworthy. Perhaps it was because of the persuasive discussion with Cam Lye, who was a more experienced pilot than I, as he had been an instructor in Canada prior to his posting to the United Kingdom. Nevertheless as captain of the aircraft, the final decision to take off was to be solely mine.

Even though there were no ground crew at Langford Lodge with experience of maintenance on B-17s, Scantleton made the decision to fly the Fortress back to Stradishall. He and his skeleton crew had the B-17 fuelled, engines run, and carried out what airworthiness checks they could do.

On the morning of March 12th, we decided to take off as it was a lovely clear day and the Met. report was favourable particularly over the Irish Sea. It was the most stupid and reckless decision made during my flying career. We turned the aircraft onto the runway for take off and I gave the motors full power. We had not gone more than a couple of hundred yards when the combined four motors set up a tremendous scream.

It gave the impression that we had four runaway propellers. I looked at Cam. Cam looked at me and we both dived to pull off the motors. By the time we had taxied to the end of the runway, we could find nothing really wrong with the motors or instruments, so we could only assume that this was the normal function of these particular motors. We decided to try another take off.

As I turned the aircraft onto the runway to make a second attempt to take off, the yellow Vauxhall control tower van came rushing across the field, lights flashing for us to stop. An 'erk' got out of the van and was pulled into the aircraft at the rear door. He scrambled breathlessly up to the cabin and said to me 'the control officer said to tell you that he has now placed an ambulance at the end of the runway'. Hell's Bells! That was the last straw. Or was it because we were in Ireland and it was just a sick Irish joke. I'll bet very few pilots have ever had a personalised ambulance placed at their disposal on take off!

The second take off was successful. With just a little sweat on the brow, under the armpits and a few other places, Scantleton turned the B-17 easterly and headed for Stradishall. The weather over the Irish Sea was clear but as they came up to the Welsh coast line, he could see that clouds were forming ahead.

Soon after passing landfall, we were in thick cloud which was intensifying the further we went. This placed us in a serious situation as we had no communication with the outside world. With an inoperable compass, we did not want to 'pussy-foot' around in case we ended up in some mountain range. We decided to forget attempting to find our way back to base at Langford Lodge in such conditions. At the first opportunity of a break in the cloud, we would go down and land at the first aerodrome we could find.

We finally found a break in the cloud and descended cautiously. After some anxious time we thankfully spotted an aerodrome. This was a fairly small drome and as we had no R/T to call up the control tower, we fired off a couple of Very lights and made sure we had the runway to ourselves and for our exclusive use. We had no wish to risk an abortive landing and have to go around again.

On landing we were directed to a dispersal pan near the control tower where we learned that we had landed at RAF Llandwrog in Wales. On entering the officers' mess that evening I was delighted to be met by Geoff Bromley, a fellow pilot who got his wings and commission on the same day as I did at RAAF Point Cook in Australia. Apart from the fact that it took an hour and a half on the following morning to get the four motors started, our return flight from Llandwrog to our base at Stradishall was surprisingly uneventful.

As if to emphasise the futile risk Scantleton and his crew had taken, the B-17 was, of course, totally unsuitable for operational purposes and was placed once more in a distant dispersal pan to sit out the war. A little over one month later it seemed to Scantleton that he was to tempt fate to excess. On 16 April 1944, the whole of No. 214 squadron was ordered to move to RAF Oulton on the Oulton Broads just north of Norwich.

All the aircraft had to be flown over to Oulton and, as this clapped-out old B-17 Mk 1 was on the squadron inventory, I was given the job once again of flying it over. Fortunately it was only a short distance between the two airfields but, about halfway to our destination, there was a loud bang and the aircraft shuddered violently. It was promptly picked up that the problem was number three engine and this was feathered immediately.

On arrival over the Oulton airfield, we found quite a number of our aircraft milling around all wanting to land. Again, with no R/T, we could not communicate with the control tower and, with a clapped-out old machine on three motors, we were not prepared to take even more risks. So we fired off a series of red Very lights, clearly indicating to all that we wanted the runway exclusively for our own use. It was subsequently found that a couple of connecting rods had snapped on number three engine, and had punctured the cylinder walls. No wonder, on making the flights from [Northern] Ireland, and then to Oulton, it had kicked up such a racket!

The gods had certainly smiled upon Scantleton. He had always been aware that his grandfather, John Scantleton, had migrated to Australia in the 1860s from Moneymore in County Londonderry, one of the six counties of Ulster that now constitute Northern Ireland.

How ironical it would have been if through my foolhardiness in flying that B-17, my broken bones had been scattered over a field in Northern Ireland, which my grandfather had left some eighty years earlier!

* * *

Vern Scantleton's forty-nine successfully completed operations was the highest in No. 214 Squadron. At the end of the war he returned to Australia and, in February 1948 at Benalla in Victoria, married Sue Roberts and together they brought up four children, Susan, Margaret, John and Kate. Vern had a calm and controlled personality which no doubt was an asset in a successful career in management with ICI.

Yet his war experiences left him like so many others with a reluctance to speak of them, and with a legacy of health effects that are now recognised as PTSD. In addition to the award of the DFC, which was presented to Vern at Buckingham Palace by King George VI, he was in later years awarded the French Legion of Honour. Vern passed away in early 2019 leaving a debt that can never be repaid.[3]

Chapter 22

A single Spitfire against 24 Japanese 'Oscar' fighters? Can there be only one ending?

Flying Officer Alan M. Peart DFC[1]

In a lone Spitfire at only 2,000 feet above the Burmese jungle, Flying Officer Alan Peart throws the iconic fighter frantically in every direction. Above him are about two dozen Japanese fighters, the feared Nakajima Ki-43 Oscars, each taking turns to swoop down and attack the lonely Spitfire. The Oscar was more nimble, could turn more tightly than the Spitfire, and was nearly as fast. For Peart, just twenty-one years old, there seemed to be only one inevitable end in sight.

*　　*　　*

In 1943–44 in the Burma campaign, a fundamental aim of the air war against Japan was to destroy the capability of the Japanese Army Air Force (JAAF). As part of this overall goal a strategic task was to supply and support by air the British 77 Infantry Brigade, known as the Chindits, in its operations behind Japanese lines for sustained periods. In March 1944 the second major Chindit incursion under General Wingate, Operation THURSDAY, was underway and deep into Japanese occupied Burma.

One of the Chindit camps, 'Broadway', was a jungle clearing about thirty miles south-west of Myitkyina, near a bend in the Irrawaddy river. However, reconnaissance flights by the Japanese soon discovered it. Success of Operation THURSDAY was totally dependent upon air support by means of supplies to ground troops, and defence in the sky against air raids by the enemy. In an attempt to provide some air cover against enemy bombing and strafing, the RAF deployed a number of Spitfires to Broadway.

On 12 March 1944 Squadron Leader W.M. 'Babe' Whitamore led six Spitfires of No. 81 Squadron RAF from the Kanglatombi airfield (known as Kangla) near Imphal in north-east India to land on the rough airstrip hacked out of the jungle at Broadway. They were closely followed by Dakota transport aircraft carrying a small servicing party, a cypher and radar unit, fuel, oil, oxygen, ammunition and other supplies. In the detachment of six Spitfire VIII aircraft was the New Zealander Flying Officer Alan M. Peart, a veteran of the squadron's North African operations.

Alan Peart was born in July 1922 in Nelson, South Island, New Zealand, and after leaving school worked as a draughtsman in Tauranga on the North Island's north coast. At nineteen years of age, in May 1941, he joined the RNZAF. On completion of his initial flying training in June 1942 he was posted to No. 610 Squadron RAF in Britain with whom he flew in operations over Europe. In November 1942 he was posted to No. 81 Squadron RAF, flying Spitfires from Gibraltar to support Operation TORCH in the invasion of French North-West Africa. During the Tunisian and Italian campaigns he claimed four victories, and was commissioned before he was posted in late 1943 with No. 81 Squadron to Burma.[2]

Flight Lieutenant Alan Peart DFC, Anzac Day, Hamilton New Zealand, April 2006. (*Private collection, Alan Peart*)

Like other pilots Peart was enamoured with the Spitfire Mark VIII and its performance.

> Powered with a Mark 66 Merlin engine, the Spitfire's Stromberg carburettor permitted negative 'G' without the engine cutting out, and it had a two-stage supercharger which provided considerable additional power at an altitude above 18,000 feet. At lower levels, however, Japanese fighters were still more manoeuvrable in a dogfight.[3]

When Peart touched down at Broadway on 12 March with Whitamore and the other four Spitfire pilots of No. 81 Squadron, they were landing on a jungle kutcha strip some 200 miles into Japanese-held territory. Like the other pilots Peart had misgivings about the location.

> The Broadway airstrip was too far from our Kangla base to permit a return after combat and there was no other alternative airstrip. The Spitfire, while a superlative defensive fighter, had a short endurance capability and therefore a short range. This meant that to refuel and re-arm, should

Broadway come under sustained aerial attack, defending Spitfires had to land there. There was nowhere else to go.[4]

The Broadway earth strip was in a clearing surrounded by tall jungle trees. Its 700 yards length was just enough to permit a Spitfire to land after negotiating a pond at one end and a morass at the other. The clearing was strewn with wreckage of aircraft and other bits and pieces, but was usable. From an air defence viewpoint it was most vulnerable being close to the enemy fighter bases.[5]

On 13 March some thirty to forty Ki-43 Oscar fighters attacked the Broadway camp and its jungle airstrip. At 14.25, with only five minutes warning of the raid, Squadron Leader 'Babe' Whitamore led five Spitfires in a scramble. Having gained a height advantage from the early warning, the Spitfires shot down four Oscars, one of them by Whitamore, and appropriately it was No. 81 Squadron's hundredth victory. It also allowed Whitamore to claim the sweepstake prize of some 900 Rupees. The squadron's total victories had thus risen to 103.[6]

Three days later, soon after dawn on 16 March, Flying Officer Peart was one of six Spitfires from No. 81 Squadron which flew again into Broadway from Kangla. They were soon in the air once more to intercept two gaggles of Zeros and Oscars over Paungbyin. Peart claimed one enemy fighter shot down and another damaged. It was his fifth victory taking him to ace status.[7]

* * *

At first light the next day, 17 March, Peart was in another detachment of six brought by Whitamore from Kangla to Broadway, the other four being Captain A.D. Maclean (SAAF), Lieutenant 'Tubby' Gasson (SAAF), Canadian Flying Officer Fell (RCAF), and Flight Lieutenant Coulter. Soon after their landing at Broadway, news came of a Japanese formation which could possibly be heading in the Broadway direction at low altitude. The real problem with the Broadway strip was that the Japanese had worked out how to attack it without any warning of their approach. If the Japanese fighters came in low enough over the hills they could evade detection by radar and catch the Spitfires on the ground, or certainly before they had scrambled early enough to allow the time to gain a height advantage.

Because of the uncertainty regarding the possible threat, there was indecision whether to send the whole Spitfire flight back into the air or only a few aircraft. If the alarm was false, they would return with empty tanks and be unprepared for a subsequent JAAF raid. Whitamore decided that, as a precaution, only two aircraft would take off immediately, himself and Coulter, leaving the others sitting in their Spitfires, one of whom was Peart. He watched them ready their aircraft.

> Both started their engines, and then Whitamore for some unknown reason changed his mind, and signalled to me to start up and go with him instead of Coulter. Babe led me out onto the strip and immediately began his take off, with me trying to follow closely behind. He had left the ground and was raising his undercarriage, while I was still on the strip, just reaching take-off speed.

The two Spitfires were only just airborne, when four Ki-43 Oscars came in low skimming the surrounding hills. The Japanese fighters flew straight over the top of Whitamore and Peart, making for the other Spitfires still sitting on the airstrip. It seemed to Peart that the Oscars passed only a few feet above him.

> Whitamore did a very risky stall turn to try and follow them, while I pushed the throttle right through the gate for absolute maximum engine power, to climb fast and try to follow. Unable to get sufficiently around to get at the Oscars, we clambered for height. We managed to reach something like 2,000 feet, and rolled out from an inverted position to find enemy fighters all around us.

The Oscars were swooping in on a strafing run aimed at the airstrip and the other parked aircraft. As the two Spitfire pilots tried to climb and turn to get behind the Japanese fighters, which was a near suicidal move so close to the ground, an even larger formation of more fighters appeared. Whitamore and Peart were pulling into a vertical climb, and half-rolling to keep the enemy fighters in sight. As they reached maximum height and pulled the Spitfires onto their backs, and half-rolled out, they were caught by the Oscars in a stall position. Peart thought there were at least twenty enemy fighters behind them.

> They were the top cover for the four initial attackers, and caught us completely by surprise. Whitamore was transmitting on his radio … so I was unable to speak to him. He was … firing at an Oscar right in front of him, unaware that three more were right on his tail firing at him.[8]

Whitamore managed to shoot down one of the Oscars, but another had dived down at great speed and was behind and firing from under Whitamore's tail. His Spitfire lost control, and appeared to fall down into the jungle.[9] The euphoria of a few days before on No. 81 Squadron's hundredth victory, and Whitamore's sweepstake win, had been short-lived. Now the swarm of Oscars turned on Peart, who estimated there were about two dozen Japanese fighters surrounding him.

I felt acutely aware that I had nowhere to go, and hoped that the superior performance of my machine would see me safely through. However … they had altitude, numbers and position … . It became the classic dogfight at low altitude with an opposition more manoeuvrable and nearly as fast. My advantage was speed and power, plus possibly armament if I had the opportunity to use it.

To prevent the fighters on my tail from getting a telling burst into me became my top priority and I hauled my aeroplane into a steep spiralling climb, whilst skidding and slipping to make myself a hard target to follow. At the top I flipped over into a steep dive at maximum power, while aileron turning with slip and skid. At the last moment I pulled the aeroplane out at maximum gravity force, and with satisfaction saw that I had lost the crop of fighters on my tail.

Even as Peart tried this tactic, to out-speed, or out-climb the Oscars, others came from altitude to latch onto his tail. In the most uneven dogfight, Peart was seemingly doomed. He was flying for his life. In the melee he managed to get behind one Oscar, to claim his sixth victory. But Peart's energy was sapping away, his brain and reactions becoming very tired. 'The business of such combat as dogfighting takes considerable physical effort with the use of arms, legs, eyes, and head turning, and it wasn't long before I began to feel really tired.'[10]

For about forty minutes, in a stretch of sky of around five miles radius and hardly more than 2,000 feet altitude, Peart put the Spitfire through everything he knew about the aircraft.

I was so exhausted that I was just looking for a place to crash-land, rather than let myself be shot down – there was nowhere else I could go. I could hardly move I was so drained. Then suddenly, … .[11]

Suddenly – nothing, the sky was empty. To Peart it was unbelievable. He had been within seconds of crashing, or being blown apart by one of the Oscars. Now all around him was clear air. Inexplicably when the JAAF pilots were in a position to finish him off, they had broken off their attacks and headed back to base. It was likely that they were running low on fuel, and one stubborn Spitfire was not worth the risk of them having to make a forced landing in the jungle. Not a moment too soon, Japanese prudence had come to Peart's aid. On landing back at Broadway, Peart's aircraft was found to have sustained serious damage, with one cannon shell lodged behind his cockpit. His elevation to Spitfire ace the previous day had nearly been his finale.

Peart found that Whitamore, as he had feared, had been shot down, estimated to be around a mile away from Broadway. However searches for him and his downed Spitfire in the surrounding dense jungle proved to be in vain. At only twenty-two years of age, 'Babe' Whitamore was dead.[12] The other Spitfires on the ground, their pilots sitting in their cockpits, also fared badly. Their aircraft were destroyed. Flying Officer Coulter was badly wounded by cannon shells and, despite blood transfusions, died later in hospital. Maclean and Gasson were lucky to escape with their lives.

The surviving pilots were flown back to Imphal, and Air Vice Marshal Vincent at once terminated the arrangement of basing a detachment at Broadway. In future aircraft would deployed from Kangla with long-range fuel tanks to give them three hours' duration including their return flight. For his remarkable fight against all the odds, Peart was awarded the DFC.[13]

The inescapable truth, however, was that Squadron Leader 'Babe' Whitamore, a renowned leader and fighter ace with seven victories in North Africa and Italy, and ten overall with fourteen probables or damaged, was gone. Whitamore was in line for rapid promotion to higher rank and his death was a great loss to the RAF fighter force, perhaps the worst in Burma up to that time. That evening at Kangla was a melancholy one.[14]

Only Peart fully realised how worse things could have been, and how lucky he was. He had been alone for forty minutes, evading more than twenty Oscars intent on destroying him. It defied all logic. Besides Peart's outstanding flying skill, chance had also played a part. His delayed take off behind Whitamore left him outside the enemy pilots' initial target range, while Coulter sitting in his cockpit on the Broadway strip was fatally wounded from the full force of the JAAF fighters' attack. If not for Whitamore's last-minute decision, Peart would have been in that position and died instead.

*   *   *

In June 1944 Peart was awarded the DFC. Later, nearing the end of the war, Alan Peart returned home to New Zealand, both physically and mentally exhausted, still only twenty-two years old but drained from the daily challenge of flying for his life. He had become a Spitfire fighter ace with at least seven confirmed victories, and up to nine other claims of damaged or destroyed enemy aircraft. However, it took him several years to recover from the toll, the stress and various tropical health conditions. In time he did, and married Jennifer and together they raised three children, Robert, Judith and Alastair. Peart attended university, gained an engineering degree, and worked on a number of national major projects, such as dams and airports, becoming a District Commissioner of Works. He passed away in September 2018.[15]

Chapter 23

Bomber training in worn-out aircraft, and that first raid to Germany's Ruhr.

Flight Sergeant John B. 'Jack' Fischer[1]

Whether flying in operations or in a training exercise, in the Second World War there were no certainties – except that disaster lay in wait in many guises for the unwary. A supposed routine training flight, or a seemingly uneventful outward leg, or an unopposed return from a mission could go wrong in an instant. Sometimes, if a flight was going smoothly, it might be tempting fate. A common RAF term in those times was, 'There's always bloody something!'

* * *

In May 1944 at RAF Blyton in Lincolnshire, bomb aimer Flight Sergeant John B. 'Jack' Fischer and his crew were training at a Heavy Conversion Unit (HCU). Fischer, his pilot Jack Fleming and their crew members had previously been flying twin-engine Wellington bombers and were converting to four-engine Halifaxes. In Fischer's estimation the Halifax aircraft used for training were in a poor state of airworthiness – 'clapped out' in his view: 'The rumour was if you got through training without an accident, you got the "Blyton medal!"'[2]

John Fisher was born in Sydney in 1922 and, after attending Sydney Boys' High School, he began training in textile design. He was tall for those times at just under six feet, fair-skinned, blue eyes contrasting with light red hair, and made friends easily. When war came he joined the Australian Army but, after six months, was 'poached' by RAAF staff looking for bomber crews. With other recruits he underwent training in Canada, then, after more training in Scotland and at an OTU in Loughborough, was posted to the HCU at Blyton.

It was at Blyton on Sunday 21 May that Fischer, his pilot Jack Fleming and their crew were briefed for a cross-country training flight of about six hours. 'The weather was pretty dull when we took off, but we climbed through the cloud and set off on our course at 18,000 feet in brilliant sunshine.'

They flew south until they were over Cornwall, by which time they had completed a little over half the training exercise. Fischer was thinking that everything was going well, when he heard the sound of the Halifax's engines change suddenly.

> The starboard inner engine raced up to over 3,000 revs per minute. Our flight engineer throttled back and the kite began to shudder from nose to tail. The pilot and engineer then decided to feather the engine and return home on three engines. Before they could feather the engine I heard the engineer say to our pilot, 'Christ, Jack! It's on fire!'

Very quickly the fire spread along the wing. The flight engineer attempted to feather the engine, and use the fire extinguisher on it, while Fischer listened anxiously to the intercom.

> Of course the engineer had a drill to go through in case of fire, and while he went about it, Jack Fleming said to us, 'Righto lads, put on your parachutes and don't panic'. If he hadn't said that, perhaps there may have been some panic, but it just held us in check.
>
> I always had my parachute harness tightly fitted just in case, for if you had it loose, when the chute opened and you went from 200mph to zero, your nether region would be flattened! We put on our chutes and opened the hatch ready to go, without there being any panic at all. We had been given the drill for baling out of a Halifax, but this was the real thing. I was to go out of the forward escape hatch, facing aft.
>
> The next thing we heard was the engineer telling Jack the engine would not feather. As it is necessary to stop the engine before a fire can be put out, we had no alternative but to get out, and we heard Jack shout, 'OK, Jump, jump, jump!'
>
> I clipped my parachute onto my harness, straddled the hatch, took hold of the 'D' ring of the ripcord, tucked my elbows in, and pulled my legs together. I was out in a flash, saw the plane disappear in an instant, waited a few seconds then I pulled the ripcord.

The small chute jumped out of Fischer's pack, pulling the main parachute after it. At which point Fischer passed out. After Fischer baled out, Fleming continued to keep the Halifax flying as straight and level as he could while the others in the crew of six baled out until there were only himself and the flight engineer left. Then he said to the engineer, 'Righto, son, give me my chute.'

The engineer put Fleming's parachute on him and ripped off his helmet, while Fleming was still trying to hold the aircraft under some control. As the engineer did this, Fleming said to him, 'Hurry up, I can't hold it much longer.' So the engineer put on his own parachute and went down to the hatch, where he waited, willing Fleming to leave the aircraft's controls. When he saw Fleming step out of the cockpit, he himself jumped out.

Meanwhile Fischer was in a free fall, and a forward descent of 200mph or more. Like nearly all airmen, when baling out from a stricken aircraft for the first time, it was his first experience of a parachute jump. There had been no practice jumps during training.

> One or more of three things must have made me pass out – I had been off oxygen for some time, at 200mph it is near impossible to breathe, and then there was sheer fright! I came to, conscious of myself swinging under the opened chute with the 'D' ring in my hand. Instead of putting it in my pocket and keeping it as a souvenir, I dropped it. And a few seconds of being unconscious meant I had not experienced the 'whap' of the opening chute, and the violent stop from 200mph to zero.

There was absolute silence. Fischer was only aware of the slight noise from air being passed through the hole in the top of the chute. He caught a glimpse of the Halifax going away from him. It climbed and banked to port, before heeling over and going down through the clouds.

> And so I floated downward. Coming up underneath me was a thin layer of cloud and, as I went through it, my descent was very bumpy. When I came out underneath the cloud I realised that I was going down backwards. By crossing my arms and pulling on the two straps that went from my harness to the chute, I turned myself around, and was now descending front on. I prepared for the landing by hunching up, and was ready to roll, but the landing was much heavier than I expected. I bounced forward onto my forehead, but was very lucky to do no damage.

As Fischer was gathering together the collapsed chute a farmer appeared through a hedge, and took him to his farmhouse. After a phone call, he was picked up by transport from the nearest RAF station. By the time he and other crew members got there they learned that their pilot, Jack Fleming, had also been found but rushed urgently direct to hospital. In addition their mid-upper gunner had landed awkwardly, and was receiving treatment for a seriously injured back. The following day Fischer heard that they had flown Fleming to another hospital.

> The engineer surmised that, as soon as Jack let the stick go, the plane went haywire, and as he got out he hit part of the fuselage. His chute must have opened, but when we saw it at the hospital later on in the day it was

ripped to shreds. It was not until we arrived back at base the following Saturday that we learned that Jack had died that morning.

It was a sorry blow to us, for they had given us to understand that he would be OK. I guess they did that so as not to add to the shock we had already received. We owe everything to Jack. If there had been any panic, or if he had failed to hold the aircraft steady, the results would have been more disastrous.[3]

*   *   *

The training accident on 21 May meant that a new pilot and a new mid-upper gunner were allocated to Fischer and his remaining crew members. After some further training on Halifaxes the reconstituted crew was posted to No. 150 Squadron at RAF Hemswell near Lincoln. Fischer found that life on an operational squadron consisted of two different worlds.

> One world was flying, and dicing with death … and in the other, when we weren't flying, we simply whooped it up. Everybody drank and nights off were spent at the local pub, or going to town to the dance, and living by the motto – 'eat, drink and be merry, for tomorrow we might die.' Quite a few crews disappeared on their first op., and it was considered that at least three had to be done before you got the hang of it.

Because their new pilot and mid-upper gunner were back from leave after completing thirty operations, the two of them only faced a second tour of twenty operations. It meant that Fischer and the others were required to join other crews from time to time as 'spare bods', so as to complete thirty operations. On one night Fischer was listed to fly as a 'spare bod' with a Pilot Officer Gow and his crew on their first operation.

> Our target that night was Osterfeld in the Ruhr, a round trip of about five and a half hours. When we got out to the aircraft for take off, it was discovered the 'Gee' radar navigational aid in the aircraft was unserviceable. You can imagine how I felt taking off with a 'sprog' crew without 'Gee'. I could map read and give the navigator fixes in daylight but, as soon as night fell it was impossible to map read unless you were lucky enough to pick up some reflected light on a river or lake. There was nothing to see down there but blackness.
>
> Nevertheless the fact that 'Gee' was not working was no excuse for aborting the operation, so off we went. Normally when approaching the target, and ten minutes before you got there, you could see the markers go down, the searchlights, and the first bombs going off. Although it did depend upon where you were in the bomber stream.

The 'Gee' navigation system was based upon a number of signals broadcast from various locations across Britain. In conjunction with maps designed for 'Gee' and the radar screen, the navigator was able to make an accurate fix of the aircraft's position. However, about halfway across the North Sea 'Gee' signals were normally jammed by German interference.[4]

Up in the nose of the Halifax Fischer looked everywhere, straining to catch a sight of the bomber stream and the target area. This night, however, there was poor visibility, and no sign of other aircraft, marker flares or searchlights.

> Goodness knows how far from the target we were for nothing was visible. Not having had a situation like this before, I didn't quite know what to do. So I told the skipper to open the bomb doors, and asked the navigator to count down to our ETA at the target. I duly pushed the button on his count, and away went the bombs, probably into some field killing a few cows.

Fischer then began to truly worry. Even though they had turned for home, they were lost. As a lone bomber, if detected by German radar, they faced near certain destruction by either predicted flak or a night-fighter.

> God knows where we were over Germany, for the navigator certainly didn't know where we are. If we were that far from the target that we couldn't see it, where would we finish up? I imagined us running out of fuel, and crashing into the sea. I don't mind admitting that over the next two and half hours or so, I was more frightened than I ever was on any other raid.

The time dragged on and, although Fischer was in a panic, he thought the crew in their ignorance through inexperience on their first operation were quite unruffled. Then, just as he feared, German radar operators detected their aircraft.

> We were targeted by predicted flak, and although the shells were bursting close enough to shake the aircraft, we just went blithely along until I shouted out, 'For goodness sake, corkscrew!' This the skipper, Pilot Officer Gow, did and in due course we ran out of the flak.

Predicted flak came from one or more anti-aircraft guns, which by means of radar control with estimated height and speed of an aircraft, would fire shells on a trajectory to meet the aircraft. In contrast barrage flak fired shells from multiple guns, with the aim of the shells all exploding at a certain height in a barrage.

Another two hours went by uneventfully until Fischer caught sight of what he thought and prayed might be the French coast.

I had my map ready to give the navigator a fix as we passed over. I could hardly believe it. We were only about ten miles from the point where we should have crossed, but we were an hour behind time. We changed course, but when we got over the UK the navigator had no idea how to get to our station!

The wireless operator made radio contact on a special frequency in accordance with a secure communication dialogue with RAF Hemswell to obtain a bearing and distance back to their home station.

When we finally came in sight of our beacon on the airfield perimeter that flashed out 'H L Hemswell' you can imagine my relief – we were home! When we got down we were so late that all the other returned crews had gone, and only the intelligence and interrogation people were there waiting for us.

The de-briefing room was usually in turmoil when all the crews came back in, all the tension being released and everyone talking about five decibels louder than normal. Now with just us there, it was dead quiet.

Pilot Officer Gow and his crew went on and completed a number of operations and survived the war. On their first operation their luck had held, but left Fischer's nerves jangling. Fischer went back to his own crew, with whom he completed twenty-one operations, eleven at night and ten in daylight, without any disastrous mishap. 'We had a few holes from flak, and came home twice on three engines. But that was all.'

Their luck had stayed the course.

* * *

In April 1945 Fischer and his crew took part in Operation MANNA, dropping food supplies to the starving Dutch population. He found it wonderful to be dropping food in place of bombs, and not being responsible for the destruction they caused. At the end of the war John returned to Sydney, left the RAAF as a flying officer in April 1946 and, in 1949, married Elin. He and Elin brought up five children, Janice, Peter, Geoffrey, Bruce and Kate.

Although he led a successful working career with a number of companies, as with so many veterans the war had left a legacy and taken a toll on his temperament. In his sixties, after years of trying to bury wartime memories, he made contact with, and visited, veterans from his old crew and his RAF base at Hemswell in the UK. After Elin died in 1981 he also re-united again with Pam, whom he had met during his service there, and they wed in 1996. Those tumultuous times, and friendships made in war-torn Britain, could never be forgotten or unwound.[5]

Part VI

1944 July to December

Chapter 24

Shot down in Germany, shot in the neck and assumed to be dead, what next?

Flight Sergeant Lloyd Christie Leah OAM[1]

On the stone floor of a guardhouse Lloyd Leah, a navigator in the RAF, lies spreadeagled. His body seems lifeless. Blood is seeping from a gaping gunshot wound on the back of his neck. A Luftwaffe officer puts his pistol back in its holster. He tells another German airman to stay with the body, before he walks unhurriedly away, as if someone else would come and dispose of another '*terrorflieger*'.

* * *

In July 1944 the crew of a Lancaster bomber of No. 460 Squadron RAF, in which Sergeant Lloyd Leah was a navigator, were young, inexperienced and at high risk of becoming typical early casualties, the inevitable statistic in new crews. Sergeant Leah was just twenty-one years old, born and brought up on his family's farm at Kangaroo Flats in South Australia.

For their sixth operation, in place of the Lancaster flown on their first five operations, they were flying a substitute plane, that of the commanding officer. On the evening of 18 July 1944 they took off from RAF Binbrook to raid a large synthetic oil refinery in Gelsenkirchen. It was to be their first operation to the very heavily defended Ruhr Valley, known to Bomber Command crews cynically as 'Happy Valley'. The initial naive enthusiasm of Lloyd and his crew on joining an operational squadron had already dissipated.[2]

With the exception of Lloyd, the crew felt that flying in a substitute aircraft was a

Flight Sergeant Lloyd Leah, No. 460 Squadron RAF, 1944. (*Private collection, Peter Leah*)

jinx, and that they were not going to return from the operation. Their usual Lancaster aircraft was unavailable due to maintenance. Their replacement aircraft's number was LL957, which Lloyd took to be a good omen as the plane shared his initials L.L., and the numbers 957 added up to his age, which was twenty one.

Apart from the captain, Pilot Officer Rex Carr, who was twenty-seven, the rest of the crew's ages ranged from twenty-one to twenty-four. The young crew's apprehension was understandable. Their training had been completed on Wellington and Halifax bombers, and their first flight in a Lancaster had come on that first operation. Only Carr, the pilot, had acquired twelve hours at the controls of a Lancaster in training.

Lloyd Leah was born on 19 June 1923 in Gawler, South Australia, and in July 1941, aged eighteen, joined the RAAF. Flying training followed in 1941–2 at South Australian bases, then in 1943 in Calgary and Edmonton in Canada, initially as a pilot and then as a navigator. After operational training with the RAF in Britain in Wellington bombers, in early 1944 he was posted with his crew to fly Lancasters with No. 460 Squadron at RAF Binbrook.

In the late evening of 18 July 1944 as Lancaster LL957 droned across the North Sea, Lloyd found that his navigator's seat and position in the aircraft was as usual relatively warm. 'It was certainly much warmer than the exposed cold tail where the rear-gunner sat, and I was able to wear light clothes most of the time.[3]

In the early hours of 19 July, LL957 approached the target and, at the designated bombing altitude of 21,000 feet, commenced its bombing run. An explosion in the oil refinery target, almost certainly from bombs dropped from a Lancaster ahead of them, spawned a huge fireball. Lloyd estimated that it rose up about 5,000 feet.

> This prevented us from dropping our bomb payload. We circled around, and made a second run at the target, successfully dropping our bombs. But on attempting to leave the target area we were caught. Blue radar-controlled searchlights coned our aircraft, which enabled a Bf110 night-fighter to attack us from the rear.

Another night-fighter raked them with its upward-firing *schräge Musik* cannon from below.

> Both of our port engines were hit and put out of action. One of the night-fighters' bursts of fire smashed through the port side cockpit window, fatally wounding our pilot Rex Carr, who received severe head injuries, and died almost immediately. The Lancaster went into a death dive. The

rest of the crew then tried to evacuate through the bomb-bay doors, but were having trouble cranking them open.

At this point Lloyd passed out, as he had lost his oxygen mask when they were hit by the night-fighter's cannon fire, and the Lancaster was still at a high altitude. It should have been the end of him.

> On regaining consciousness at a lower altitude I found that I had fallen into the cockpit of the aircraft, which in its uncontrolled dive was now steeply inclined. As I could not hear the other crew members near the bomb-bay, I believed that they had evacuated. Rather than try and climb up the plane's incline to the bomb-bay, I decided there was only time to get out through the gaping hole which had been the port side cockpit window. I was attempting to do this when an explosion within the Lancaster blew me straight through it.
>
> The next thing I knew was when I regained consciousness, and groggily realised that I was hanging from a tree. I believe that the blast must have knocked me unconscious. I could not recall pulling the rip-cord on the parachute, I can only surmise that it must have snagged on some metal or glass on the broken window, as I was hurled out.

As his wits returned to him Leah saw that he had come down not far from a Luftwaffe airfield and close to what looked like one of its security guardhouses. He was near the western outskirts of Venlo in Holland, and some eighty kilometres from Gelsenkirchen, although he did not know this at that time. His only thought was to get down from this tree, or he was done for. 'I was unable to dislodge the parachute from the tree, so I managed to free myself from the parachute harness, falling to the ground and breaking my left ankle.'

He was very close to the perimeter fence of the Luftwaffe airfield. In a state of shock, and staring at parked aircraft, his mind raced. Could he steal one of those planes and fly it westward? Luckily, before he could act on this outlandish thought, he heard the sound of guards and their dogs from the airfield in pursuit of his landfall. The guards had either observed him and his parachute descending, or glimpsed it caught in the tree and were closing in.

Lloyd stumbled away despite his throbbing ankle and managed to climb a tree in an attempt to avoid detection. It proved to be futile. The dogs picked up his scent very quickly, and found him soon enough.

> On orders from the guards I climb down from the tree. With my broken ankle I am marched, or rather dragged to the guardhouse by a German sergeant. At the guardhouse he pulls me down a flight of stairs to a lower room. Then he shoots me in the back of the neck, and leaves me on the

floor for dead. But I am not. Fortunate to still be alive, I cautiously open one eye. This scares the wits out of a young corporal standing nearby, who of course believes that I am dead.

Meanwhile an officer in the guardhouse had heard the shot and rushed to investigate. Realising that Lloyd was not dead, he ordered an ambulance which drove Lloyd to a local hospital, probably run by the Dutch underground in Venlo, where a local Dutch surgeon operated on him. They saved his life.

> While recovering in the hospital, I was contacted by the Dutch Resistance through one of the nurses. Their message was that although they could arrange for my escape and return to Allied lines in France, it would be too arduous given my medical condition. It would probably be in my better interests to be interred in a PoW camp.

Together with other injured or sick PoWs Lloyd was moved first to a PoW camp in Silesia, Stalag Luft VII, only a few miles from the Russian front, then to another camp at Lambsdorf, close to the Czech border, and with the Germans in retreat from the Russian advance, to Stalag 383 near the Swiss border. These periods in PoW camps, and transfers often in cattle trucks, stretched through the severe winter of 1944–45.

> It was bitterly cold, the coldest I have ever felt. On one occasion the temperature was said to be -20F. Nerve damage caused by the bullet wound to my neck, and associated nerve re-growth, resulted in so much pain in my arm that I had trouble sleeping and had to hold my forearm near vertical to gain some relief. Able-bodied prisoners often had to march to the next camp, and many died doing so. If I had been forced to march, in my weakened state and a damaged ankle, I certainly would not have survived. After leaving the hospital at Venlo in Holland the nearest person I had to a doctor was a slaughterman with first aid training while in Stalag Luft 7 in Silesia.

From Stalag 383 Lloyd was moved yet again to another camp midway between Ravensburg and Nuremberg in Bavaria. When news came of another planned move Lloyd and another fellow PoW managed to escape and live rough until they made contact with advancing US forces. Then by 'commandeering' a car they drove through Allied held territory to eventually reach Paris.

> Once in Paris I had difficulty obtaining passage from France for Britain. Finally I was able to see the Australian Consul, who arranged for a plane to take me to Britain – as the only passenger! I was admitted to RAF Rauceby Hospital near RAF Cranwell in Lincolnshire.

Rauceby was a hospital under the control and management of the RAF, and home of the Guinea Pig Club, which was an association of RAF and Allied aircrew who underwent experimental surgery and treatment.

> Several surgeons at the hospital inspected me and were of the opinion that they could not operate on the damaged artery on my neck which served my left arm. I was referred to Dr Fenton Braithwaite, who was the foremost surgeon of 'last resort' so to speak at the hospital. Braithwaite operated and tied off the artery in my neck, which was believed to be one of the first such procedures in the world at the time.

The operation for arterial bypass surgery was successful and Lloyd was in fact only the second person in the world to have this ground-breaking surgery. When fully recovered he was discharged and demobilised from the RAF in September 1946, after which he returned to Australia by ship. When he was re-united with his mother, Lydia, Lloyd learned of another remarkable occurrence related to his survival.

> On the day and at the exact time of my operation at the Venlo Hospital in Holland, which saved my life, my mother experienced a mental image of the unfolding events over breakfast at her home at Gawler, South Australia.

Without any knowledge of her son being shot down or of his situation, her vision was of looking down onto a hospital operating theatre, and of Lloyd having surgery on the operating table. In the course of the vision a nurse wearing a green orderly uniform, turned and looked up at her, and stated that Lloyd was going to be all right.

> A few days later this vision was recounted by my mother to the post-master of Gawler when he delivered a telegram to my parents, which advised her and my father that my plane had failed to return from its last mission. I was posted as 'Missing', and presumed dead. The post-master was so astonished at the time by the recounted vision that he wrote down the date and details. On my return from the war, he reconciled the events, dates and times of the vision against the actual event in Venlo Holland with me.

The post-master and Leah were astonished to realise that his mother had experienced some kind of extra-sensory perception, at the precise time when his operation was taking place in Venlo Hospital. Yet at that time, before she received the telegram, his mother did not even know that he was missing.

*   *   *

Lloyd Leah was the only one of the crew of Lancaster LL957 to survive. Fortune had favoured him, just as he had sensed on seeing the aircraft's number, LL957. Leah led a successful career in insurance and farming. He was active in local government, chairing Stirling Council, and in 2013 was awarded Australia's OAM medal for his service to conservation and the environment. In 2015 he was awarded the French Legion d'Honneur for his war service. Leah passed away at age ninety-three in 2016, leaving two sons, Peter and Andrew.[5]

Chapter 25

Blasted into the night sky over Stuttgart – 'Can I walk to Switzerland?'

Flight Sergeant Keith Campbell[1]

Keith Campbell, 2016. (*Private collection Keith Campbell*)

E ach morning at around 09.00 at Bomber Command HQ at High Wycombe, Air Chief Marshal Sir Arthur 'Bomber' Harris would meet with some twenty of his senior staff in their daily morning conference to decide on operations for that night. On 24 July the decision made was for a raid of around 700 aircraft on Stuttgart and, by late morning, teleprinters were chattering out the operational order and related plans to the various Bomber Command groups at airfields up and down Britain's eastern flank.

Later that day briefings for the night's raid on Stuttgart were then held by each Group in the early evening for aircrews of each squadron. The weather forecast was for 10/10ths cloud cover on take off, to break up into small amounts over southern England and France. It was forecast to become variable 5/10ths over Germany, perhaps 8/10ths over Stuttgart, up to about 16,000 feet.[2]

Because Stuttgart was a major industrial centre with automotive factories, military bases and an important rail interchange, the city was bombed repeatedly throughout the war. Between 16 and 29 July 1944 bombing raids struck Stuttgart on five nights. By mid-July 1944, to counter the constant attacks, Stuttgart had established very strong air defences including eleven medium (88mm) and thirty-eight light (20 to 40mm) anti-aircraft gun batteries, as well as a nearby Luftwaffe night-fighter base. The city's location in a narrow valley also made it difficult to pinpoint.

*   *   *

At RAF Driffield, close to the east coast of Yorkshire, Group Captain Forsyte DFC told the assembled bomber crews of No. 466 Squadron what the target for the night would be. Bomb aimer Flight Sergeant Keith Campbell, just twenty years old, listened to the pronouncement – 'Ops are on'.

> It was Monday 24 July 1944, and everyone was expecting another short trip. When we heard the petrol and bomb load no one could guess what the target was, as we all had tanks and wing overloads and were carrying HE (High Explosive). Group Captain Forsyte soon settled the many guesses and announced our target was Stuttgart.[3]

Campbell was a member of the crew of Halifax bomber LV833, P-Peter, in No. 466 Squadron RAAF. The other crew members of P-Peter were: pilot and captain, Flying Officer R.J. 'Jim' Walsh DFC; navigator Flight Sergeant Keith Smith; wireless operator Flight Sergeant Pat Conroy; flight engineer Sergeant Bob Palmer; rear gunner Flight Sergeant Mat Whitely;, and mid-upper gunner Sergeant Howard Lloyd. That night they also had a passenger, a 'Second Dickey', Pilot Officer W.D. Croft.

Croft was a new member of No. 466 and was flying with P-Peter for operational experience before going on a raid with his own crew. While a 'Second Dickey' was usually viewed as an unlucky encumbrance, perhaps a more important passenger in the crew's opinion was 'Peter Junior', a toy rabbit mascot, who flew every mission. It was a common practice for many crews to take a mascot which they looked upon as a lucky talisman. Flight Sergeant Campbell liked to keep 'Peter Junior' close by, tucked into his bomb-aimer's position.

Keith Campbell was born in Tamworth, northern New South Wales in Australia on 18 September 1923, joined the RAAF Reserve at eighteen and, a year later, in May 1942 was called up. In November 1942 he left for training as a bomb aimer in Canada, followed by further training in Britain before joining No. 466 Squadron at RAF Leconfield, Yorkshire. From Bomber Command bases at Leconfield and Driffield, before that night's operation, Campbell and his crew in P-Peter had completed thirty-three operations. Earlier in 1944 the number of operations to complete a tour had been increased to forty. He was well aware that inevitably the odds on them completing a thirty-fourth, and even reaching forty were lengthening each time they flew.

> Things went along normally – we went out to the kite, P-Peter, as usual – with 'Peter Junior' our pet rabbit mascot in the nose. We checked everything and went outside for our final smoke. The padre came around and wished us a good trip. Soon it was time to set off, so we took our place in the line to move up to the runway. Then the ground crew, only a

few of them as it was about 22.00 hours, gave us the 'thumbs up' and we were in the air. In a few seconds we were circling around, waiting until all twelve aircraft had taken off and gained height before setting course for Stuttgart.

The twelve Halifaxes flew south over England at about 15,000 feet, and then at the planned turning point climbed to 20,000 feet on a course over France. With no moon the night was dark and, as forecast, as they flew on over occupied Europe the cloud below them began to break up.

Occasionally one of the boys reported sighting one of the 700 bombers close to us. All of the equipment was working perfectly and P-Peter was behaving well. Once over Germany the flak defences were very active; there were several bursts very close – we could hear shell fragments rattle against the bomb-bay. As usual I was leaning on my chute, in the nose looking down in the bomb-aimer's position. When moving around to see the targets more clearly, the left clip of my harness clipped accidently onto the hook in my parachute. Don't know why I always used my 'chute' to lean on, perhaps it was a feeling of security that its nearness seemed to give.

In some ways when in the target area, the bomb aimer lying in the aircraft's nose, was a second pilot giving the pilot instructions such as 'right a bit, left a bit' on the bombing run, as the pilot was unable to look down on the Pathfinder flares and markers.

Heavy flak was encountered over the target, in loose barrage form, stepped up from 16,000 to 22,000 feet.[4] Despite the flak, Campbell's guidance took them smoothly over the markers.

The Pathfinder Force had been spot on, and we bombed on the markers OK, hoping as usual that our bombs would land in the middle of some flak battery. We turned after bombing and getting our photo, then Bob Palmer, our engineer, said he was going back to check 'bombs gone' as by this time we were past the main defences. I only saw one fighter that night, an Me 210, but he didn't bother us.

Bombing drill completed, Campbell turned around to get back to the H2S navigation aid.

I was just about to unclip the 'chute when there was what seemed to be a heavy dull explosion behind me, and someone saying 'bloody hell … '. The next thing I knew I was in mid-air, floating down swinging on the end of a single strap of my harness!

An explosion, which Campbell at the time thought to be a stray flak shell scoring a direct hit on the Halifax bomber, blasted Campbell straight out of the nose of the aircraft.

The explosion had blown the kite to hell. Only for the fact that my chute was on, otherwise I would have continued down to earth much faster than is good for one's health. I have no recollection of opening the 'chute, and I must have been temporarily knocked out, and the wind opened it. My helmet with its intercom plug and oxygen tube must have pulled out – damn lucky as they usually get hopelessly tangled. They can easily strangle you or break your neck.

It took a long while to come down, and it was a fantastic experience. I could see the last of the raid, all the flak and searchlights at the target, the fires in the city, Pathfinder flares burning out, and strings of bombs bursting. It looked like a fairyland somehow, everything seemed so unreal. Saw several fighters fly past, going up to intercept the rest of the chaps, and an occasional burst of tracer, like a miniature meteorite, streaking across the sky.

There was complete silence except for the creaking of the harness, and it was hard to realise what had actually happened. Luckily the wind was blowing away from Stuttgart, and I seemed to be slowly floating down, suspended in space by a single strap with a layer of thin clouds lazily coming up to meet me.

At first I mistook the clouds for the ground, and made several 'perfect book landings' only to find I went right through what I thought was the ground. Finally, when the real earth was about thirty feet away, it seemed to rush up at an alarming speed. Before I had time to do a 'book' landing I was sprawled out in a wheat field, which was nice and soft luckily. I gradually realised that I was alive, and this was not a fantastic dream.

Campbell quickly remembered the drill on coming down in enemy territory. He removed his harness, and bundled it up with his parachute. After taking out the torch from his 'Mae West' life-jacket, he placed the life-jacket and bundled parachute into a depression in the ground, before covering everything as best he could with stalks of wheat. He just had to hope it was not discovered too soon.

My next thought was a cigarette, so I had one, and found my compass. I set off in a south-west direction to put as much distance between that spot and myself as possible. It was approximately 02.15 hours on the 25 July when I landed, so I had a few hours to walk before dawn. I left the wheat paddock and wandered across more fields until I found a road.

In one direction the road headed south-west and Campbell began to walk that way. The chance of encountering local people, vehicles or troops was a risk, but he decided it was worth it. Eventually he came to a small village. Should he stay on the road, or backtrack and make a detour of unknown length? In the dark he could become totally lost.

> I decided to walk through the village. At the village pump I was very glad of a drink and a wash, as I was rather thirsty and equally bloody from a few small cuts and grazes, received when I made my rather hurried exit from the kite. After washing I felt I was a bit more presentable again. I continued on, and then saw two 'Jerries' approaching. Didn't quite know what to do, so promptly jumped into a ditch.

Praying that the two Germans had not seen anything, Campbell waited until they had passed. Then he resumed his walking until dawn began to break when he found a wood with fairly thick undergrowth. He lay down under the cover of some bushes, and made himself as comfortable as possible. Exhausted, he went straight to sleep.

> I woke up at about 10.30 am, and felt a lot better. Then everything came back in a rush – instead of waking up in my bed, I was in the middle of Germany. And not very happy about things. I thought of the rest of our kites, and the crews who would have arrived back at the squadron. As usual someone would ask, 'Anyone missing?' The Intelligence Officer would say, 'Yes, P-Peter isn't back.' Some chap says 'Bloody bad show, another good crew gone.' And so my squadron career ends after thirty-three trips. And then I thought about the rest of the crew – it was only too obvious what had happened to them. Fortunately it was all over in a very few seconds.

Campbell lit up another cigarette and took stock. His typical escape kit included:

– Maps and compass
– Money
– Rations, which also contained three bars of chocolate, gum, sweets, Horlicks tablets, and other tablets of various medications
– Water bag
– First Aid Kit and a handkerchief
– Cigarettes (around 40) with matches and lighter
– A saw and a knife
– The torch from his Mae West

Halifax LV-833 P-Peter of Flight Sergeant Keith Campbell, No. 466 Squadron RAF, 1944. (*Private collection Keith Campbell*)

In the event of capture he had his RAF identity card. He was also rather well off for clothes – being dressed for the cold at 15,000 to 20,000-feet flying altitude, with thick flying sweater, battledress, another sweater, flying underwear, flying and ordinary socks, flying boots and scarf.

> After that I took stock of my 'injuries', which I was very pleased to find consisted of only a few scratches and bumps. Then I cut off the tops of my flying boots, leaving an ordinary looking pair of shoes, removed my rank and brevet from my battledress, and settled down to study my maps. I had to decide on a plan of escape.

Being aware of the approximate position of the aircraft after completion of the last night's bombing run until the explosion, and by studying his maps and compass, Campbell was able to estimate his location. He thought it to be about thirty miles south of Stuttgart, but could not pinpoint the wood in which he lay hidden. Campbell's calculations of where had landed were probably very accurate. He did not know it at the time, but Halifax LV-833 P-Peter crashed twenty-seven kilometres (seventeen miles) from Stuttgart at Plattenhardt.

He spent the rest of the day in a quandary, wondering what to do, and waiting for nightfall. Darkness would be his only friend.

> I finally decided to make for the Swiss border as it was the closest neutral country. However, I realised that it was practically impossible as I had no knowledge of German, very little food, and the German police would be looking for the crews of planes shot down. I didn't set out again until about 22.00 hours as it was mid-summer, and consequently just getting dark. I found another road going approximately south, so I followed it for about half a mile when two men, probably farmers, turned a corner and walked

towards me. It was no use turning around and going back, as they had already seen me.

Campbell kept on going. He did not know whether he should do a 'Heil Hitler' or not, as they got nearer. His escape attempt could soon be over. In the end he casually passed them without a word, and they did not seem to think anything wrong or out of order.

> About two hours later I heard the sirens go, and spent the next half hour watching the boys prang Stuttgart again. It was very interesting to see a big raid from the ground. First the multi-coloured flares, then the searchlights picking out the kites, the flak barrage and noise of the HE exploding, the fires and smoke caused by the incendiaries, and the tracers streaking across the sky – and the tragedy of a plane going down in flames.

Campbell was distracted from watching the pyrotechnics of the raid when he saw some lights and figures emerge from a farmhouse perhaps a hundred yards away. They, too, were watching the raid, so he waited until they went back inside before continuing. He had become very thirsty and had no water, so kept on hoping he would run across a stream, or pass through another village with a water pump.

> A few more hours of walking passed and I found a small stream, so had a drink and a wash. I filled my water bag and ate a square of chocolate, with a few Horlicks tablets.

He carried on until dawn, passing through several small villages where everyone was asleep, until just before dawn he found another wood. Breakfast was another piece of chocolate, Horlicks tablets and water, then Campbell went to sleep hoping for the day to pass. Hunger and tiredness were now his constant companions.

> I woke about 10.00 hours and had another 'meal' – the same again. While I smoked a cigarette, from my maps I at last managed to locate the road, along which I had been walking, and where I now was. I tried to get to sleep again, but couldn't. I sat for about an hour and got thoroughly sick of doing nothing, so decided to explore the wood. I collected my belongings and pushed on.

After coming out of the wood Campbell found another stream, had a wash and replenished his water bag, before following its course in good cover and into another wood. A half hour later he emerged to see a fairly large town lay ahead of him. What should he do now, it blocked his path? Was there some way round it?

I decided not to risk going through the town, so I retraced my steps for about half a mile, and then went off at right angles to try and go around the town. On this new course I came to some fields at the edge of a wood – I immediately wondered what might be growing there. It proved disappointing however – cabbages. Still it was something to eat, so I picked one and ate it. I was surprised how good it did taste, so I put one inside my battledress jacket for future eating.

He now found that the fields meant that he had approximately half a mile of open country to cross. Although the fields were heavily cultivated, mainly wheat and cabbages, he could not see any farm workers. He took the risk and walked on, grabbing ears of corn to eat as he went.

I was very hot as I still had my battledress and all my flying clothing on, and it was a glorious summer day. So I threw away my flying boot tops, which I had kept as a comfortable pillow. When I came to a main road, I continued to walk along it. As there was a wood adjacent to the road, I thought that if I saw anyone I could easily divert off into it. After walking for about two miles I saw another town and a wide river ahead, so I walked along the bank of the river for a while. I was feeling tired again so sat down, had another look at my maps, and removed some of my heavy clothing.

In the warm sun he lay down against the bank of the river, and exhaustion soon sent Campbell off to sleep. After a short time the shouts of some children, who were swimming in the river about 100 yards away, woke him. He picked up his gear and climbed up the bank, as they swam in his direction. One of them, maybe after seeing his white sweater, which he had shed and thrown on the ground, began pointing and shouting. Soon all of them were shouting at him.

They may have just have been saying 'Hello', but he left in such a hurry that he left his white sweater behind. It might betray him as an RAF flyer but he was better off without it, he thought. He walked as quickly as he could across more fields and followed some farm tracks. There were farmers in the fields and some women cutting wheat and tying it into sheaves. Campbell kept walking and no one said anything to him.

I was still quite close to the river, and passed another group of swimmers. They waved and shouted, so I waved and shouted some kind of noise back at them. This seemed to be OK, and no one took any further notice of me. I kept on.

Campbell walked for another two days and nights, keeping to woods for cover wherever he could, or little-used roads. He saw very few people and doubted if they noticed him. One old chap said something to him, so he grunted in reply which seemed acceptable. On the next night he picked up cabbages and potatoes from another field, and in another wood lay down and fell asleep at about 03.00 hours,

> I woke up at 09.00 hours feeling extra hungry. Breakfast that morning was raw potatoes and cabbage, with a square of chocolate. I ate the last three sweets, and felt a little better. So I set off and came to a road which I followed for about three miles. The traffic became fairly heavy, passing military trucks, cars, bikes – some waved to me, so I waved back.

Campbell was in trouble. This could not last. At any moment he could be confronted and, unable to speak German, he would be asked for his papers. He was on a road with quite busy traffic, and decided to get away and make for the next wood. It was too late.

> A civilian lorry passed me and the driver signalled to me that he would give me a lift. I shook my head at him as he passed by, but he stopped anyway. As he was only about ten yards away, I felt that I couldn't do anything but keep on.

To turn away and retrace his steps would only arouse suspicion. Could he keep walking and just mutter something unintelligible again?

> When I was level with the driver he said something to me that I didn't understand. But I replied in French, trying to make it seem that I was a French worker. Unfortunately another chap with the driver said something in French – he knew the language better than me. The two of them had a little conference and then asked me more questions, and finally taking out their identity cards and pointing at them, then at me. I only had my RAF card.
>   If I behaved I was likely to get on better, as the civilians weren't too well disposed towards the RAF. I gave him my RAF card which he couldn't read anyway, but he kept it. Then he said in very halting English, 'You RAF – Englander Ja? Flieger?' I answered 'Ja', and he pointed at his lorry. So I resumed my journey by motor transport.

In the lorry with the driver and his passenger was a little girl. Campbell thought her to be about five years old.

> I thought it would be a good thing if I gave her some of my remaining chocolate. This put my stocks up considerably and when I shared what was left with the driver and his mate they were very surprised and managed to say 'thanks' in English. After driving on for about half an

hour we arrived at Tubingen where the driver stopped on the outskirts of the town.

The other chap went into a beer garden and came out with three bottles of beer, one of which he held out to me and said 'beer?' So I didn't lose by investing half a block of chocolate. It was excellent beer, ice cold and tasted A1. After finishing the beer, they took me to a house, which had a large swastika on it, so I thought, 'Here's where the Gestapo get me.' They escorted me to the door, exchanged 'Heil Hitlers', and asked for someone there.

They were redirected to the railway yards where, once again, the three of them alighted and the driver pulled out a packet of Chesterfield cigarettes, offering one to Campbell. Ten minutes or so went by before a police officer in a green uniform appeared. He was holding a revolver.

I was handed over to him, with a long explanation. It must have been a good report on me, as he put away that wicked looking revolver. But I noticed that he left the flap of his holster undone. He indicated that I was to go with him, and after a while we managed to have a very difficult conversation in bits of French, English and German – helped out with signs.

He was quite a good type, but made it clear that I was 'his prisoner', and patted his gun! I was quite happy about being a prisoner, as by then I was very hungry, tired, dirty, and couldn't have carried on much further by myself. I had covered about forty to fifty miles, but would still have had a long way to go, and very little hope of getting to Switzerland. The show was over.

Following the usual interrogation process, Campbell was sent to a PoW camp at Bankau in Poland. In January 1945, in the face of the Russian Army's advance, the camp was evacuated and, in the depths of a very severe winter, Campbell and the other PoWs were marched to another camp at Luckenwalde some fifty miles south of Berlin. Then, in May 1945, they were liberated by the Russians, and Campbell was flown back to Britain by RAF aircraft and, in August, repatriated to Australia.

* * *

Sixty-two tears later, in 2006, Keith Campbell was astonished to learn from the Historical Branch of the UK Ministry of Defence that his Halifax bomber was not hit by flak. It collided with another bomber of No. 466 Squadron. Twelve Halifax bombers had been despatched, and those two were reported as missing. The rest of Campbell's crew were killed, as were all the crew of the other aircraft.[5] By the freak chance of being ejected violently from the bomber, his parachute opening by some fluke spontaneously, and hanging from a single strap, Campbell was the only survivor from both crews.

Maybe as Halifax LV833 P-Peter was shot down, the toy rabbit mascot 'Peter Junior' brought Campbell his bizarre good fortune. Yet once on the ground it was his spirit, resilience and persistence that enabled him to survive his days on the run, and the deprivations of PoW captivity in the freezing winter of 1944–45.

In late 1945 Keith Campbell returned to Australia, left the RAAF and, in 1948, married Berenice. With that same resolve and determination that he displayed in the war, he forged a new life and successful career in hotel and catering management, and with Berenice had two children, Fiona and Peter.[6] His son's name would always be a reminder of LV833 P-Peter, his toy rabbit 'Peter Junior', and his miraculous escape, and all his life Campbell considered himself very lucky to be alive. After Berenice died in 2013 Keith remained fit and active, living independently until at age ninety-five he passed away in July 2019.[7] It was seventy-five years almost to the day since that fateful operation on 24 July 1944 to Stuttgart.

Chapter 26

The pilot's dilemma – 'All the crew have baled out, but is it now too late for me?'

Pilot Officer K.E. Tanner[1]

On 17 September 1944 a daylight bombing raid was begun by No. 463 Squadron RAF on German positions at the port of Boulogne in north-west France. Because of rapid gains made by Allied ground forces advancing from Normandy, more than 100,000 German troops were cut off in garrisons in Biscay and Channel ports such as Boulogne. Those German forces refused to surrender, and dug in to make their positions more defensible as individual fortresses. Under Hitler's orders they were to fight to the last man. To lessen the likely casualty toll on Allied troops, Bomber Command was called upon to bomb the German defenders into submission.[2] Boulogne was under the command of Lieutenant General Ferdinand Heim with 9,500 troops and supplies for several months.[3]

Allied bombing raids on Boulogne had commenced on 8 September. In the operation mounted on 17 September by No. 463 Squadron, Lancaster LM675, piloted by Pilot Officer K.E. Tanner, took off at 08.15 hours from RAF Waddington in Lincolnshire. The outward flight and approach to the Boulogne target area was without incident. Although there was a slight haze, visibility was fair. With the red target indicator clearly in sight, Tanner held the Lancaster steady at 8,000 feet as it released its bombs at 09.41. In that instant Tanner felt the heart-stopping thumps.[4]

> Immediately after 'Bombs Gone', we were hit by heavy flak, causing a hole in the port wing approximately 11 feet by 6 feet, and severely damaging the ailerons. The aircraft went out of control in a diving turn, during which the no. 3 fuel tank blew out and exploded behind the aircraft. I ordered the crew to abandon the aircraft, while I maintained some moderate control of the plane at 4,000 feet, during which time the Wireless Operator, Mid-Upper and Rear Gunners endeavoured to get out of the rear door.

Those three crewmen found the rear door jammed and its handle broken off, so they had to move forward to the front hatch. This was also partly jammed, adding further difficulties for the crew trying to bale out. All the time Tanner strove to keep the Lancaster airborne.

> Eventually all members of the crew apart from myself squeezed themselves out. Throughout these extremely difficult circumstances, my crew behaved in an exemplary manner, and showed calm and coolness throughout. During this time I maintained a reasonably controlled descent, with the port engines fully opened, starboard engines half-throttled, full aileron and rudder bias.
>
> I estimated that the crew got out between 2,000 and 3,000 feet. At 1,500 feet I too attempted to bale out – unsuccessfully as the aircraft was diving and uncontrollable.

Unable to get to the hatch, Tanner faced the dilemma experienced by many bomber pilots of fatally damaged aircraft. Having done his utmost to control the plane, so that his crew were able to bale out, he was seemingly trapped. He had to think fast – very fast, or he was doomed. He clawed his way back into the cockpit seat with just one thought.

> 'Can I somehow crash land this thing?' I wondered. At 800 feet I regained some limited control of the aircraft and, having no other alternative, I attempted to make a forced landing in the quickest possible time.

There were only seconds left before impact with the ground. Tanner desperately tried to guide the plummeting bomber towards some open ground.

> With my starboard outer engine on fire I eventually landed in a field that was obstructed with anti-invasion posts. I found that the undercarriage and flaps were serviceable, and allowed me to make a successful touch down on the grass.

Luck must have perched on his shoulders as the Lancaster's wheels somehow avoided collision with the anti-invasion posts.

> Towards the end of the aircraft's landing run, to avoid further danger of more posts and obstacles in my path, I swung the aircraft to port coming to rest on the edge of a wood. As the starboard outer wing and engine were fully aflame, I made a very quick getaway.

In defiance of all probabilities, Tanner had crash-landed the Lancaster near Rolet, south-east of Samer in the Pas de Calais area of France. In an obstacle-strewn terrain he brought the aircraft to a halt, only a few yards from a wood, which would have torn it to pieces, and almost certainly prevented his evacuation. Meanwhile, all the crew landed safely in the vicinity.

The navigator, Flight Sergeant R.M. Dent,[5] in his report stated:

> Our pilot's captaincy and leadership displayed throughout these intense moments gave us confidence and inspiration. We considered the aircraft impossible to fly, and how he effected a landing was, in the opinion of all of us, a miracle, and we never expected after we baled out that the aircraft could be landed.

On the night of 17 September Bomber Command dropped 3,391 bombs on Boulogne. The raids on Boulogne continued until 26 September, when Lieutenant General Heim and his men surrendered. The onslaught by Bomber Command, part of Operation WELLHIT, led by II Canadian Corps, had helped to cause the German forces to despair, and view further fighting as useless and in vain.[6] The bombing raids on the Biscay and Channel ports clearly saved many lives and casualties in Allied ground forces. Against all the odds Pilot Officer Tanner overcame the pilot's dilemma, and saved his crew and his own life.

Chapter 27

Surviving the Arnhem disaster – Thirteen days in No Man's Land

Flying Officer Frederick Stephen 'Fred' Dyer[1]

O n 17 September 1944 the Allies launched two operations, an airborne assault, Operation MARKET, and a ground assault, Operation GARDEN, to provide outflanking bridgeheads in Holland for a rapid advance by Allied ground forces. The objective was to enable a faster drive to the Rhine and into Germany. Troops were dropped by parachute and glider across three natural water barriers to secure bridges over the Maas river near Grave, the Waal at Nijmegen, and the Neder Rijn at Arnhem. However, by 21 September, fierce German counter attacks, in greater strength than Allied forces, meant that Operation MARKET GARDEN was in disarray and close to defeat.

Re-supply by air to the cut-off Allied troops, particularly at Arnhem, was being severely curtailed by enemy air defences. Enemy anti-aircraft fire, through a combination of heavy flak, light flak, machine-gun and rifle fire, was being hurled into the air at the Allies' transport aircraft. In spite of increasing losses of aircraft and airmen, the air supply drops continued, in the main by Stirling and Dakota transport aircraft. The intensity of the flak became like a blizzard, cascading into the sky.[2]

* * *

Flying Officer Fred Dyer, No. 233 Squadron RAF, 1943/44. (*Private collection, Stephen Dyer*)

At RAF Blakehill Farm, south-west of Cricklade in Wiltshire, Flying Officer Fred Dyer was a navigator in a Douglas C-47 Dakota of No. 233 Squadron RAF. Dyer was born on 1 August 1921 in Adelaide, South Australia, and, after volunteering for the RAAF, began training in 1942. Further training in navigation followed in Canada and the UK before he was posted to No. 233 Squadron in June 1944. He was five feet ten inches tall, of slim build, with dark hair, and possessed a cheerful personality that combined both energy and a certain calmness.[3]

At 10.15 hours on 21 September 1944 Dyer learned that he and his crew were to fly their plane in another re-supply drop operation later that day to Arnhem in Holland. At 13.09 Dyer's Dakota took off with a load of oil and mortar bombs in fifteen panniers.

> We had four Army men aboard to push the load out when we reached the Dropping Zone (DZ). So in all there were eight men aboard – Mike Aden and Ken Dorville, who were the two pilots, Jack Hickey, the Wireless Operator, and myself, the Navigator. On the outward flight everything went OK until we reached the DZ at Arnhem at 16.05 hours, where we had to run through a lot of flak.[4]

Despite being bracketed by flak, they were able to drop their load of panniers in the drop zone by the usual method of the soldiers pushing out the containers. Pilots Aden and Dorville then turned the Dakota for the return home. As Dyer looked down on the wreckage of aircraft that had been shot down, he thought he felt their own plane struck.

> I think we were hit, but I assumed not seriously, and we began the return trip. About ten minutes after leaving the main Arnhem area, at 5,000 feet we received several more hits from an Oerlikon gun on the ground. We were hit in the port wing and in the fuselage. One shot came through the floor just in front of Mike Aden's feet, and out through the top of the cabin.
>
> Several minutes later the Army men at the back alerted me to flames that were coming through the fuselage floor. After telling Mike I tried to put out the fire with the extinguisher, but the flames had a firm hold, and I had to abandon the attempt. Mike decided to try and reach the lines of the Allied forces before making a crash landing. When we were down to 2,000 feet, Mike told us to get the Army chaps into crash-landing positions.

Before going back into the cargo area to speak to the four Army men, Dyer clipped his parachute pack onto his harness.

I went back to the aft door, where Jack Hickey was standing. I tried to reassure the Army men, and told them that we were going to crash-land. They said that it was too late, and pointed over my shoulder. I turned around, and saw that in the last few seconds the forward part of the plane's fuselage was being enveloped in flame and smoke.

The fire was spreading very quickly, black smoke filling the Dakota aircraft, which was losing height rapidly. Hope for a crash-landing under some control was clearly gone.

Jack and I decided the time had come to abandon the aircraft, and I told the Army chaps to jump out with us. I went out, and Jack followed me, but the others failed to do so. By the time we jumped we were only at about 800 feet. Just as we left the aircraft, it was engaged by heavy machine-gun fire from a position about half a mile away from us. As our crashing plane was out of range, they fired only a few bursts in our direction. It only took us about 20 seconds to reach the ground.

The two pilots, Aden and Dorville, were unable to leave the burning Dakota, and perished with the plane as it crashed into the ground. Dyer and Hickey left the aircraft at a height around 50 per cent lower than the recommended safe altitude of 1,500 feet for baling out.

We hit the ground at about 16.10 hours, both landing intact about fifty yards apart in a small clearing of a large pine forest. We hid our parachutes and Mae West life-jackets in a ditch, and ran off in a westerly direction, wanting to get away from our landing position as quickly as possible. We heard rifle shots from the same direction as the machine-gun fire, which hit a couple of trees near us. Then we hid in some thick undergrowth to work out a plan and, after about an hour, things quietened down.

To assist their escape once on the ground, Dyer and Hickey carried various items suited to survival in Holland. A small package contained a compass, some Dutch guilders in cash, and local maps printed on silk. Rather than paper maps, silk was used to better withstand water damage. Although they were unaware at the time of exactly where they had come down, they had landed near a small country town, Hooge Mierde, near Eindhoven in Nazi occupied Holland, about eighty kilometres (fifty miles) south from Arnhem, and not far from the eastern border with Germany. Given that they were clearly in close proximity to German forces and a battle zone, Dyer persuaded Hickey that they should first try and contact a local farmer, and hope he and his family would prove to be friendly.

They began to walk through the pine trees, hopefully towards the positions of British forces. Some shots from some distance away, assumed to be from German troops, made them run deeper into the forest. They thought and hoped that it was unlikely that they had been identified as Allied airmen. Coming upon a clearing, they saw a barn and farm-workers in fields, who were harvesting potatoes and loading them into a cart pulled by a horse. Dyer was in two minds about approaching them.

> As twilight gathered the farm workers walked northwards in our direction. As they came nearer, they were going to pass about hundred yards from us. When we saw that we had been observed by a young boy, we decided to walk towards them.
>
> They were Dutch, as we were hoping, and one of them spoke a little English, so we were able to gather that we were indeed in Holland, and about thirty miles from the British Army front line to the south. They took us to a barn, and after about fifteen minutes, to the farm house, which was in the north-west of the clearing.

There the farmer, Jarard, his family and workers talked together for a while, discussing what they should do about these two British airmen. Finally, they motioned Dyer and Hickey into the house, and gave them a meal of bacon and eggs.

> After this, we were taken back to the barn for the night, where we hid in the straw. Because I had been working in the aircraft in my shirtsleeves, when I baled out I left behind my jacket. So the eldest daughter gave me a pair of old overalls, and a red woollen scarf. We spent a very chilly night, but slept fairly well as we'd had a busy day.
>
> During the next day a man who spoke English came to see us from the local 'Common Office'. He told us that we must remain in hiding as there were many German troops around. Also there were about 200 German supply workers stationed in the nearby village of Hooge Mierde, which was only about five kilometres (about three miles) away.

In the first few days it seemed safe enough for Dyer and Hickey to walk from the barn to the woods, which were about 100 yards away. This was because the farmer wanted them to hide in the woods during the day so that, if they were found by the Germans, they would not know that the two airmen were being helped by him and his family. He was still taking a grave risk in harbouring the two airmen. If the Germans found them in the barn, the farmer and his family would face deportation to a concentration camp or execution as collaborators.

Walking to the woods also gave us a change of surroundings, as well as a little exercise, as the barn itself was too full of hay for any moving around. One night we decided to stay in the woods because we could hear brisk fighting to the south. We thought the barn offered good cover and observation positions if the fighting came north, and could be attractive to the German troops. The noise of battle seemed to die out next day, so we returned to the farmhouse, where we dried our sodden clothes from a night of incessant rain, before returning to the barn.

There was no knowing how long they must hide. It appeared to Dyer that the Allied armies' advance from the south had slowed, and was being held up by German forces.

We hollowed out a deep shelter in the barn's straw that enabled us to lie about four feet below the surface. Besides giving us a feeling of greater safety, it certainly hid us, and it was much warmer at night. We descended into our pit at dark, which was about 19.00 hours, and came up in the mornings when the farmer gave us the 'all clear'. It meant that the fine pieces of straw worked their way beneath our clothing, irritating us constantly. The stiff straw was forever poking our faces, noses and ears.

During the day, from an opening at one end of the barn, the two airmen could see on the horizon the church steeple of Hooge Mierde, and beyond it the church steeple at another small town, Laage Mierde.

We spent most of our time gazing at those church steeples. We also slept a lot during those first few days, but we soon weren't tired enough to sleep during the daytime, and just lay in the straw looking out at the sky and the steeples. The farmer and his family fed us well enough, bringing mainly hot potatoes, cheese, milk and half-cured ham sandwiches to us in the barn. Sometimes an apple each.

They were told by the farmer that the number of Germans in the vicinity varied a lot. At one time there were 1,000 or more in the village, with mechanised forces and artillery dispersed in the woods for cover. At another time there were only a few dozen. On 23 September they had seen another re-supply operation by RAF Dakotas go north to Arnhem. Night and day the air was almost constantly buzzing with aircraft engines. It seemed to Dyer they were all Allied planes.

We saw several large American Fortress and Liberator bomber formations go overhead, and heard in the night quite a few other RAF bomber forces pass over. On occasions we caught sight of roving Spitfires, and once saw two Spitfires diving with cannon firing near Hooge Mierde.

During the last few days of September we heard artillery firing and shells bursting in the east, north and south of us, the nearest being about a mile away. One night a huge explosion shook the barn, and we subsequently found out that it was the Germans blowing up a bridge.

On 29 September Dyer and Hickey learned from Jarard that the German forces were preparing to withdraw, and were raiding houses of the local Dutch population, and among other things looting clothes, horses and bicycles. While those raids were happening, their farmer and guardian hid his horses and bicycles in the forest in case they were raided. Twenty refugees from nearby villages arrived at the farmhouse seeking shelter.

Because of the increased threat of German troops raiding the farmhouse, once again Dyer and Hickey fled to the forest and hid during the day, but were able to sleep in the barn again at night. However, on 30 September the farmer informed them that German troops had moved so close to the farmhouse that it was too dangerous for them to leave the barn. Next day, 1 October, Dyer observed a squadron of Spitfires strafing German artillery positions not far to the south for around twenty minutes.

The days were passing, and as the conflict came closer to the farm, which they had come to see as a sanctuary, Dyer and Hickey faced a dilemma. Did they stay where they were, and hope the battles passed them by, but take a risk that they might get caught up in the fighting? And by staying in the barn they were putting the Dutch farmer and his family at even greater risk.

The other two options seemed to be either to flee away from the fighting, which would mean going deeper into German-held territory, or should they try and find a way through to British forces? For three days, as the sounds of battles came closer and closer, they had confined themselves to the barn. They waited, uncertain of which option to take.

On 3 October we decided to try and walk towards the British Army's lines, and so borrowed more overalls, scarves, caps and overcoats, for warmth and disguise. Jarard, our main guardian at the farm, and an English-speaking local man, set out with us, so as to try and get us started in the right direction.

Mid-morning the four men set off. The uncertainty of where either side's forces were deployed was making them apprehensive. Anyone moving around and not in an identifiable uniform could easily be shot on sight by either side. It was the thirteenth day since Dyer and Hickey had baled out. Dyer wondered if it would it be an unlucky day? 'We had only got as far as Hooge Mierde when we saw an armoured car of the British Army.'

They had to take a chance, and hurried towards the armoured car, which was scouting ahead of the front lines, shouting to its troops that they were British airmen. Luckily they were not shot on sight, and were able quickly to prove their nationality. Dyer reflected that it was indeed a lucky day!

> After handing our borrowed clothes to Jarard, we rode back in the armoured car towards Reusal, eight kilometres (five miles) to the east, where there had been heavy fighting for the last four days.

If they had tried to walk the eight kilometres on their own, even assuming that they chose the correct easterly direction, it was highly likely that they might have been killed in crossfire, shelling, bombing or strafing by aircraft. In the armoured car with the protection of their own British troops they avoided contact with any German forces and made it to Reusal safely. 'There we were stupefied to learn that Arnhem had been evacuated.'

From Reusal the two airmen were driven to the Divisional HQ where they were given mugs of tea and issued with jackets and greatcoats before continuing on to Brussels. Next day Dyer and Hickey boarded a flight back to Croydon, England. It had been thirteen days since they had taken off from RAF Blakehill Farm.

*   *   *

At the end of the war Fred Dyer returned to Adelaide, where he was re-united with his wife Martha, who had been born in Scotland, and whom he had married in 1943 shortly before leaving for training in Canada. They had a son, Stephen, and built a new life together. Fred completed a degree at the University of Adelaide and became a teacher and deputy headmaster. Martha studied at a business college and worked in a number of senior positions in financial administration. Fred Dyer's quick thinking in baling out of his stricken aircraft, and his involuntary thirteen days of survival in no man's land, proved lucky for both him and Martha.[5]

Chapter 28

Dumped in a ditch, semi-conscious, one arm hanging half severed – night is falling, and so is oblivion

Flight Sergeant Henry 'Harry' Howard[1]

In a raid on the Dortmund-Ems Canal on 23 September 1944, the Lancaster of bomb aimer Harry Howard aborts its first bombing run due to poor visibility. On a second run the Lancaster is split in half by another Allied bomber in a mid-air collision. In an instant, with a combined velocity of more than 500 mph, metal of the two aircraft tears and rips through metal. The disintegrating Lancaster hurls Howard out into the freezing night air, in a violent ejection that slices Howard's right arm open to the bone.

*   *   *

Sometime in the early hours of the morning of 24 September 1944 in the Operations Record Book (ORB) of No. 463 Squadron RAF at Waddington airfield in Lincolnshire, someone wrote against Lancaster LM309 the status of its sortie: 'Aircraft missing – no messages or signal received'. On the evening of 23 September at 19.15 hours Lancaster LM309 had taken off with the rest of the squadron to bomb the Dortmund-Ems canal and its aqueduct. The entry in the ORB was the typically understated remark recorded for any aircraft that did not return to base and which had not made it back to another airfield in the UK. The bomb aimer in that Lancaster was Flight Sergeant Henry 'Harry' Howard.[2]

Harry Howard was born in October 1920 in Melbourne, Australia, and, on joining the RAAF, he was nearly six feet tall, slimly built and with a fair complexion. He really enjoyed being around people and, with a humorous personality, loved engaging in conversation. After initial flying training in Australia, Howard flew to Britain on 1 January 1943 and, following further operational training, joined No. 463 Squadron at Waddington.[3]

Flight Sergeant Harry Howard (front row extreme left, cross-legged), No. 463 Squadron RAF, 1944. (*Private collection Gretta Howard*)

His first mission was a raid on the night of 18/19 September 1944 on the German port of Bremerhaven, which had some of the strongest air defences. Howard and his crew completed their bombing successfully in a raid that destroyed and damaged a number of German navy ships and a U-boat, and survived their first operation. On 23 September their second mission was to be the Dortmund-Ems canal and its aqueduct in Germany's Ruhr Valley. As was normal in the operations of Bomber Command, this was no easy introduction to the elusive goal of completing thirty missions.[4]

The night was rainy and cloudy, making visibility poor, and so, as they came into the target area of the Dortmund-Ems canal, Howard asked his pilot, Flying Officer P.J. Lundquist, to circle around again. Instinctively, Lundquist turned the Lancaster around. The Germans' fighter flares lit the bomber's silhouette on the clouds, making them feel vulnerable to attacks from the German night-fighters, which flew below them. The upward-firing guns, *schräge Musik*, of some Luftwaffe fighters were particularly lethal in targeting bombers from below.[5]

As Howard's Lancaster circled around, however, another of the squadron's bombers was hit by flak or a night-fighter's fire. One of the stricken bomber's wings collided with Howard's Lancaster, splitting the aircraft in two. Howard was sucked out of the Lancaster, and, in the shattering collision of the two aircraft, his right arm was nearly torn off by either a fragment of metal or a flak splinter. It seemed to Howard as if his arm was hanging only by skin and sinews. But luck had smiled on him, because, in his bomb-aimer's position, he had his parachute clipped on under his stomach for comfort. As he was violently ejected from the aircraft, his ripcord had caught on something so that his parachute billowed out automatically.

Howard floated down and began to gather his senses. His right arm hung limp, numb and lifeless. Once on the ground he was in shock and began to fear for his life. This was not so much from German troops, but from a fear of execution by civilian mobs, who frequently dealt out vengeance on Allied 'terror fliegers'. After landing he crawled into a ditch, bewildered and in shock. Would he bleed to death and first light find him dead? Shivering with the cold he fell unconscious.

Next morning he awoke and realised that, if he was to stay alive, he had to force himself to move and find help. Besides the shocking condition of his lacerated right arm, Howard was also in excruciating pain from his injured back and hip and had obviously lost an unknown quantity of blood. Once more luck was with him. A sympathetic farmer came upon Howard, and took him back to his farmhouse, where he gave him some food, and telephoned the authorities. In due course he was taken to a PoW hospital and treated for his injuries.

In all, Howard spent about five months in two different hospitals before being transferred to a PoW interrogation centre in Frankfurt. Although he was not physically beaten, Howard was left in a small room with no human contact and hardly any light. The food, if it came, which was not often, offered little in sustenance or nutrition. It was all designed to weaken and disorientate Allied prisoners so that, in desperation, they might spill information. After what he had been through, all he could do was console himself on still being alive.

Howard was questioned twice, and each time resisted a subconscious urge to talk. His interrogators asked him about the new navigation equipment, and how it worked. He answered over and over again, 'Don't ask me, I don't have a clue!', 'I don't know', or responses to that effect. After about two weeks, Howard was taken out of solitary confinement and transferred to another form of camp, where he mixed with other Allied PoWs and the food and conditions were better. He quickly learned from other inmates that it was designed to relax the PoWs, get them talking freely, as there were German spies posing as PoWs in their ranks, with the express purpose of reporting their conversations.

The next transfer took Howard to a true PoW camp at Bankau on the Polish border. When orders shouted in German by the guards were not immediately followed, the guard dogs were frequently turned on the PoWs. With Germany being increasingly squeezed between the Russian Red Army in the east, and

Allied forces in the west, food for the PoWs at Bankau was reaching starvation level. A typical daily ration became one loaf of bread between eight to ten men, and a mug of thin, watery soup. For those men like Howard, still in a recovery state from horrendous injuries, the pitiful food rations barely kept them alive.

If they were very lucky they might get a piece of margarine, or a spoonful of jam, and a cup of coffee made from acorns. Some Red Cross parcels did get through and, although a parcel had to be shared between three to four men, they did lift dampened spirits. Then the Red Cross parcels stopped coming, and one morning the PoWs were woken earlier than normal. The Russian advance had broken through the German defences and was approaching Bankau. The Germans had packed up the camp, and began the relocation of all PoWs in a retreat from the Russian Red Army. They set out to walk for about 300 kilometres (188 miles).

At one point on the walk the column of PoWs was confronted by a horde of angry civilians from a nearby village. The villagers held torches and brandished rustic weapons, intent on hacking Howard and his fellow prisoners to death. Even as their German guards fired into the air above the villagers' heads, the mob was throwing petrol bombs at the PoWs. Eventually the mob dispersed and the column was hurried on before there was another attack. The march went on westward for five to six weeks, until about fifty kilometres (thirty-one miles) south of Berlin they reached another camp, Stalag III-A at Luckenwalde in Brandenberg.

While it is believed that during the war more than 200,000 prisoners of various origins passed through Stalag III-A, of whom many were sent to work as slave labour elsewhere in *Arbeitskommando* groups, the camp usually housed between 6,000 and 8,000. It has been estimated that perhaps up to 5,000 inmates died in the Luckenwalde camp.

Although Howard had survived the horrendous march from Bankau to Luckenwalde Stalag III-A, he was very weak and could hardly move. Food rations at Stalag III-A were no better than Bankau, such as a kilo of bread between fifteen PoWs, or a bucket of potatoes to be shared between twenty-five. They heard that the Russian advance was nearing the camp and, on 22 April 1945, he was woken to the sound of gunfire and screams. Emerging from their prison huts they saw dead German guards and Russian troops advancing through the camp with rifles raised. Howard felt a wave of sheer terror. Was this the end? Would they just be shot in the chaos?

In the mayhem of the Russian capture of Stalag III-A, Howard again found a way to survive. The Russian troops kept them imprisoned in the camp, giving them no information. Their treatment remained harsh and food was still scarce and of minimal nutrition. In desperation Howard and other PoWs devised ways to break into camp food stores, foraged for potatoes and searched for left-over vegetables in the horses' feeding bins, despite the threat of being shot by the Russians if they were caught. Days went by, then weeks, and their eventual fate remained unknown. Some prisoners tried to break out without success. Then, at last, without any warning the day came when they were traded to British forces in exchange for Russian PoWs. A week later they were back in Britain.[6]

*   *   *

On repatriation Harry Howard returned to Melbourne where he married Betty Groves, and they raised four children, Peter, Claire, Terry and Marie. Harry built a new life and a career in government stores and transport. He remained a gregarious personality and, while calm and determined, loved a laugh. Yet his ordeals in the war, his severe injuries, and the deprivations of life as a PoW left their mark. He was susceptible to depressive bouts where he would get very angry and become quite introverted for two to three days. To his family it was clearly the legacy of what he had endured – and what he had overcome.[7]

Chapter 29

Pilot dead, no-one else can fly, one engine gone, hammered by flak over Essen … yet baling out seems like suicide!

Flight Sergeant G.W. Walters[1]

On a daylight raid on the Homberg oil refinery in the Ruhr Valley, Lancaster T-Tare of No. 44 (Rhodesia) Squadron RAF is struck by a heavy burst of flak. The pilot is hit and collapses unconscious, or is thought to have been killed by flak shrapnel, and the flight engineer is also wounded in the leg. Bomb aimer Flight Sergeant Walters, although not a pilot, takes over the controls. With the greater part of the aircraft's instrument panel destroyed, and one engine put out of action, the Lancaster and its crew appear to be doomed.[2]

* * *

Aircrew of Bomber Command were extremely reluctant to bale out over Germany and occupied Europe. Being machine-gunned by German fighters while hanging from a parachute was a not uncommon occurrence. Once on the ground, lynching by a civilian mob as a 'terror flieger', torture and execution by the Gestapo, or a slow death as a PoW were the likely fates and, understandably, feared.

Whether shot down over enemy territory, or trying to nurse a damaged aircraft back to base, airmen had a deep desire to somehow find a way back to Britain. Whatever the difficulties and ordeal to do so, there was a belief that anything would be better than imprisonment by the Germans. While officers were sometimes treated humanely, other ranks were less so. The Geneva Convention allowed other ranks to be put to any work not directly related to war production – in effect used as slave labour.[3]

Baling out was usually seen as a last resort and airmen would hang on in a damaged aircraft as long as they could. They would cling to a hope that they could get back to their home airfield, or any RAF airfield or, a last resort if necessary, bale out over Britain or over the sea. No better example of this is the crew of a Lancaster bomber of No. 44 (Rhodesia) Squadron.

Although No. 44 Squadron was renamed in 1941 with the addition of the name of the African colony, Rhodesia, recognising the contribution of airmen from Southern and Northern Rhodesia, its make-up also included many airmen from such as Australia, the UK, New Zealand and South Africa. In April 1942 Squadron Leader Nettleton, a South African, had led the audacious daylight raid of six Lancasters on Augsburg, for which he was awarded the VC. The squadron had a fine pedigree and tradition, from its formation in 1917 as a home defence fighter unit until its disbandment in December 1919. It reformed as a bomber squadron in March 1937, and in early 1942 was the first squadron to become operational with the Lancaster.

On 1 November 1944 at 13.30 hours, eighteen Lancasters of No. 44 Squadron left their base at RAF Spilsby, near Great Steeping in Lincolnshire, to undertake their first-ever daylight operation as a full squadron.[4] It was a raid to attack the Homberg oil refinery in Germany's Ruhr. To fly into a maelstrom of flak in the night skies of the Ruhr's 'Happy Valley' was daunting in itself. To do so in daylight was terrifying to contemplate, in some minds perhaps verging on suicidal.

Lancaster IM650 T-Tare, piloted by Flying Officer J.H.T. 'Jack' Howarth, a quiet retiring Rhodesian, took off from Spilsby at 13.42 hours.[5] In Haworth's crew were:[6]

Name	Role
Sergeant M.F. 'Mark' Seller	Flight Engineer
Flight Sergeant G.W. Walters	Bomb Aimer
Sergeant A.W. McAllister	Rear Gunner
Flight Sergeant G.W. Gardner	Wireless Operator
Sergeant B.J. Saunders	Navigator
Sergeant T. Mackay	Mid-Upper Gunner

The outward flight to the Homberg target area passed without significant incident. It was a misleading lull, for the arrival of the bomber stream in the target area was met by an intense box barrage of flak. Its intensity was as if to make up for the heavy blanket of cloud which cloaked the target and prevented sightings of aircraft by German air defences. Fortunately, the cloud also concealed the bombers from enemy fighters. Because of the thick cloud, a Pathfinder force dropped Wanganui flares, which used lightweight parachute markers.

Between 16.08 and 16.12 hours, at altitudes between 16,000 to 17,000 feet, the Lancasters of No. 44 Squadron released their bomb loads on these

Wanganui markers.[7] Eleven aircraft suffered damage from the hailstorm of flak. A concentrated wave of flak cascaded onto Haworth's bomber, causing T–Tare to shudder as it absorbed the fragments of bursting shells and deafening the crew.

Direct hits into the cockpit shattered many of the instruments and badly wounded Haworth. Within a few minutes the crew realised that Haworth had died, or that is what they thought. It was a crew's worst nightmare. They were flying without a pilot. The flight engineer, Sergeant Seller, carried on doing what he could to keep the Lancaster airborne and in level flight.

It seemed that they were in a situation without any options. Still in a firestorm of flak from the air defences of Happy Valley, T–Tare was damaged seriously and their pilot was dead. To bale out, even into the blizzard of flak, seemed the only option. Yet not one of the crew relished the thought. The rear gunner, Sergeant McAllister, at first thought that he had no choice in the matter anyway. He was trapped in his rear turret.

Flak damage had caused his turret to lose power, preventing him from rotating his position to either jump out or step back into the fuselage, where there was a rear hatch. McAllister grabbed an axe that was available for just such a situation and used it to free himself. Finding that the hatch was also jammed, he wielded the axe again to break it open.

Meanwhile bomb aimer Flight Sergeant G.W. Walters, having moved Haworth's slumped inert body to one side, took over the Lancaster's controls. There was no time to examine Haworth properly. Luckily, the airspeed indicator and altimeter appeared to be still functioning effectively. However, the remaining instrumentation was beyond use. In addition, one of T–Tare's four engines was out of action. Fortunately it had not caught fire. Still the stark reality was that Walters had received very little training in flying, had no experience of being in control of a Lancaster on an operation and would be unable to land the aircraft.

Despite his rudimentary knowledge of piloting any aircraft, Walters told the crew that he was prepared to attempt to fly T–Tare back to England, where they would have the chance to bale out over home soil. Every one of the crew instantly responded in the affirmative. But first they must get out of the target area and escape the waves of flak.

Buoyed by a swirl of emotions, hope, desperation and the trust of the remaining crew, Walters turned T–Tare onto a westward course for home. As they flew on towards the setting sun, the cloud prevented them seeing any landmarks on the ground. To add to their difficulties, flight engineer Seller revealed that he had been wounded in the leg by flak shrapnel. Despite this, he was able to carry on assisting Walters, managing the engines, and monitoring the aircraft's speed and height.

Walters kept the Lancaster eating up the miles, relying only on his airspeed indicator and altimeter. They had to pray that no enemy fighters found them as their rear guns were out of action and they were incapable of taking evasion manoeuvres such as corkscrewing. Time must have seemed excruciatingly slow. Their luck held and, eventually, T Tare began to cross the English Channel. Their wireless operator, Flight Sergeant Gardner, sent a signal to RAF Spilsby, to the effect that, because the pilot was dead, once they crossed the English coast all the crew intended to bale out.

The aircraft's course plotted by the navigator, Sergeant Saunders, was charted to take them across the Kent coast. Walters and Seller held T-Tare true to the heading, and very soon they sighted the coast's White Cliffs. Once they were over land, Walters instructed the crew to bale out. However, first they faced a dilemma. What should they do with Haworth's slumped body? Within the cramped, dark and noisy confines of a Lancaster, and now with the urgent imperative of baling out, no one could be one hundred per cent certain that he was dead. Was there a faint chance that he was unconscious? In any case, no-one wished to leave Haworth to go down with T-Tare to a fiery end.

It was decided to bale him out on a static line. They strapped a parachute on Haworth and let him go. Then, one by one, Saunders, Mackay, McAllister, Gardner and Seller dropped through the Lancaster's hatch. Once the last of the crew had jumped out, Walters turned T-Tare back onto a course to take it over the sea, and then baled out himself. Saunders, Mackay, McAllister, and Gardner landed safely, but soon learned that Seller had not. His parachute, possibly damaged by flak, had failed to open, and he had fallen to his death.

As the flight engineer, Seller had been so pivotal in supporting and encouraging Walters in his initiative to try and fly T-Tare back to England. Now he also had lost his life in a most tragic way. Saunders, Mackay, McAllister, and Gardner waited anxiously to hear if Walters had managed to bale out, and whether he was still alive. Walters did land safely, and was subsequently awarded the Conspicuous Gallantry Medal (CGM). He had saved the other four crew and himself from baling out into an unknowable fate in Nazi Germany.

T-Tare was recorded as crashing at 17.45 hours in southern England. It is not known where Flying Officer Haworth's body made landfall.[8]

Chapter 30

Surviving those first few demanding operations – then an unimaginable and unforeseeable disaster

Flight Sergeant Richard Nairn[1]

For aircrew in RAF Bomber Command, serious injury or death could come at any minute, and in any number of unpredictable ways. For freshly trained aircrew during the first days and first few operations with a Bomber Command squadron everything was new and full of a mixture of excitement, tension, nerves, enthusiasm, as well as at times anxiety and fear. In each airman, of course, the mix of emotions varied according to their psychological make-up and personality but it was overlaid with a layer of that sangfroid typical of the RAF.

Surviving those first few operations to gain experience and 'know-how' under fire, which no amount of training could imbue, was critical. Some said that only after about ten operations would you begin to learn the intangible 'smarts' to stay alive, and have any chance to complete the goal of a tour – thirty operations. Yet disaster could strike in unimaginable ways.

*　　*　　*

In November 1944 Flight Sergeant Richard Nairn, wireless operator in a new crew of a Lancaster of No. 103 Squadron RAF could not have imagined the disaster that would befall him and two other crew members. Richard Nairn was twenty-eight, five feet nine, dark-haired with brown eyes and had left his job as an advertising representative in July 1942 to join the RAAF in Sydney. After initial training, he arrived in Britain in December 1943 to undertake operational training. Straight from completion of bomber training, on 7 November 1944 Nairn and his crew arrived with three other new crews at No. 103 Squadron, RAF Elsham Wolds in north Lincolnshire.

Some of No. 103 Squadron's aircrew, who had just completed thirty operations flying Lancasters and were about to go on leave, told Nairn that

Flight Sergeant Richard Nairn, No. 103 Squadron RAF, standing beside a Lancaster at RAF Elsham Wolds, 1944. (*Private collection, Andrew Nairn*)

operations were a 'piece of cake'. In their first days Nairn and his crew undertook two cross-country bombing exercises and he speculated when they would be rostered for their first operation.

> We began our daily visits to the flight offices to check the listed flying duties for the day. These were indicated on a blackboard in chalk, simply with the pilot's name, and his aircraft's call sign. Upon obtaining this information we then went to breakfast on bicycles, and then for pick-up by jeep for a visit to our allotted aircraft to check all equipment. After this we went to the mess by jeep for lunch, and to collect any mail, or write letters.[2]

Since the whole airfield, including offices, hangars etc., was dispersed over a wide area, it was necessary for all aircrew to travel by bicycle. The only exceptions were for aircraft inspection and operations, when aircrew were transported by jeep.

On 11 November the name of Nairn's pilot, Flying Officer D.M. Furler, was chalked on the flight office blackboard, together with Lancaster LM 131. Nairn learned that the target on their first operation was the Coisse oil refinery at Dortmund.

After lunch we went to the flight offices to collect our parachutes, Mae West life-jackets, and any other clothing, and escape kits. Should we be shot down over Germany, we were advised of certain escape towns where an airman might find sanctuary, such as the Baltic ports of Lübeck and Rostock (red-light areas recommended!), and Schaffhausen on the Swiss border.

Airmen's escape kits could comprise such as the following: food concentrate, e.g. tablets; a fishing line; pain-injection syringe; escape money (usually guilders or francs); a pipe with a hidden compass; silk maps of the operational area etc. A penknife was slotted into a flying boot so that, on the ground, after hiding the parachute, an airman could cut the stitching of the flying boots, leaving only the 'shoes'.

From the flight office Nairn and his crew went to the briefing room, where thirteen other crews gathered.

The map of the target and route were revealed, Dortmund – a round trip of about five and a half hours. On the faces of other crews I saw expressions of anxiety or relief, perhaps reflecting experience of past raids over this area. After this we were told the objects of the operation, with the Squadron's Navigation Officer plotting the course to avoid flak positions, and our rendezvous over the English coast.

Other briefing information included: 'window' dropping point; pathfinder flares; Very flares colours of the day; bomber code sheets; 'Gee Box' readings of geographical shapes en route and in the target area; 'Q' signal sheets; details of German Freyburg and Wurtzburg radar etc. As always, radio silence was to be absolute to avoid any signal being picked up by the enemy. Further briefings followed from the squadron officers responsible for wireless operation, bombing, gunnery and meteorology. Nairn's Lancaster was one of fourteen detailed for the raid on Dortmund.

Once our navigator plotted the course to Dortmund on our maps, we boarded a jeep and were driven to our Lancaster LM131 in its dispersal bay. We climbed aboard for our first operation through the door on its starboard side. The doctor arrived in his jeep to dispense Benzedrine 'wakie-wakie' tablets, if requested. We did not avail ourselves of this aid, probably because of it being our first operation. However, we were already very tired due to the day's preparations prior to boarding the aircraft, and some of the crew were exhausted.

At 15.54 hours Flying Officer Furler lifted LM131 off the runway into the winter sky.[3] Nairn thought that the fully-laden bomber with its full bomb load struggled to take to the air. Once airborne he switched on the IFF signal (Identification Friend or Foe), for protection from Allied fighters, land and sea anti-aircraft batteries, before they made rendezvous with the main bomber force at 12,000 feet. To Nairn that was a sight never to be forgotten.

> From the astrodome there were bombers as far as the eye could see at every quarter – above, ahead, below, behind and either side. And these were only some of 250 bombers on this operation. All crew members were fully occupied during the flight, with the navigator plotting our course and watching his 'Gee Box' for any speeding blips indicating fighters, the skipper banking from side to side to help him and the gunners in searching the sky for Luftwaffe night-fighters. Any observations of lights or exploding aircraft were logged.
>
> Every half hour I would log the call signs from the squadron. Over enemy territory we dropped bundles of 'window' dependent upon nearness to German radar. We climbed slowly up to 20,000 feet, and began our approach to the target. Each bomber was dropping a flare on the target and, as soon as we dropped ours, I switched the radio over to R/T to receive bombing instructions from the master bombers flying below us, at about 10,000 feet.

On the way to Dortmund the bomber stream had encountered sparse broken cloud, whereas over the target the first waves of aircraft bombed through variable cloud ranging from 50 to 100 per cent cover.

> Upon our approach to bomb, the skipper alerted the crew, 'Bomb doors open'. We were now ready for the straight and level fifteen seconds run over the target. On the master bomber's instructions the bomb aimer switched on the camera and released the bombs.
>
> Immediately our Lancaster was relieved of the bomb load, she gave a violent sighing jerk upwards and we sped away from the target area and its radar-directed flak. The view of the target at our bombing height of 20,000 feet prior to closing the bomb doors was brighter than daylight.

As Lancaster LM131 hurried away from the target area, any release of tension felt by the crew did not last long. On their return journey Nairn noticed that there was a minimum of conversation, and the search was on again for enemy night-fighters. The crew's anxious scanning and peering into the gloom proved happily to be unproductive and, on reaching the English Channel, Nairn was able to receive signals very clearly from the squadron's base.

> After flying through the allotted corridor to avoid our own anti-aircraft guns, we soon arrived over Elsham Wolds to await landing instructions.

Upon landing at 21.42 hours we were taken immediately to meet the intelligence officers for debriefing, and to receive our rum and Ovaltine which, after our excitement on our first operation, had the desired result of loosening all our tongues to a maximum.

At the end of our debriefing, and our returning of escape equipment etc., we picked up our bikes and rode to the mess for our egg and chips. Usually after a few yards I would ride into the ditch beside the road – probably caused by a combination of exhaustion and the rum-laced Ovaltine!

Next day after breakfast Nairn and his other crew members again cycled to the flight office to check if they were listed for the night's operation – and possibly to receive from the adjutant any cigarettes which had belonged to the crews who did not return the previous night. Some crew also visited the aircrew library, which was an important part of training only accessible by aircrew. Nairn was one of those who always sought out the booklet in a red cover published by the Air Ministry, which listed the silhouettes of new enemy aircraft.

Their next operation, the second, on 18 November was to Wanne Eickle, a major rail junction on the Dortmund-Duisberg railway line. This time Furler was at the controls of Lancaster ND861 as they took off at 15.19 hours, expecting a flight of almost seven hours there and back.[4] Nairn thought the outward flight and bombing over the target went as planned.

On our return flight, however, when over France I was surprised to receive a faint signal from the Squadron, so far from England. The signal from my memory was four blocks of four letters per block in Bomber Code, and it stated that due to thick fog we were diverted to a choice of any of three airfields.

Because of the faint and unexpected signal so far from the coast, I felt it would be wise to check the signal closer to home for any possible correction. This, however, proved to be impossible because, with so much radio interference from other returning bombers in the same predicament, it seemed all hell had broken loose. By this time we were coming up the east coast of England in a thick brown soup of a fog – visibility nil. At some point the skipper said that we only had about one quarter hour of fuel left, so there would not be time to check the signal.

Flying Officer Furler, as pilot and captain, was faced with making a quick decision on the three available airfields. Nairn recognised that there could be no more time spent hoping for a break in the weather and a return to Elsham Wolds.

We had a choice of two airfields in the south of England, and one in Scotland at Dyce outside Aberdeen, with which the skipper said that he was familiar, but only on Oxford training aircraft.

Although Furler also knew that Dyce airfield was surrounded by hills with a runway a little short for a Lancaster bomber, he chose that option and headed northwards. Nairn could only assume that Furler had re-assessed that they had sufficient fuel to reach Dyce.

If Dyce airfield was fogged in, we would have to bale out, leaving the aircraft to fly on a course back out over the North Sea until the fuel ran out. However, as we neared Dyce, the fog cleared, and we now had a perfect starry night. With great relief we landed safely. We were received by the duty officer, who told us that we would not receive our rum ration as Dyce was a dry station. Nevertheless, we did get our hard-earned egg and chips.

In the morning, before we could make a visit to Aberdeen town, we received a signal to return to the Squadron immediately. We were met on arrival by our Signals Officer, a Squadron Leader, who asked to see my log which I had logged correctly but wrongly coded. However, he seemed relieved that we were safe.

The previous night had been chaotic, due to the confusion caused by other airfields also being fogged in. Dyce had been a good choice, thought Nairn.

Some aircraft did not receive any signal, so they returned to Elsham Wolds, overshooting or crashing on the runway. One bomber just missed the Sergeants' Mess. So, with many wrecked aircraft on the diverted airfields and our own airfield, my error was minimised and only required a written report to our Group 1 Base. Our Signals Officer consoled me saying, 'Funny things happen in the air!'

The next operation, on 21 November, the third for Nairn and his crew, was a raid on a major railway marshalling yard at Aschaffenburg.[5]

When we arrived there over the target area, it was as if all hell had broken loose down below. We tuned into our master bombers' wireless transmissions and opened the bomb-doors ready for the fifteen-seconds straight-and-level bombing run. We received instructions to bomb the 'greens' which were just released. After about fifteen seconds the skipper called the bomb aimer, 'Have you dropped those bombs yet?' He replied that the 'greens' were observed, but with some cloud and decided not to bomb.

So we closed the bomb-doors and began another circuit of the target, which allowed the Germans' radar-controlled flak batteries to pin-point our aircraft. By this time we were over the target again with the bomb-doors open, ready for our second fifteen-second run. Our rear gunner was screaming that the directed flak was on to us. He could see it, and hear it, as it seemed to be coming directly at him.

As soon as the bombs were dropped, to avoid the flak, the skipper dived, reaching a speed of over 350mph. My cheeks felt as though they had dropped down to my boots. On our return flight to Eltham Wolds, as expected, not a word was spoken. We landed at 22.12 hours, and after our debriefing and return to the mess on our bikes – and my usual prang into the ditch – we all agreed that this trip should equal two operations. Then came the sequel. Although the bomb-aimer had done a good job on the second fifteen-seconds run, because of the flak, excitement and our violent evasive action, he had forgotten to switch on the camera.

This could have meant, in theory, that the bombs may have been dropped elsewhere, such as in the English Channel or in the North Sea. Lack of photographic evidence of bombs being dropped onto a target could result in a crew's operation being classified as not completed. Nairn was relieved when they heard that the operation was resolved in their favour, because luckily their debriefing information tallied with the other bombers' reports.

The tension, tiredness, nerves etc., although not consciously apparent to myself, was shown distinctly in my log writing. As we had neared the target, my writing became progressively wobbly, but on our return it soon straightened up as we neared the English Channel. The strain could be seen in other different ways. For example, I observed one aircrew member who each day seemed to be letter writing quietly alone. I noticed that his hair during my few weeks in the squadron changed to a distinct light grey. I was told that he had just completed twelve operations.

The next operation, our fourth, was Freiburg, a seven-and-a- half-hour round trip, where, on its outskirts we were told, were billeted some divisions of enemy troops who were preparing to attack French forces over the Vosges mountains. For this operation our aircraft was N-Nan, which was having engine trouble with its port inner motor. The ground crew had been working on it for many hours, and were exhausted. Eventually, whilst boarding the bomber, I saw their tired faces, when they looked up at me. Their expressions were as if to say, 'I hope this bastard doesn't come back.'

The operation proved to be successful and effective. Nairn read newspaper reports that the operation inflicted extensive casualties. 'Now after getting through our first four operations, we were given our first leave. The skipper, bomb-aimer and myself decided to drive to London in a tiny four-seater Austin car.'

Close to Bassingbourn in Cambridgeshire, the three airmen were motoring south at night on the Great North Road towards London. In fog and the usual blackout conditions their car headlights were switched off, as were street lights, making it a strain to peer ahead and follow the road. It was not unlike the pea-soup fog that they had encountered when they had to divert to Dyce. Suddenly, with a massive bang and tearing of metal, they collided with the rear of a truck, which was loaded with scrap metal and had broken down. It was as if their little Austin car had smashed into a stone castle wall. The impact hurled their puny vehicle into the ditch at the side of the road.

> The skipper suffered a broken collar-bone, our bomb-aimer was left half-blinded in one eye. I sustained a broken leg, and head and face injuries, including a two-and-a-half-inch fracture on the left-hand side of my face. It left me with a whistle in that ear, and numbness in my upper jaw. After some weeks in hospital I returned to the Squadron, and found that the remainder of our crew had been allotted to other crews. Our mid-upper gunner, navigator and engineer, having been allotted to new crews, had gone missing on various operations. Our rear-gunner, who had been transferred to the squadron leader's crew, returned from an operation badly shot up.

Nairn also learned that the other three new crews, with whom they had arrived on 7 November, were posted as 'Missing' on various operations. So perhaps their disastrous road accident, which despite their injuries, Nairn and his two comrades so luckily survived was in reality a moment of serendipity.

> While I had been away recovering from our road accident, the squadron's adjutant had a nervous breakdown and been transferred out, and the doctor also because of a drink problem. I felt this was understandable, because of the obvious strain to these two officers from waiting night after night for the return of airmen, knowing that some would not come back. And some of whom they would have gotten to know well.

Sometimes there were periods when crews went missing every night. It was common for airmen to speak of seeing the empty chairs in the mess each morning – of those who had been shot down during the night.

At some point I heard that our engineer was shot down over German and Russian front lines, and was nearly lynched by German civilians. I myself did not fly again, and finished up doing a commando course on a station near Weston-Super-Mare, to prepare for a posting to the Japanese theatre of the war!

Luckily that did not happen, and Nairn returned to Sydney in July 1945. He married Betty Hughes and they had two children, Andre and Margaret.[6]

Chapter 31

'Tail-End Charlies' can be lucky … and fearless.

Sergeant Ricky Dyson[1]

Rear-turret gunners of RAF bombers suffered the highest casualty rate of all bomber aircrew, which caused them sometimes to be disparagingly referred to as 'Tail-End Charlies'. Yet they were highly valued by other crew members. To sit in a cramped gun turret with its front panel of thin perspex, exposed to freezing temperatures, for interminable hours, expecting to be hit by flak or enemy fighter fire at any moment, required a unique kind of courage. In the later years of the war the perspex panel was often removed to provide greater visibility, particularly night vision, and so fully exposing a rear gunner to the icy air and wind.

To provide some protection while sitting for several hours in a freezing turret where, in place of the perspex panel, there was just open air, rear gunners were issued with special clothing. In addition to normal clothing, rear gunners were provided with electrically-heated inner and outer flying suits, as well as many layers of gloves in silk, chamois, wool, and electrically-heated leather. For their feet they were issued heated slippers within sheepskin flying boots which, together with a seat-type parachute, made for difficult entry to, and movement in the turret. Most critically their bulky protective clothing hindered their exit from the turret when baling out.

Many rear gunners disliked and distrusted this cumbersome attire. Rear gunner Sean Drumm, of No. 630 Squadron at RAF East Kirby, said that no rear gunners on the squadron would wear them. 'Mine went on fire. I looked down and there were sparks coming from the flying boots. I got out quickly and got the suit off. I wouldn't wear one again, nor would anybody else. We used to dress in long johns and vests and overalls and then a thick brown inner suit and an outer suit followed by the flying boots.'[2]

Rear gunners were often the first to be riddled with bullets from a night-fighter's machine guns, or blasted apart by cannon fire. Their need for constant alertness to warn of an approaching enemy fighter, and gunnery skills to defend against attacking fighters, were often the difference between life and death for the aircraft and its crew. Because of this their steadfastness and bravery to do such a job, meant that, despite their nickname, they were held in great respect by the rest of a bomber's aircrew.

*   *   *

For rear gunner Ricky Dyson on 26 November 1944 there would be another pivotal moment in his war service. It was not the first such day. In May 1940 he had fled from the German Blitzkrieg with the other ground crew of No. 59 Squadron from their airfield near Amiens in France, first on a farm tractor and then on foot, along with thousands of other troops and civilians making for the Channel ports. Dyson survived the German onslaught, staying alive in the death and destruction of the chaotic retreat, reached Boulogne, and became one of the lucky ones escaping on a paddle-boat back to Britain.

Shortly after that time Dyson counted himself doubly fortunate to still have his life, for two weeks later, on 8 June, the aircraft-carrier HMS *Glorious*, in which he had been serving in the Fleet Air Arm in 1939, was sunk by the German battlecruisers *Scharnhorst* and *Gneisenau*. Of some 1,500 sailors and airmen only forty-six survived. Back in England after evacuation from France, he re-joined No. 59 Squadron and, in due course, went through training for aircrew and gunnery school.

In August 1944 he began operations as an air gunner, first with No. 9 Squadron. Subsequently he served with Nos 106 and 44 Squadrons and in November 1944 was with No. 189 Squadron at Fulbeck where, on the 26th, a rear gunner in a new Lancaster crew, he learned that they were rostered for a raid on Munich.

Sergeant Ricky Dyson, No. 189 Squadron RAF, on post-war visit to RAF Fulbeck crash site and memorial. (*Private collection, M. Dyson*)

I was flying on Lancaster PB745 Q-Queenie, piloted by Flight Sergeant Doug Presland, and I was replacing the normal gunner who was recovering from a head wound. We took off in poor visibility at 23.59 hours, carrying a full load of high explosive, cluster and incendiary bombs, and a full tank of fuel.[3]

The night was cold and wet, heavy with low cloud. A bomber stream from No. 5 Group, comprising 270 Lancasters and eight Mosquitoes, was setting off to raid Munich. On take off, Lancaster Q-Queenie was climbing for about eleven minutes. At 1,000 feet the bomber began to turn when disaster struck. Q-Queenie was on a wrong heading and too low. The Lancaster bomber tore through a hillside of fields and hedges, before a massive explosion collapsed the whole aircraft into a disintegrating inferno.

Dyson was knocked unconscious in the impact, and came round to find himself still sitting in his rear gun-turret which, with a rear section of the aircraft's fuselage, had been ripped from the Lancaster, and catapulted away from the main burning wreckage. Once conscious Dyson quickly realised what had occurred.

The rear turret with me inside it had broken away from the body of the aircraft and been hurled about fifty yards away. With full fuel tanks and a full bomb load we had crashed into high ground. The aircraft had exploded and burst into flames on impact, showering debris over a wide area.

Part of the fuselage behind Dyson's turret was also on fire, blocking any escape that way. Unless he got out at once he would be burned alive. He struggled out of his flying suit and grabbed an axe held in the turret for just this situation. Dyson hacked at the turret's perspex canopy, breathing in smoke and flames that were engulfing his turret from behind. His first strokes only chipped at the toughened perspex panel until ever despairing blows broke open a small opening. He scrambled through, falling to the ground on to his back, then ran into the dark while behind him his gun-turret filled with roaring flames. In his headlong dash for safety Dyson collapsed into a hedge.

Aircraft wreckage was scattered over the area and was burning furiously, with incendiaries exploding, and unexploded bombs lying both in and about the remains of the Lancaster.[4] Dyson looked back at the burning Lancaster and, on hearing cries for help, instinctively rushed back to see if he could rescue any of his crew members. He found the pilot, Presland still trapped in his cockpit, one leg severed below the knee, and flames licking at his body. Amidst the smoke, fire and exploding ordnance, Dyson managed to pull Presland free and dragged him some way from the aircraft.

Then he went back again and, beating at the flames, pulled out first the bomb aimer, Sergeant Billy McClune. Next he found the navigator, Sergeant Alan Probert, who was seriously injured and with his clothing on fire, about fifteen yards from the aircraft. Dyson put out the flames with just his hands, receiving burns on both hands while doing so.[5] Now badly burned himself, Dyson tried but failed to rescue the mid-upper gunner Jack Fender, and he himself was found eventually by the rescue parties wandering around, suffering from shock. 'The pilot, Doug Presland, and the mid-upper gunner Jack Fender, had severe burns and other serious injuries, whereas mine were only slight. The horror of that night was printed on my mind for ever.'[6]

Fender was freed by firemen, and both he and Presland survived after prolonged hospital care. All other crew members died of their injuries. Dyson received extensive treatment for burns to his face and hands, followed by extensive medical treatment, before being sent on recuperative leave. In addition to clinical care, psychological assessment would follow but for Ricky Dyson the war was not yet finished.

Chapter 32

Boxing Day night in Burma, one engine burnt out at tree-top height ... the dark impenetrable jungle below lies in wait

Pilot Officer W.G. 'Bill' Taylor[1]

Pilot Officer Bill Taylor drops the Mosquito fighter-bomber down to treetop height, and opens up the twin engines to full speed. It was Boxing Day, 26 December 1944, and his Mosquito was one of four, each carrying four 250lb bombs in the bomb bay, and long-range fuel tanks below each wing. They had taken off at dusk to attack the Japanese HeHo air force base in Burma's south. On the approach to Heho the four Mosquitos are met by a wall of anti-aircraft fire. At only fifty feet over the Japanese base Taylor sees the tracer fixed on his starboard wing, which quickly erupts into a stream of black smoke and flames.

* * *

As the end of 1944 approached in the Burma campaign, Allied forces on the ground were on the offensive on three fronts. In the centre, General Slim's Fourteenth Army was driving south towards Mandalay. In the air, there was another offensive, the battle for air supremacy. Allied ground forces were crucially dependent upon their air forces maintaining air superiority so that they were able to rely upon transport aircraft for supplies.

On 26 December 1944, Pilot Officer W.G. 'Bill' Taylor, with his navigator, Warrant Officer K.F. Putman, took off at 16.04 hours from Kumbhirgram airfield in Assam in north-east India.[2] With three other Mosquitos of No. 45 Squadron RAF (The Flying Camels), they were on an operation to bomb the Japanese Heho airfield. Heho airfield, around 200 miles south-east of Mandalay in the eastern Shan state, was an important air base for the Japanese Army Air Force (JAAF).

Bill Taylor had enrolled in the RAAF in Sydney Australia in November 1941, undertook flying training in Canada and the UK, before, in September

1943, being posted to India. There, in February 1944, he joined No 45. Squadron (The Flying Camels). The bombing raid on HeHo on 26 December 1944 would be Taylor's ninth operation.

Pilot Officer Bill Taylor, No. 45 Squadron RAF, India 1944. (*Private collection, Sue Cox*)

> Our planes could carry four 250lb bombs in the bomb bay or two 500lb bombs, one on each wing, and were armed with four machine guns and four 20mm cannon in the nose. On this occasion, as we had to travel across the Burma valley and into the hills on the far side, we carried extra fuel in tanks under the wings in place of some bombs. The fuel in the wing tanks would be used first and, once empty, the tanks would be dropped.[3]

The under-wing fuel tanks extended the Mosquito's range beyond its typical 1,700 miles.

It was not only beneficial to get rid of the extra weight and drag of the under-wing fuel tanks: once empty they were a critical weak point. After the fuel was used up the tanks would fill with gas and, if hit with a bullet, could explode and blow a wing off. 'We took off late afternoon so we could arrive just after dusk. Up to this time there were no Allied airstrips in Burma. If you got shot up you'd had it.'

A crash landing or baling out into the dense Burmese jungle was close to being a suicidal act. It was an absolute last resort. Compared with doing the same over occupied Europe there was no comparison. An air search for survivors or a ground rescue operation were both usually non-viable. At the pre-flight briefing, Taylor was surprised to hear that for the first time a strip at Kalemyo had just been opened, inside Burma but not far from the border with Assam, and it was available for night landings in an emergency.

The four Mosquitoes' outward flight to Heho went smoothly, fuel tanks were discarded, and their course was bringing them on target. As they began their approach they dropped down to near treetop height.

> We did a wide half circle around the airfield so that after the attack we would be on our way home. All was set, so we opened up to full speed and made our attack at about fifty feet. We were flying line abreast and I was in number three position. When we reached the aerodrome the Japs opened up on us with a wall of small arms defence. One gunner

got me in his sights and, as they were firing tracer bullets, I could see them passing over my starboard wing.

Coming in so low over the JAAF airfield, with each Mosquito's two Rolls Royce Merlin twelve-cylinder engines at full throttle, the four fighter-bombers were pushing their top speed of around 370 mph. It should have reduced the likelihood of being hit by anti-aircraft fire. Even though the Japanese gunner had locked onto his range and trajectory, Taylor felt that he couldn't go up as he would fly into more of the gunner's bullets, and he was too low to drop his height further.

Pilot Officer Bill Taylor, No. 45 Squadron RAF, with medals 2018. (*Private collection, Sue Cox*)

I just had to keep on going. He soon lowered his sights, and hit my starboard engine setting it on fire, and we could see a great stream of black smoke pouring out the back. In a matter of seconds I feathered the engine, pressed the fire extinguisher, reduced power on the good engine so the plane wouldn't flip over on its back, cut the switches and petrol to the starboard engine, and dropped the bombs.

Although the fire extinguisher did put out the fire, Taylor and Putman could see that the main wing spar was badly burnt, and the damage unknown.

Despite relying on only the port engine, Taylor had the Mosquito still flying under his control. However, even if he could keep the aircraft in the air he was confronted with two huge and immediate dilemmas. He had to conserve fuel to have a chance of making the return flight, yet he must climb to get over the surrounding hills some of which were around 5,000 feet high. HeHo airfield sat at around 3,800 feet, so Taylor needed to climb at least 1,500 feet. To gain height meant more power, and that would use more fuel. With no alternative he made the decision, took the Mosquito climbing over some close hills, and headed west.

We were now out of firing range from the ground, and the smoke from the starboard wing had stopped which was a good sign. We flew down a few valleys and eventually cleared all the hills, and set course for Kalemyo, which we had been told at the briefing before take off had night landing facilities. In fact this was the only landing strip we had in Burma at this particular time.

On only one engine they did not have sufficient fuel to return to Kumbhirgram in Assam. Kalemyo in Burma's north-west, and not far inside the Indian border, was the only option. It was a particularly daunting challenge for Taylor's navigator, Putman, who was not long out of training. Looking for anywhere to make a forced landing in the blackness of the jungle below was an impossibility. 'We headed west and, as it was a clear night, we felt confident that we could pick up the meeting of the Irrawaddy and Chindwin rivers.'

The conjunction of Burma's two major rivers was the key for finding a course to Kalemyo. But their single engine and dwindling fuel must last out. Otherwise the vast Burmese jungle would devour them. The blackness of night stretched ahead. Assuming they could find Kalemyo before the fuel ran out, Taylor was also concerned that the Mosquito's landing equipment could have been damaged, and be inoperable.

> On the way I discussed with Putman what could happen, if and when we landed. It was possible that the starboard tyre could be punctured, and also the air pressure line to the brakes could be damaged.

Putman would be in charge of the undercarriage on landing, and might have to make a split-second decision. Whether the landing wheels and other associated equipment were undamaged, and able to be operated, was unknowable. Visibility remained good and they found the junction of the Irrawaddy and Chindwin.

Putman's navigation proved to be excellent, and in due course they came to Kalemyo, still with enough fuel to pull around and acquaint themselves with the airfield. The very real likelihood of not finding Kalemyo, and running out of fuel had been avoided.

> We circled around and fired the colours of the period – there are two colours used for identification, which change every six hours. Then we fired a red flare indicating we were in distress. Very quickly they flashed back LL, which meant 'Standby'. I then noticed transport lights of vehicles moving towards the strip, which indicated that they had no night-flying lights or other facilities for the runway.

Taylor now faced a choice.

> We could do a belly landing where anything could happen, or take a 50/50 chance with the undercarriage and do a normal landing. Being captain it

was my decision and I chose to do a normal landing, and my navigator agreed. He was to have his hand on the undercarriage handle when we touched down, and if I felt any movement to the right, I would call out and he was to lift up the wheels.

At the end of the airstrip where we would make our approach they placed three trucks diagonally on either side of the air strip with their lights on. They then flashed a green light and in we went. I had to approach at 10mph faster than usual to gain better control. As it was built for Hurricanes, single-engine aircraft, I knew I could have trouble pulling up.

At 20.20 hours Taylor put the Mosquito down at Kalemyo. Although the wheels and undercarriage appeared to hold firm, the end of the strip's runway was coming up fast. He had no idea what lay beyond the lights of the three vehicles. The end of the runway was just totally black night, and Taylor wondered if the brakes were going to hold up.

Luckily all went well and I stopped right at the end of the strip. We got out and were met by a Wing Commander, who told me that I shouldn't be there, as the strip was not yet operational! How lucky we were that someone had made a mistake at the briefing!

Without that mistaken advice before take off, Taylor and his navigator would have been forced into a choice of a crash landing or baling out into the dense Burmese jungle. Neither of those would have offered much of a future.

On Taylor's eventual return to Kumbhirgram he received the following commendation in his log book from Group Captain E.O. Whiteley, Air Officer Commanding, No. 221 Group: 'Pilot Officer Taylor saved his own life, the life of his crew, and caused no further damage to his aircraft, only by his own flying ability and exceptional airmanship.'[4]

As in so many improbable survival incidents, luck had played a crucial role. Incorrect instructions at the pre-operation briefing, to the effect that, if necessary, pilots could put down in a night landing at Kalemyo had inadvertently saved the lives of Taylor and Putman.

Post-operation reports of the raid confirmed that two enemy aircraft were seen at HeHo, one 'Oscar' fighter at the north end of the runway, and one 'Dinah' reconnaissance aircraft at the south-east end of the dispersal area. Twelve 500lb bombs were dropped and the 'Dinah' was left in flames.[5]

* * *

Operations by No. 45 Squadron continued until August 1945 when, after Japan's surrender, the Australians in the squadron were sent to Calcutta to catch a ship home. It was in poor condition but, given a choice between going home and waiting, they chose to go. After stops in Fremantle and Adelaide, the ship entered Sydney Harbour on a sunny Sunday, 28 October 1945. Waiting for Bill Taylor were his mother and sister-in-law. Sadly, his father had passed away while he was overseas.

Bill later married and had a son and daughter. War had taught him to be careful and value all that life has to offer. His life had been saved by the bizarre chance of an incorrect briefing in regard to Kalemyo, which proved to be his salvation. He didn't march on Australia's Anzac Day – most of those he flew with lived in Canada or the UK, and the Australians he knew were scattered far and wide. He lived in Sydney, in his later years cared for by his daughter Sue and other family members, until he passed away in July 2019.[6]

Part VII

1945

Chapter 33

New Year's Day hangover – a Lancaster crew hangs together, and hangs on

Flying Officer M.G. 'Merv' Bache[1] and
Flight Sergeant John M. 'Jim' Jay[2]

In a daylight raid on 1 January 1945 the Lancaster of Flying Officer M.G. 'Merv' Bache is on its bombing run approach to the Dortmund-Ems canal at Ladbergen in northern Germany when it takes two direct hits from flak. Despite the bomb doors being blown off, catastrophic damage to two engines, and to the aircraft's instrumentation, Bache holds his course and releases the bombs. With the aircraft cruelly damaged and the port inner engine ablaze, he turns the crippled bomber back towards Holland. The aircraft is doomed, yet no one in the crew relishes baling out over Germany.

*   *   *

On that New Year's Day of January 1945 at RAF Waddington in Lincolnshire, Flight Sergeant John 'Jim' Jay, nineteen years old and a rear gunner on Lancaster PA169 PO-H, was woken at 03.00 hours. He and other air and ground crew who had left the New Year festivities, many after midnight, were woken in their beds in the early hours and pulled from their sleep. It seemed that they had only just shut their eyes.

Although there had been no hint during New Year's Eve of any operation being planned, an early morning departure had been ordered for a daylight raid by No. 467 Squadron on the Dortmund-Ems canal aqueduct at Landbergen. While the Lancaster would be carrying nine 1,000lb and four 500lb bombs, the crew would be forcing eyelids to stay open, and some would be carrying hangovers.

At around 07.30 hours ten Lancaster bombers began to take to the air.[3] At 07.34 hours Flying Officer Bache lifted Lancaster PO-H off the runway, with his crew trying to shake off the effects of those seasonal festivities.

Flight Sergeant John 'Jim' Jay, rear gunner (extreme right), and crew of Lancaster, No. 467 Squadron RAF (RAAF), at RAF Waddington, January 1945. (*Private collection, John Jay*)

The crew of Lancaster PO-H comprised:

Crew Member	Role
Flying Officer M.G. 'Merv' Bache	Pilot, and Captain
Flying Officer L.E. 'Jack' Patison	Navigator
Flight Sergeant S.H. 'Sam' Nelson	Bomb Aimer
Flight Sergeant C.J. 'Cec' Dreger	Wireless Operator
Flight Sergeant L.C. 'Les' Court	Mid-Upper Gunner
Sergeant E.R. 'Ernie' Wilson	Flight Engineer
Flight Sergeant John M. 'Jim' Jay	Rear Gunner

Like most of the crew, Jay himself had not got to bed until the early hours and felt pretty tired. It was their fifteenth operation, halfway towards the 'Holy Grail' of thirty. Another raid on the Ems canal triggered a recollection by Jay of a lucky escape on 6 November 1944 on a night operation to bomb the Ems-Weser canal.

> Night suddenly changed to day! Jerry had worked out our course and height, somewhat below a thin cloud cover and laid a laneway of parachute flares. I could see Lancasters all round in the reflected light from the cloud layer, with fighters darting through, firing and vanishing below, to go around for another attack.

We couldn't evade as we were virtually on our bombing run and the bomber stream was all around us. The Lancaster to port was attacked, but I was too fixated on my area of cloud with a possible fighter flashing through to notice the result. We were also attacked but without damage. We lost four aircraft, twenty-eight men.

There were no target indicators laid down and no clear target, so we headed for home but were diverted to a Yankee drome where they were astounded not only at our 14,000lb bomb load but that we brought it back and landed with it.

On 1 January it was a raid to the same general area, but this time the operation, to the Dortmund-Ems canal at Landbergen, was in daylight – a daunting prospect. The outward leg to Dortmund went without incident until, on their closing approach to the target, they were hit by flak. Two direct hits into the bomb bay blew the bomb-bay doors off. Another hit was into the port wing-root.

Surprisingly, at first Bache did not discern any apparent effect on the handling of the aircraft and, with his mind set on completing the mission, he pressed on to bomb normally at 11.17 hours from 11,700 feet. The target area was clear and visibility good. As they had experienced only moments earlier, the anti-aircraft fire was very accurate. Immediately after bombing they were hit again by flak. At once Bache knew this was different and looked back at the two port engines.

> It was in the port No. 1 tank, from which we lost most of the fuel. The inboard side of the port motor was ripped away and brown smoke and flames were pouring out. This engine was promptly feathered and the fire extinguisher switched on, causing the fire to go out reasonably quickly. The port outer engine was also hit, but did not catch fire. The effect was that power was lost from this motor, and revs were fluctuating from 2,200 to 2,000 per minute.[4]

In the rear turret of the Lancaster rear gunner Jay felt the hit, and the aircraft lurch to starboard.

> Despite the port outer engine being also hit, there was still enough power for my rear turret. In addition the trimming wires were shot away, and we had developed a forty-degree starboard bank, and Sam Nelson had to tie a loading cable to the rudder bar to hold it even in this position. We had bombed at around 12,000 feet, but quickly lost height and when we crossed the Rhine we were at 7,000 feet. Here we copped a lot more flak – this about fifteen minutes later, with our airspeed down to 130mph.

Heavy and light flak continued from the Rhine onwards. We lost use of the port rudder and the front turret, had a shell through the cockpit, and the bombing panel blown out under Sam's nose. We also lost the master compass unit through the roof, whilst Les and Cec stood beside it waiting to bale out and, of course, the wings and tailplane were absolutely peppered.

I was deathly frightened today. I never saw such flak. We could even see the flames of the explosives. I just sat there in my turret waiting to be hit, my knees and stomach trembling uncontrollably. Every now and then I'd scold myself for being scared, and stop it, but a few seconds later it would go again. And we took it for twenty minutes solid from 9,000 feet down to 3,600 feet.[5]

They were in a lone, mortally-damaged bomber struggling in daylight to stay airborne. Jay in his rear gun turret fully expected an interception by German fighters. If so, they would be easy prey. In this condition the maimed Lancaster flew on, all the time losing height. In a forty-degree bank to starboard, Bache was sustaining unbelievable effort, energy and skill to keep the aircraft flying and heading west towards Allied lines in Holland. Yet he knew that they would have to bale out shortly.

I warned the crew, and they put their parachutes on in readiness. We struggled along like this with the aircraft in about 40-degrees attitude bank, and yawing from side to side of our track, gradually losing height. Our best airspeed was around 125–130mph, and we were well behind the main formation.

A Tempest fighter aircraft was sighted and, upon us firing our last Very flare, it circled us above and astern and stayed with us until a point near the Maas river. Two Spitfires were also seen circling, while we were preparing to abandon our Lancaster. The crew were warned to be ready to receive abandoning instructions as soon as our height was down to 3,500 feet.

Somewhere between fifteen and twenty miles short of the Maas river, the port outer motor cut out and would not feather, but continued to windmill. The port inner engine, which had been windmilling from Landbergen, was restarted in an endeavour to obtain sufficient power to cross into Allied lines. It gave us about two to three minutes service at 1,000rpm, and then we were compelled to cut it, in view of vibration and the possibility of the whole engine falling out or blowing up.[6]

They had been flying through flak for about forty minutes and had crossed the Maas river. Holland and, possibly, Allied troops were below them. For Bache the moment to order the crew to bale out was getting very close.

The crew took up parachute positions, the flight engineer in the bomb-aimer's compartment, the navigator in the flight engineer's position, the wireless operator and mid-upper gunner at the rear door, and the rear gunner in his turret. During this time we were being repeatedly hit by flak in the front turret, in the bombing panel, through the floor and roof of the cockpit near the pilot's instrument panel, and in other parts of the aircraft.

Shortly afterwards, being reasonably certain of our position from checks by our navigator and bomb aimer, I ordered, 'Jettison hatch and open doors'. The bomb aimer opened the front hatch inwards, so there would be no possibility of jamming it, and so delaying jumping, and propped it against the sighting head in the perspex nose. The mid-upper gunner opened and checked the rear door, and held it closed until I gave the order to jump. When I gave the order, all the crew baled out.[7]

In the rear turret, Jay found that he had lost power. Since the only practicable way for a rear gunner to bale out was to rotate the turret, and fall out from there, he had to manually winch his turret 180 degrees. He had only seconds remaining to get out if he was not to go down with the aircraft. Jay eventually baled out somewhere between 3,500 and 1,800 feet.

Because of the violent slipstream of the diving Lancaster, I had to push myself hard away from the turret, and went out, I think, at about 2,400 feet. Next thing I was aware of, there was a not too violent jerk. I held the ripcord in my hand, and my boots just kept on going. The jump was nothing – think I'd exhausted my reserves of fear, and actually it was a relief. To know we were free of flak, and all we had to do was jump.[8]

Bache listened to his crew's communications as they baled out, although he could not be totally sure that they had all jumped. As the bomber hurtled downwards, there would only be a matter of seconds before it smashed into the ground. He had to assume that the intercom silence meant that all the crew had got out.

After allowing fifteen to twenty seconds to elapse from the last acknowledgement by the crew, I put my left foot on the right rudder pedal, lowered my seat, and with my left hand held full-right aileron, before stepping into the flight engineer's position. The aircraft started to roll and threw me onto the floor. I grasped the hand rail in the bomb aimer's compartment and hauled myself forward. Then, as I was halfway lowering myself through the hatch, the slipstream held me for a moment. But I managed to push myself clear, and pulled my ripcord almost immediately.[9]

Bache baled out probably below 2,000 feet, very close to the recommended lower limit of 1,500 feet. His descent was brief, before he hit the top of a pine tree, then landed heavily.

Jay saw the skipper come out of the Lancaster and watched the plane crash and blow up before he himself came down in a small wood, and was unhurt. Within a few minutes a bunch of children came running towards him.

> When I came down I wasn't sure whether I was in Allied or German territory, and when a number of children ran towards me, shouting and waving, my mind flew to briefings on German 'Werewolves' – adolescent fanatics with an appetite for stray troops and airmen. I drew my revolver. In the event I realised I couldn't shoot children, and put the gun away.
>
> As they came closer to me I was tremendously relieved to see they were laughing and quite unthreatening. I was even more relieved when, over a rise in the land, a number of adults appeared behind them. I realised how close I had come to murdering their offspring. I was not yet twenty myself and so rattled that I had difficulty releasing my parachute harness – the easiest of mechanisms to operate.
>
> The skipper then appeared and, led by the Dutch kids, the two of us moved off. About a mile further on we met up with Jack Patison, our navigator, and Les Court, our mid-upper gunner, and some Military Police from the British Army's 51st Highland Division. They took us to a little place called Overloon, where we got a cup of tea. Cec Dreger, our wireless operator, and Ernie Wilson, our flight engineer, joined us there. Cec had a broken ankle, and Ernie was helping him hobble along. From there we went to Eindhoven hospital for a check-up, where they found that Ernie too had broken his ankle.[10]

Later they learned that Sam Nelson, their bomb aimer, had also made a safe landing. All seven crew had parachuted from the crashing Lancaster at a dangerously low altitude, the first to go probably at around 3,000 feet. The last two, Jay and Bache, at around 2,000 feet or lower, had parachuted down only four miles west, and one mile north of German lines, in a spearhead salient of the British Army. However, they were also standing in the middle of a minefield, where only two months ago there had been a major tank battle.

It was extraordinary that a crippled Lancaster, flying on only two engines in daylight, made it as far as Holland without being shot down. It was also remarkable that all seven crewmen of such an extensively damaged bomber were able to parachute to safety. That they were able to land behind the Allies' front lines was largely due to the flying skill and brave determination of their pilot Bache. The crew's trust and support of Bache was also indispensable. He reported that the crew were perfectly disciplined in the best possible manner throughout the operation, and in baling out from the aircraft. On return to RAF Waddington Flying Officer Bache received an immediate award of the DSO.

*　*　*

In addition to their own skill and fortitude, Bache and his crew later learned that their good fortune on the morning of 1 January probably owed much to the Germans' Operation BODENPLATTE. After several months of planning and postponements, the Luftwaffe launched Operation BODENPLATTE, using all the fighter aircraft that could be mustered from across Germany. At about 08.20 hours (GMT) Luftwaffe fighters attacked sixteen Allied airfields across Holland, Belgium and France.

Of about 900 German fighters some 600 survived to return to their bases between 09.30 and 10.30 hours GMT. This meant that while Flying Officer Bache urged Lancaster PO-H to struggle on to Allied lines between 11.20 and 12.00 hours GMT, those returned fighters would have been re-arming and re-fuelling. And, of course, relative to the scale of Operation BODENPLATTE, a single RAF bomber flying low and slow towards Holland would have had little priority. Bache, Jay and their other crew members were lucky in more ways than one.

Flight Sergeant Jay subsequently completed another ten operations with No. 467 Squadron, twenty-five in total by the end of the war. One weekend, while on leave, he visited a relative in Edinburgh where he was invited to a dance organised by a local insurance company. There he met a Scottish girl, June, and from there on he used every day of leave he had to travel to Edinburgh to see her. When Jay was repatriated to Australia, he and June corresponded for five years until, in 1950, June joined him in Sydney. Soon after they married, brought up a family of five sons, and currently live together independently in their Sydney home. The unpredictability of chance in 1945 had smiled upon them.[11]

Chapter 34

No ordinary day – baling out at 15,000 feet and into the Battle of the Bulge

Flight Sergeant Russell Stinson[1]

In the early hours of 6 January 1945, on a raid to bomb a parachute factory in Berlin, the Mosquito of navigator and co-pilot Flight Sergeant Russell Stinson is flying straight and level on the last few miles to the target in Germany's 'Big City'. As yet there is no flak, then an amber light on the instrument panel begins to glow. They are being tracked by anti-aircraft radar. Stinson is in the nose section setting the readings in the bomb-sight and, with the bomb doors open, holds the release toggle. Suddenly there is a terrific smashing sound and the Mosquito bucks and rolls.

Stinson is bucketed from side to side in his bomb-aiming position. The starboard engine has burst into flames from a direct flak hit. Stinson struggles back to the cockpit next to his pilot, Flying Officer Frank Henry. Most of the starboard engine and leading edge of that wing had disappeared. The aircraft is wrecked and losing height. Instruments and navigation aids are gone, and there is no light or power. Luckily oxygen supply is still flowing. Although the Mosquito has dropped to around 16,000 feet, it remains too high to bale out without oxygen equipment for Stinson and Henry to hope to survive.

They must get lower to escape. Suddenly Henry yells 'fire' as flames sweep across both wings and under the cabin. Escape through the bottom exit, the recommended procedure, is impossible. The Mosquito goes into a steep twisting dive. Ejection of the cockpit's housing is the only option. They must get out that way, before the pressure of the aircraft's plummeting spin traps them in their cockpit.

* * *

The morning of 5 January 1945 began as an ordinary winter's day in Britain, or so it seemed to Flying Officer Frank L. Henry and Flight Sergeant Russell A. Stinson, pilot and navigator respectively of a

Mosquito fighter-bomber in No. 571 Squadron RAF.[2] As part of the Light Night Striking Force (LNSF) in No. 8 Group, No. 571 Squadron had been formed with Mosquito B.XVI bombers on 7 April 1944 at RAF Oakington, Cambridgeshire. With each Mosquito capable of carrying a 4,000lb bomb, the LNSF flew night-bombing operations, including harassing and diversionary raids against targets in Europe, particularly Berlin.[3]

That winter's day, or more precisely the night and day of 5/6 January, would be twenty-four hours when, for Henry and Stinson, the extraordinary would begin. The early morning was cold and wet with occasional weak sun, something Stinson had not seen for weeks in the

Flying Officer Russell Stinson in his later years. (*Private collection, Geoff Baldwin*)

British winter of 1944–45. Early in the morning he and Henry were notified that an operation was being planned for the evening.

> During the morning Frank and I took our Mosquito K-King on a night-flying test, which was a normal practice before any operation. Shortly after take off our port motor began to splutter and lose power. Returning to base, our mechanics checked the problem but, unfortunately, K-King was taken into the hangar for major repair work. At about 15.00 hours we were briefed on an operation – a trip to the 'Big City', Berlin. Our new aircraft was to be G-George, the newest in the flight.[4]

Stinson was of medium height and stocky, with a thick thatch of reddish hair. Born in 1924 and brought up in Sydney, he attended Shore School, excelling in mathematics. Stinson lied about his age at the outbreak of war to enlist in the RAAF. Following further training in Canada, he joined the RAF in Britain as a navigator.

From 15.00 hours on 5 January the Mosquito crews of No. 571 Squadron were kept in the briefing area because of security. Bad weather resulted in delay until, at 20:30 hours, they were again in the main briefing room. Improved conditions were forecast and departure was scheduled for later that night.

> Around midnight there was a new briefing, same target but en route, a 'siren raid' was to be carried out. We were given our normal pre-

operations meal, bacon and eggs and chips. The weather was supposed to improve further for our return.

A 'siren raid' consisted of flying toward a large populated area and turning away when nearing the area, causing the air-raid sirens to be activated. This meant large amounts of 'Window' had to be dropped. 'Window' was aluminium foil strips which appeared on the German radar screens with the appearance of a large bomber force, but able to be created with a relatively small force of about seventy aircraft.

At 02.00 hours in the early morning dark of 6 January as Mosquito ML942 G-George taxied out to the runway, Stinson peered into rain, low cloud and poor visibility.

At 02.10 we were airborne, climbing in heavy cloud towards Orfordness in Essex. Frank and I both remarked that George felt different to our old King, but for no apparent reason. At 15,000 feet we broke through thick cloud, before going above scattered cloud and into a full moon.

This low cloud was all over Europe meaning that the German night-fighters would probably be grounded, thought Stinson hopefully.

At 25,000 feet we were over the Dutch coast and the German radar had jammed my set. Luckily I had been able to get some good navigation results to help my flight plan. At 27,000 feet we levelled out, heading for the Ruhr. This meant dropping Window out of the aircraft every sixty seconds, which at this height on full oxygen I found quite exhausting.

Nearing Essen we changed course northwards towards Hamburg and the coastal cities. Up to now the trip had been uneventful, and George was running perfectly. Close to Hamburg we turned 180 degrees towards Hanover, still dropping Window as part of the 'siren' raid diversionary tactic. There was no change in the weather.

There was an absence of flak or searchlights, and Stinson was relieved that from there on there was no more need for dropping Window.

I was only able to check our position with a rough check on the Pole Star, due north, which was very bright, and as we approached Hanover we set course for Berlin. Our target was a parachute factory. At 03.50 hours in our approach over Berlin, I moved into the nose section of George. My navigation had been spot on. I began to set the readings in the bombsight. We were now on the most dangerous part of the operation, flying straight and level for some five to six miles so as to bomb accurately

I had already opened the bomb doors, and I was holding the bomb-release toggle in my hand. Frank called out 'Markers ahead!' Although there were no signs of any flak, Frank said that our anti-aircraft 'boozer', an amber light on the dash, had begun to glow, meaning that we were being plotted by anti-aircraft radar of the ground air defences.

A 'boozer' was a term used for a warning device in aircraft used by Bomber Command crews which lit up when enemy radar was tracking their aircraft. It was an ominous, although not unexpected, indication that the Berlin air defence radar had them pin-pointed.

> Everything still seemed normal when suddenly there was a terrific smashing sound, and George seemed to buck and roll. I was flipped over in the nose section, but I could see that the starboard motor was in flames. Frank was yelling for help. What had happened?

The Mosquito had received a direct hit in the starboard engine from anti-aircraft fire. Stinson felt totally confused.

> Somehow Frank manages to take George into a shallow dive. With great difficulty I crawl back into the cockpit, and grab the Grosvenor lever, which spreads foam onto the burning engine. The combination of foam and the Mosquito's dive puts out the fire. During this panic I realise that I have somehow released the bomb toggle, allowing our 4,000lb cookie to fall away. Luckily this lightens the plane, helping Frank to regain some control. We are now in a shallow dive in a south-westerly direction – according to the Pole Star.

Stinson can see that part of the starboard engine and the leading edge of the wing have been shot or burnt away.

> Our compass is going mad. Our instruments and navigation aids are gone with the loss of the starboard engine. Only the compass, airspeed [indicator] and altimeter are left working – hopefully. We have no light, only a tiny hand-held torch. Fortunately our oxygen has not been damaged. But we are now completely exhausted, cold and terribly shocked. We know that George is a wreck, and at some stage we have to bale out. We are still airborne but losing height. Yet we do not want to bale out until we are below 15,000 feet.

Their Mosquito had been hit by the flak at well above 20,000 feet, and was losing height as they headed west.

> The propeller of the damaged engine is windmilling, making extra drag on the aircraft. I pull the feathering knob, but there is no reaction. We are very quiet, no doubt shock and fear are taking over. Our main hope is to get as far as possible back over friendly land. It is 04.20 hours, at 16,000

feet still above the cloudbank, which appears like a large white sheet in the moonlight.

Since being hit we have been a sitting duck, but fortunately the bad weather and cloud has grounded the Luftwaffe night-fighters. Even in a shallow dive, keeping the Mosquito airborne and flying west is exhausting Frank. The good engine has been at full power since Berlin. Its oil pressure and temperature are at their limits. Suddenly Frank shouts, 'Fire!' Flames are sweeping across both wings and under the cabin. This means escape through the bottom exit is impossible.

Putting my chute on my chest I reach for the cockpit release. The top flies away … now to get out. I pull my oxygen line away, but getting my chute over the rear cockpit housing is difficult due to pressure from the steeper dive we are now experiencing. At last I free the chute, but I cannot get any leverage with my feet. In desperation I pull the ripcord.

Stinson blacked out for a few seconds. As well as being warned not to bale out above 15,000 feet, aircrew were advised that baling out without oxygen at that altitude for those who had to, had a low survival rate. Crews were also told that baling out from the upper cockpit of a Mosquito was very dangerous because of the large tail plane. The inferno engulfing George meant that Henry and Stinson had no choice.

The next thing I remember was floating earthward – great relief. In the distance I could hear the screaming roar of the crashing plane, then silence. What had happened to Frank? Just below was the cloudbank, and falling through it was like falling through a heavy fog. Suddenly 'bang': I had landed on the edge of what appeared to be a frozen lake.

I rid myself of the parachute and other equipment, although I didn't hide them as regulations required. The question was what to do? It was bitterly cold, heavy snow, sleety rain and extremely dark. I began to move away from the ice into heavy timber and undergrowth and eventually came across a narrow bitumen road. My right knee seemed to be injured, and it was now 05.30 hours.

Terrified, freezing cold and exhausted, Stinson felt that he had no choice but to move, and began to walk along the road.

After a short time a small light appeared in the distance. Approaching the light, it looked to be shining in a farmhouse. I hoped there were no dogs around? Who was inside, and where were they? Cold, fear and desperation made me push open the unlocked front door. Inside were two old people and three children listening to a radio in front of a large fire. I imagined the radio voice was English. I was yelling 'Parlez Anglais?' But their reaction was negative. Then the older girl said 'Yes, a little'.

At first they thought Stinson was a German paratrooper whose dark blue uniform was a similar colour to the dark blue of the RAAF, and that the Australian badge on his shoulder was Austrian. Stinson managed to explain that he was an Australian, who had baled out of an RAF aircraft.

> I gave the chocolates and money from my escape kit to the children. The older people appeared to believe my story and through the young girls said they would send for help. I was taken down the cellar ladder to the 'stock yard'. They secured the trapdoor, and it was now daylight. My 'friends' in this cellar consisted of a number of fowls, two large pigs and a Friesian cow. It turned out that the rest of their livestock had been taken by the Germans.

The father and mother of the three children had been taken by the Germans as forced labour. Stinson could see that lack of food, and cold weather, was taking a heavy toll on older people and children such as these who were left.

> The only warm spot in the 'pen' was in the hay below the fireplace above, but still very cold and damp. Fear of the future was getting to me. Would help arrive, or the 'Hun'? About midday the cellar trap-door opened and one young girl, bucket in hand, appeared, followed by two men in farming clothes – one youngish, the other old and frail. The older man spoke English, and it was at this moment I noticed the younger man was carrying a revolver. My heart sank.
>
> The old man approached me and asked me for my identity, I gave him the 'meat tags' around my neck. I smiled, and said 'friend'. At this point the young man, Andre, departed, thank God, and the girl began milking the old cow. In excellent English the old man explained where we were – near Belle Croix, in Belgium, close to the German border. My chute and dinghy had been found and secured. The man explained that tank battles were going on just south-west of us.
>
> He said that most of the locals were against the Germans, but were afraid to help any Allied airmen for fear of Gestapo reprisals, so I must move on. Andre would return and help me to safety. He then left; no handshake or goodbye. The girl returned with a cup of warm milk and a hardboiled egg – most welcome. About 2pm Andre returned, carrying a large bag and a haversack.

The bag and haversack contained escape clothes for Stinson, an old cap, rolltop jumper, overalls, gumboots and a large service greatcoat. The civilian clothes were shabby and unwashed, and to be worn over Stinson's uniform in case of capture.

> My flying boots and an old blanket went in the haversack. I could only just manage to understand Andre's English, but he was saying that we would go to a friend at Amel, about twenty-five miles away, that afternoon, as there was little activity in that area, and the weather was very poor. Upstairs, the family had glasses of cognac on the table as a farewell. Then after hugs and kisses from the children, we began our trip.
>
> Outside was an old motorbike with a sidecar, similar to those made by the Germans. I worried whether Andre really was a friend? It was snowing lightly, cold, and there were pine trees everywhere. We got into the sidecar, where Andre covered me with a large waterproof sheet; told me to keep quiet and out of view, calling me 'Kid', very much American slang, and we were off.

The trip was slow and rough, although to Stinson as a hidden, unseeing passenger the sidecar often seemed to become airborne, and then to land with a terrible thump.

> The temptation to peep out was great, but I resisted. It appeared that we had been travelling on some back tracks, because there had been no sound of traffic. Suddenly the engine stopped, and there were voices. It was late and getting dark. Then I heard 'Out, Kid', and on emerging I was greeted by a man and a woman.
>
> They were Andre's friends, and we were in a large farm shed. Through the door I could see, in the distance, a large stone house. The man and the woman both spoke excellent English, welcoming me as their guest. My home was the farm shed, which also housed the bike. Andre left so he could explore our next journey. The couple explained that we were in undulating open farming country, so that the next leg of the journey would be very dangerous.

The couple told Stinson that terrific battles were in progress in their vicinity. The Germans had stopped the Americans in the south and the British in the west, but the US Army had made some advances near Givet on the river. The fighting was part of the ferocious Battle of the Bulge, which raged from 15 December 1944 until 26 January 1945, as the German Army mounted a major offensive against the Allies through the Ardennes forests. It was Hitler's last desperate gamble to halt the Allies' invasion of western Europe. In the most severe European winter for many years, Stinson had parachuted down into the midst of this brutal and decisive clash of armies.

These people feared the Gestapo, and told me that if the Gestapo came, they could not help. But if Andre, who they thought was one of the best, could get me to their friends at Rochefort, my chance of freedom was very good. They then left, closing the large shed door. Once again I was alone: a horrible feeling. Later that night Andre returned carrying a lovely roast pork meal, which I really enjoyed. It seemed like I would be lucky to have just one meal a day.

While I was eating, Andre explained that we would not be able to make Rochefort, forty miles away, as the Germans were sending reinforcements from the north. So the best we could do was to meet his contact near Erezee, twenty miles away, which might need some walking at night. Andre helped me make a bed in the hay, then left. I dozed on and off all night. At one stage I could hear the drone of aircraft. Perhaps it was an RAF raid somewhere?

When Stinson awoke next morning, 7 January, the weather seemed to have improved.

Peeping out the hayshed landing window, I could see broken sunlight. This was a large farm, with many buildings and a large mansion. The falling snow was much lighter than yesterday. The country was undulating, with small paddocks but no sign of livestock or machinery. Maybe these were in the other sheds. There was only hay in mine. To keep warm I jogged around the shed. How I would have liked to pop outside.

Then the door opened and a lady entered. She looked much older than she had seemed yesterday. She was carrying a basket with corn meal, milk and dark bread. She explained that this was the best she could manage for some breakfast, but to me anything was welcome. She told me of reports on the radio about heavy battles. It seemed that the German lines were still holding.

Stinson asked her, 'Where is Andre?' She replied that he must be patient, and that Andre would return, and that he should to eat.

When I had eaten the meal I went back upstairs to check on what was going on. A grey sun, cold, but no snow. Later in the morning three low-flying Ju88s screamed over the shed, but otherwise all was quiet. Where was Andre? But again I knew I had to be patient. Then at dusk Andre returned.

Unfortunately, he said that our planned next move was not possible because the Gestapo had eliminated his friends in Erezee, which would make our stay difficult, and large numbers of troops created more problems. We would have to bike some way, then walk. Andre opened the shed door and we left in the bike and sidecar. This time he did not cover me, but told me to keep down and hang on as he would have to go fast, and he took off like a rocket.

The road was rough and slippery, and Stinson wondered how he would manage to stay in the sidecar.

After a few miles Andre suddenly turned off the road and stopped behind a clump of hawthorns. It was getting dark, and we were near a main road alive with German troop-carrying vehicles. It was my first sight of the enemy at close quarters so to speak – something new for an airman!

Andre said that when it got dark and there was a break in the traffic we would cross. So we had to be ready to take our chance. We sat there hardly speaking, listening to the roar of the military traffic and the singing of the passing soldiers.

They sat motionless, waiting for silence, and the night to fully descend.

Then Andre kick-started the old bike into life, and we were off, over the road, then through what appeared to be a drain, with mud and slush spraying everywhere.

However, Andre was keeping the bike mobile, and seemed to know where he was going, and I just hung on and hoped. We had not gone very far when we stopped near an old gravel pit. No more bike – we went on by foot. The moon had now come up, and this helped me to follow Andre, who was setting a very brisk pace.

They walked for three or four hours until, suddenly, Andre pushed Stinson into what seemed to him to be like a very large hole.

This turned out to be the cellar of Andre's friends' home. It was all that remained of a burnt-out building. We stopped there for the rest of the night. We shared a bottle of cognac. No chance of sleep. I was absolutely done for. My feet were burning and every bone ached. Andre seemed quite fit. The noise from the battles in the distance was deafening, and there was a penetrating glow like that of a bushfire. Yet my fear seemed to have gone, and all that was left was hope.

Before dawn on 8 January we were on our way, again on foot. A man appeared from somewhere and spoke to Andre, telling him where to find a bicycle, and that the Americans were advancing on Rochefort. A short way down the road we found the bike. It had a small trailer attached so that Andre could pull me along. Riding the trailer was an art, as it was very narrow and unstable. Dawn was breaking, the weather had improved, and we could see hundreds of vapour trails in the sky. The country road we were on was a bog of snow, slush and mud, but this was what confined the vehicles and heavy armour of both armies to the main roads.

Inevitably in such conditions their progress by bicycle and clumsy trailer was very slow. Around midday they approached the highway to Namur. Stinson was about to have another close-up view of the enemy.

Traffic was heavy, with military and all kind of armoured vehicles. We ditched the bike and took cover in a muddy ditch about half a mile from the road. This was to be our home until dark, as long as we were not detected. There was continuous gunfire in the distance, and German fighter-bombers flew overhead. Troops were erecting tank traps and laying mines on each side of the road. Andre said that we must find a way across the road.

He had noticed that troops who had been laying mines had not come near a small gully which traversed the road, so this would be our way across. We were very fortunate that, for some reason, no one came anywhere near our hideout. Late in the afternoon covered trucks collected the troops although it appeared that some guards were left along the road. Andre said that, after dark, we would follow the gully on foot.

For Stinson the thought of a long walk in gumboots through mud and slush, with a constant fear of stepping on a mine, or wondering if one of the guards might hear them, left him even more on edge. 'Once it was night-time it was "Let's go, Kid" from Andre. We had to keep close and silent. Then when we neared the road, more lights appeared, and more traffic. We stopped.'

They dropped to the ground, their thoughts willing the German vehicles not to stop.

After they passed, we went across the road. Everything seemed to work, maybe more through luck than anything else. After walking for about half an hour over what appeared to be farmland we stopped.

Andre said we had about two miles to go to his friends' place. I wondered if I could make it. The next hour seemed never-ending. Then suddenly, we stopped once more, and a figure seemed to emerge from the ground. We were at his friends' home in Rochefort. It was not really a home but instead a magnificent underground bomb shelter, impossible to detect from above.

The bomb shelter was situated on a farm about two miles from Rochefort. It had originally been built by a wealthy wine merchant, and had food, beds, and was completely self-contained. The present owner of the farm was a middle-aged widow called Daphne, who had been born in England.

> She had helped a number of Allied airmen. She gave us some food, and some dry clothing. She told us the Americans should take Rochefort tonight or early tomorrow. Shortly afterward Andre told me he had to leave, and my future would now be in the hands of Pierre. This was a terrific shock, bringing tears to my eyes. I would never see him again. How to thank him? We shook hands, hugged each other, and he left. May God look after him, I thought.
>
> Daphne told me that I would be her guest until Pierre arrived, hopefully after the Americans had taken the town. By listening to a French station on the radio, she told me that the Americans had crossed the river Meuse at Givet, and that Rochefort was under siege. The Germans were moving to a line along the Namur highway. Although the shelter was three metres [ten feet] underground, you could still hear the rumble of the armour. I was lucky to get some well-earned sleep.

Early in the morning of 9 January the whole area began to shake, with the noise of gunfire and the roar of engines.

> It was unbelievable. This was the Battle of Rochefort, part of the Battle of the Bulge. Daphne seemed calm, and remarked 'if we survive, we are free'. She then gave me some food and explained that Pierre would only come when the fighting had passed and it was safe. This meant staying put for some time. The battle seemed to get closer and closer, and at one point a heavy vehicle, perhaps a tank, passed very close to our hideaway. Friend or foe, I listened and wondered? By about 2 pm everything went reasonably quiet.

Later that afternoon Daphne told Stinson that she must visit the town, and give people help if needed, but that he must remain in the shelter.

> When Daphne opened the shelter door and left, there was a strong smell of cordite. About 10 pm Daphne returned. She was a complete wreck. She had been helping evacuate the injured. The Americans had won the battle and gone. We were free, but evidently Daphne's lovely town had been destroyed. Daphne changed and we had supper. She told me Pierre would come next day. I went to bed.
>
> In the early morning when we went outside it was a lovely fine day, and Yankee planes and tanks were everywhere. It was hard to realise that there was no more need for fear. Suddenly coming toward us was an old French-type jeep, driven by a man in uniform. This was Pierre, a

gendarme stationed at Marchennes in France, once the HQ of the French Resistance. He had been contacted by Andre and asked to take me to the RAF base in Douai.

Daphne took us downstairs and gave us some food. While enjoying our meal, Pierre asked me to take off my escape clothing and put on my flying boots and tunic, which he said would help when we were stopped by American military police. Daphne seemed rather upset that her home, although having escaped much damage, was being taken over by the Americans. I said goodbye and gave her many thanks, but unfortunately forgot to get her address.

Stinson got into Pierre's old jeep and they drove off down a dirt road more resembling a ploughed paddock than a road, with smoke everywhere like a heavy fog.

Approaching Rochefort we saw a burnt-out Tiger tank with its charred crew – not nice. This was very much the norm until we reached Gavet, where we saw not only Germans but dead American troops and their destroyed tanks and vehicles. It was hard to comprehend that fighting was still going on further north.

We crossed the Meuse at Givet on an improvised low-level pontoon bridge. The trip from here on went past many towns and villages, with people waving everywhere. We were pulled up many times by MPs, but when they realised who Pierre and I were, they waved us on. It was hard to realise that there were no more hideouts. I will never forget the scenes around Rochefort and Givet after the battles. Thank God I was an airman.

While we were purring along in the old jeep, Pierre told me that he had a big surprise for me when we got to Marchennes. We arrived about 4 pm to be greeted by Frank Henry, all spick and span. Apparently Pierre had contacted RAF Douai beforehand and had arranged for Frank to be brought to the police station to meet us. Today was 10 January, and I must have looked pretty shocking, as I had not shaved, and had very few washes since 6 January.

The first thing I had was a good clean-up: bath, shave, and Pierre's wife gave me some clean underwear, and washed mine. What a great feeling to be clean again. Pierre took us into a large room with an open fire, saying 'when you have told all your stories, we will eat, then party'. Frank explained that he had been interrogated in Douai, and that our reports of our shot-down Mosquito should be similar, and I agreed.

So Henry recounted how he had baled out, and where he landed. When Stinson was trying to free himself from the Mosquito's cockpit, he accidentally kicked

Henry in the face, causing him to lose control of the plane. This knocked him back as he attempted to get out and the fire was spreading everywhere. Suddenly the plane rolled, and luckily he just fell out. Henry believed this was at about 3,000 feet, as he landed very quickly. He came to ground in someone's garden in a village about twenty-five miles from Stinson's landing place in Luxembourg. He was rescued by a local policeman, who eventually handed him over to the American forces in France.

> The Americans contacted the RAF at Douai, who sent help, and on 8 January Frank ended up in Douai. He was told that I had been rescued by the Resistance and that they would get me safely to Douai. So for two days he had been relaxing and enjoying himself, while I tried to flee from the Battle of the Bulge!
>
> Just then, a door opened and Pierre said 'come in' to a very large kitchen, in which there was a large table covered with food, and where we met Pierre's wife, and three other people. These three, two men and a lady, perhaps in their 40s, had been active members of the Resistance. The local police station at Marchennes was HQ for the Resistance in northern France and the lowlands.
>
> It was a wonderful meal, roast duck, and his wife was a very good cook, although very quiet and spoke little English. Pierre said food was still very scarce, but that the Americans were very generous. After the meal we returned to the open fire. Pierre's friend spoke of their experiences in the Resistance which, although perhaps a little 'stretched', were amazing and interesting. All the time Pierre was very attentive with the drinks. It was a merry party which broke up very late.

Next morning, 11 January, an RAF staff car arrived and took Henry and Stinson to RAF Douai, where they had lunch, then in the afternoon to the RAF HQ at the Grand Hotel in Brussels. Early on 12 January Henry and Stinson were driven by jeep ten miles south to an RAF base at Avers, which was the airfield for Brussels, served by RAF transport aircraft, Douglas C-47 Dakotas. It seemed that negotiating a lift on board one of these aircraft, followed by a short safe flight to Britain was all that remained of their rescue, no more life or death situations, thought Stinson. He was wrong.

> When we arrived at Avers we were each issued with a large, wide, leather belt, attached to a light rope, 15 or 20 feet long. We were told this would help us board the plane. Because German aircraft were still making low-level raids over the area, the transports had to keep moving. After landing they turned and came back slowly along the grass, and the cargo was dropped down a ramp without the C-47 stopping, and then collected by

Army trucks. The aircraft continued on back to the airstrip, and without halting took off again.

Henry and Stinson were instructed to position themselves where a C-47 transport plane was moving back towards the airstrip, on the starboard side of the aircraft, and be prepared to begin running.

> When the plane was approaching the take-off area, the pilot signalled, and we put on our belts. To board the plane was an art. The starboard motor was cut to stop any slipstream and two aircrew, in harness onboard, raised the ramp about four feet off the ground. With the transport aircraft moving at about 10mph, we threw the ropes attached to our belts to the airmen on the plane's ramp. They caught our ropes, then, as we ran, they pulled us aboard. We managed to do it – it was crude but effective. But I never want to board an aircraft this way again!
>
> Once we were aboard, the engines roared and we were on our way. The bare metal floor of the cargo section was slippery, so we had to attach our ropes to metal rails for some stability, then sit on the floor. The five transport crew all wore harnesses attached to the railings. While we flew at 1,000 feet down the coast to Boulogne, then across the Channel, the cargo door remained open.

On landing at the transport crew's base at South Cerney in Gloucestershire, Henry and Stinson were greeted by their own CO, Wing Commander Don Bray, who flew them back to Oakington.

> Immediately after landing at Oakington, Frank and I were taken separately for a 20-minute circuit in a Mosquito, which was official policy for anyone who had been in a crash. Then we went back to our quarters.

It was exactly a week since the two of them had taken off on that ordinary day, and for Stinson it had been in to and out of the extraordinary Battle of the Bulge.

Within a few days Henry and Stinson were once again operational with No. 571 Squadron flying night raids over Germany. On 22 February they sat down to their 'pre-ops' midday meal – the usual bacon, eggs and chips. During the morning they had learned that they were rostered on an operation that night and had completed a night-flying test in their Mosquito C-Charlie. Henry, however, thought the aircraft to be 'a bloody old wreck'.

Over their meal Stinson noticed that Henry appeared to be on edge, as if something was worrying him. Was it some personal anxiety, or the worn-out condition of C-Charlie? As he listened intently to the operation briefing,

Stinson felt his own trepidation rise when he heard that the target for the raid was the 'Big City'.

> Berlin again was no surprise – another 'Siren Raid', with more Window to drop. The Met weather report was good, no moon, light winds and little cloud. The route was south via Beachy Head in Sussex, then over the Ruhr, Bremen, and Hanover to Berlin. The target of the main force bombers approaching from the North Sea was Hanover. Our diversionary 'Siren Raid' had an ETA [Estimated Time of Arrival] over Berlin at 22.30 hours.

Once the briefing was over Henry and Stinson were driven in a truck with other aircrew to dispersal where, onboard the Mosquito, their first check was of the bomb fuses. Pins were removed from the 'cookie' bombs, rendering them active. Stinson placed the pins in the navigation bag, He was well aware that it meant that any mishap on take off could result in a massive explosion.

> When both motors began to roar, I suddenly heard Frank shout out the f*** word. Our port motor was losing revs, about a 1,000. With 'cookies' on board there was no way of taking off with that loss of power, so Frank turned off both motors, and the ground crew arrived.

The ground crew sergeant told them there was no back-up aircraft and there would be a delay while the engine was checked. About fifteen minutes later they were given the OK by the ground crew and the motors started. As they taxied for take off again, Stinson did not hear any oaths from Henry.

> This delay meant that I had to re-plan my route and log in an effort to catch up with the main group – being a lone duck has no future. I decided to follow my flight plan until nearing Bremen, then turn due east to join our group on the Bremen – Hanover leg.

Doing this meant flying near Osnabruck, where Germany's AA (anti-aircraft) gunners' school was located, causing it to be designated as a prohibited area. Stinson dropped more 'Window' than normal to counter German radar, and he thought everything seemed to be going to plan.

> It was now time to test my navigation, and I told Frank to steer 095. Shortly after this flak appeared off our starboard wing. Fortunately the range was well out, probably AA recruits, and it soon died down.

Farther away to starboard Stinson could see a heavy glow of fires, where the main force had bombed Hanover.

> I was relieved as it appeared my navigation was somewhere near the mark, and we should soon catch up with our own group from 571 Squadron.

Suddenly Henry yelled out over the intercom, 'Snapper!', which was the codename for a night-fighter. Straight ahead of them Stinson could see exhaust flames.

> The night-fighter's interception approach had overshot and missed us. Our 'Boozer' light was bright red, indicating that we had been tracked by radar. Frank turned and dived hoping to evade another attack.

Unfortunately it was too late. The whole plane lit up, as tracer shells seemed to envelop the port wing. Another night-fighter had attacked them. Had the 'Boozer' radar warning light been on for some time and had they overlooked it? Stinson opened the bomb doors and released the 'cookies'.

> Our port motor had been hit and was in flames. Frank pushed the feathering button, and I pulled the 'Grosvenor' lever to release the fire extinguisher foam onto the wing. Luckily this worked, putting out the fire. We were now into a steep dive from about 25,000 feet when I noticed that the starboard motor was also feathered.
>
>   Frank pushed the feathering button for the starboard motor and this together with our accelerating dive restarted it. Gradually Frank managed to get us straight and level. With all our instruments seemingly in one piece and working, I thought escape was still possible. Our panic is hard to explain.

On the one good engine they headed away in a southerly direction. Stinson had little doubt that Osnabruck anti-aircraft gunners had notified Luftwaffe night-fighter command in the area of the lone Allied intruder aircraft and its course.

> To this day I still question my decision to plot a revised course near to Osnabruck, so as to join our group on the Bremen to Hanover leg. However, the alternative would have been to fly alone on the original route, perhaps with a worse fate.

Henry and Stinson's Mosquito was flying at about 20,000 feet on its one engine. Stinson had them on a course of 190 degrees and, in theory, he thought they might have enough fuel to still be able to make it back to base.

> However, although we had overcome our panic, we were still a lone duck. Then Frank told me, with no option for me argue, to find an airfield in Allied occupied territory, and quickly. He was done in, he said, and did not want to have to bale out. My only choice was to put out a 'Mayday' call, so I transmitted 'Terrier Charlie to Base', knowing full well we were well out of range. Amazingly a female voice replied from Brussels, Hillsbrook Base, giving us a course to fly, and they would keep in touch.

This seemed to buck up Frank and I also felt much relieved. After our last ordeal and narrow escape in January – no more parachute jumps, thank you! The controller in Brussels called us again, and said she would contact us every ten minutes with our required course. I checked my map and was happy that we were heading for Brussels. The next call in perfect English instructed us to fly a different course of 090 for thirty miles, and land. Frank was excited at this until I told him this new course would take us further into Germany – the Huns were alerted to our plight and trying to dupe us. Fortunately Frank believed me, and from then on we kept strict radio silence and a close eye on the 'Boozer' light.

After flying on one motor for about an hour, with many contacts from Brussels, we were handed over to Hillsbrook control tower. They told us to fly a course of 270 and they would light up the runway and its approaches once we were down to 1,200 feet. When the lights went on Frank had a new lease of life. He yelled out, 'Put your belt on, I am going in!' We were halfway down the strip, and about 150 feet high, when everything went black – no runway lights. We hit the ground and bounced. Frank yelled out, 'Wheels … !' – then bang!

Flying Officer Russell Stinson and Flight Lieutenant Frank Henry in front of Mosquito J-Johnny, sitting on top of a 4,000lb 'cookie' bomb, March 1945. (*Private collection, Geoff Baldwin*)

The next thing Stinson knew was when he woke up about midday in a white nightgown in bed, surrounded by a number of nurses in white uniforms.

These nurses turned out to be Belgian nuns, as I was in a Roman Catholic hospital. A senior sister speaking English, while the other nuns looked on and giggled, told me that I had been brought there by RAF ambulance from the crashed plane. Evidently I was unconscious with facial damage and my head and teeth, which seemed loose, were still aching. A doctor had reported on my condition to the RAF.

In the evening Frank and another RAF officer arrived, arranged my discharge, and took me to the Grande Hotel and its HQ. This time I was given a comfortable bed upstairs. Next morning, Frank arrived with some breakfast which I found hard to eat, although I felt better. He gave details of our crash landing.

We had bounced well down the runway, and then over a railway cutting, before ending up in a small park. When he shook me and I did not reply, he thought I was dead. The plane had been completely wrecked, apart from the cabin, miraculously, and Frank was uninjured. My head must have hit the front instrument panel. I stayed in the hotel all day, just lolling around.

Next morning I felt much better still, although I had a slight headache and a very sore mouth. I went downstairs to the office, and signed the visitors' book, and was told we would be in the hotel for a few days.

Stinson reflected on the secret pact that he and Henry had made when they were limping towards Brussels on one engine. They agreed that they would not mention in their official report what actually happened. After being hit in the port wing and engine, in the panic Henry had pushed both feathering buttons by mistake which caused the Mosquito's violent dive. Ironically the sudden steep dive probably took them away from the night-fighters and avoided another attack.

* * *

At the end of the war Russell Stinson with his wife Dorothy Banks-Smith, whom he had met in England, travelled back to Australia and took up farming in NSW, raising three children Susan, Julie and Robert. He served as a councillor in Coonabarabran Shire and when he and Dorothy reached sixty years of marriage they received a telegram from the Queen.[6]

* * *

Chapter 35

Dangling from a parachute, lined up in the sights of a Luftwaffe night-fighter, has this thirty-first operation tempted fate too far?

Flight Sergeant Richard A. 'Dick' Deck, bomb aimer[1]

In January 1945 Flight Sergeant R.A. 'Dick' Deck is in a Halifax bomber on a raid on Magdeburg, a city as strongly defended as Berlin. It is their thirty-first operation, one more than the stipulated target of thirty. After bombing the target the Halifax is attacked from below by a Luftwaffe night-fighter. The fuel tanks in the starboard wing of the Halifax catch fire. On the pilot's order Deck bales out and as he swings on his parachute another night-fighter sets his sights on him. He hears the engine drone growing louder, then he sees the green light on its nose, as it rapidly closes on him. Deck resigns himself to becoming just another statistic.

* * *

At RAF Leeming in Yorkshire in January 1945 for the crew of Halifax MZ427 E-Easy it was not getting any easier. On their supposed penultimate – twenty-ninth – operation on 12 January with No. 429 Squadron RAF, after almost reaching the target at Flensburg, they were forced to abort because of damage to their blind-bombing radar equipment. This meant that their record remained on twenty-eight completed operations and they still needed to complete two more to finish their tour of thirty. A few days later, on 14 January, they carried out a

Flight Sergeant R.A. Deck, No. 429 Squadron RAF, January 1945. (*Private collection, Alan Deck*)

'gardening trip', mine-laying in the sea off Norway's port of Oslo, leaving just one more operation to be completed.

Their flight commander made a submission to Group HQ to give them credit for a completed operation for their early return from the aborted mission to Flensburg on the 12th. Flight Sergeant Deck, bomb aimer of E-Easy, hoped unrealistically that the submission might be approved quickly. Nothing was forthcoming. The thought of post-tour leave remained tantalisingly close. They were put on the battle order for 16 January to Magdeburg. Deck knew that they faced a long dangerous trip to complete their tour of thirty operations.

> This would in effect be our thirty-first operation, and therefore the last trip of the tour. Plans were in place for a celebration upon our return, and everybody wished us luck. We knew and realised that Magedburg was one of the hottest targets in Germany, and some old timers even preferred a Berlin trip to Magdeburg.[2]

E-Easy's crew were well respected in the squadron and renowned for ensuring they always had enough fuel to make the return leg on long-haul operations. It made them a 'special crew', a favourite choice for extra-long operations such as a 'gardening trip' or a raid on Magdeburg in eastern Germany. The seven crew of E-Easy were:

Crew member	Role
F.H. 'Bud' Biddell	Pilot
Charles 'Chuck' Chapman	Navigator
R.A. 'Dick' Deck	Bomb-Aimer
R.H.S. 'Roy' Bourne	Wireless/Air Gunner
R.H. 'Ron' Streatfield	Flight Engineer
Fred 'Pete' Peters	Mid-upper Gunner
Roy 'Phil' Phillips	Tail Gunner

In the afternoon, a little before the operational briefing's commencement time of 15.45 hours, Deck sat with the rest of the crew of E-Easy and, as he put it, 'sweated it out' prior to their thirtieth operation, or was it their thirty-first? 'I had just received some mail. Chuck Chapman said that he would send his mother a cable the next day, saying that he'd finished flying after our last operation.'

The thought of the alternative situation, when a family received a cable stating that their son or husband was missing, was left unsaid but always in the back of men's minds.

The squadron had an energetic young bombing leader, Steve Glass, who was also flying on the Magdeburg operation, and he and Deck had a friendly wager as to which of them could get the most H2S fixes, hand in the best log, and not have a fix more often than one every two minutes. Following the briefing, in the early evening Deck and the crew were driven out to E-Easy.

> Out at the kite Jimmy and his ground crew boys had E-Easy all tuned up, and everything working to perfection. They were proud of this slick kite with the words 'European Express' painted on her nose, and ours was the only crew that Jimmy liked to be flying in E-Easy. We talked and joked with them before taking off, but hinted seriously as to the high risk of this particular trip.

The weather for take off was fair to cloudy, with slight rain and moderate visibility. E-Easy carried two 1,000lb bombs and twelve incendiary clusters. Pilot Bud Biddell took E-Easy into the night sky at 18.59 hours.[3] They were soon crossing the coast, and Deck watched as they descended to a low level for the outward leg to Magdeburg.

> Flying over the North Sea at a few hundred feet above the waves in the darkness had always had its bad points, but tactics required it. The element of surprise when arriving over Jerry-land paid dividends. We had often gone across in this way so we were used to it, but when Phil the tail gunner reported seeing two kites collide and explode, it reminded us that it could happen to us too.

One of the Halifaxes from No. 429 Squadron had bogged down on take off, and three others aborted en route, which left just ten from 429 for the attack on Magdeburg. When Deck calculated that they were close to the point where they must climb for height and break radar and wireless silence, he turned on the H2S radar.

> I got some good fixes off Heligoland, and was pleased at the performance of the set. A fix every two minutes was easy and over the mainland we went towards Hanover, turning shortly after towards our target. Everything was going smoothly.

They found the weather over the target area was clear, making for good visibility, and Deck could see the target markers, plentiful and well concentrated.

> The target was well lit up with fires and flares, and the street detail was visible. The flak was considerable, but we waded through and bombed accurately, and started on the route for home. We knew some enemy fighters were in the area as the gunners reported seeing many fighter flares, and once they spotted a Junkers night-fighter crossing our nose.

Meanwhile Chuck Chapman and I were working hard as heck trying to keep us on track. Chuck was transferring all his wind readings to Roy the wireless operator/gunner (WAG), who was transmitting them to England. We were passing south of Brunswick, heading west, when suddenly there were four distinct bangs heard on the starboard side.

E-Easy had been hit. Peters, the mid-upper gunner, could see that the inner part of the starboard wing was on fire. Ron Streatfield, the flight engineer, checked the petrol cocks to determine the source of the fire, while Biddell feathered the starboard inner engine. Deck heard Streatfield report that the fire was in the main fuel tanks.

He said that they were impossible to extinguish. Bud told us all to prepare to bale out. We answered in turn accordingly, and immediately dropped our work and put on our 'chutes'. I don't think any of us panicked – everything went smoothly and quietly. Chuck and I lifted our seat, and opened the escape hatch.

I gathered up the chocolate and chewing gum, gave half of it to Chuck, and took the rest and put it where it would be safe in my clothes. As I stood by, it seemed that I checked my parachute and harness a hundred times. Peering out of my little side-window near the bomb-sight I could see the raging fire, which by now was over a good part of the starboard wing, and part of the fuselage too.

Biddell was switching between diving and stalling the maimed Halifax, trying desperately to extinguish the flames in the bomber's slipstream. E-Easy had lost a lot of height, and was now below 10,000 feet. Deck thought that the situation looked hopeless.

Ron warned Bud that the fire was spreading, and that eventually the kite would explode. From the time Bud told us 'Prepare to bale out', five to ten minutes ensued, although it seemed more like twice as long, until Bud ordered, 'bale out!', and wished us luck. First went Chuck. I watched him drop into space and darkness. Then Roy the wireless/air gunner dropped out.

I switched on my mike and reported, 'Navigator gone, WAG gone, bomb-aimer going.' Not waiting for a reply, I pulled the mike-lead out of its socket, and with my right hand always grasping the parachute release handle, I sat down on the floor. I shoved my legs out until the rushing air outside the plane was enough to pull the remainder of my body out.

I did all this as quickly as possible so that I wouldn't have time to think of anything else. It turned out to be one of the easiest things I've ever done. No sooner was I out than I realised I was just hanging in the dark starlit sky with no apparent motion at all. The noise of Easy's three remaining engines faded away and the realisation of the happenings of the last few moments dawned heavily upon my mind. Firstly I was thankful that the chute had opened, and prayed to God for help and guidance.

Fighter flares were being dropped around Deck and he felt horribly exposed.

I thought of what Jerry fighters do to British flyers as they float helplessly in parachutes – they shoot them. Then what I had feared seemed imminent – the uneven drone of a German night-fighter reached my ears. I looked up at my chute. It loomed huge and white – visible I thought for miles. The Jerry fighter was approaching, and I could see a green light on his nose. It appeared as though he was coming straight at me, and I've never prayed so seriously in my life as I did then.

Deck hung there, waiting for the burst of machine-gun that would obliterate him. But inexplicably nothing happened.

The fighter turned and climbed above me, and I never heard him again. I think he must have been blind – or else a human being. I did a lot of thinking as I hung up there, waiting for the ground. Nobody had said what had hit us. I was under the impression that it had been a spot of predicted flak. I worried a lot about that because the only time predicted flak is so accurate is when a kite gets off by itself away from the main stream.

It was my responsibility to ensure that we were on track and in the stream. It was all over now and I had to think of what lay ahead, and how I would evade capture when I got on the ground. It was also becoming damn cold up there. I'd left my gloves in the aircraft, and my hands were turning blue.

It felt to Deck as if he'd been dangling for ages, yet he seemed no closer to the ground. He even wondered if he was heavy enough to bring the parachute down.

As I was getting cheesed off with such a slow descent, I reached up to pull the straps on one side to release some of the air from the chute. But that was too much like hard work so I gave it up. Looking down at the ground I tried to get a picture or some idea of the country I was going to land in.

I knew that the white was snow, but the black areas looked to be patches of water, and I thought I'd have to be careful to steer away from them.

Finally my nearness to the ground became clear when, out of the dark silence of the night, I heard the barking of a dog.

Deck sensed the wind change, and detected breaths of warmer air. The patches of black and white began moving at a great speed, and Deck prepared himself for a 10mph impact with the ground.

I fell to the ground easily and safely at the bottom of a hilly slope, in a small open field cushioned with a thick layer of snow. I lay motionless for a moment, and then rolled onto my stomach, before crawling up towards the billowing pile of silk, my parachute which was flapping in a light breeze. I drew it all under me, and then released the harness from my body. I lay there for a few minutes, thinking over the situation, and wondering just what was on the other side of the hill.

The night was calm, dark and a clear sky full of stars, and the ground was covered with about twelve to fifteen inches of snow. But to his right Deck could discern a large black silhouette of something set against the horizon.

My plan was to head south-west towards Switzerland but, before setting out, I thought I would lie low for a few days, until the Germans had given up the search for me. You see they knew a kite had been shot down, and they would have the *Volkssturm*, their home guard searching for me.

It was around 22.00 hours, and Deck needed to move as far as possible from the crash site before daybreak, and find somewhere to hide both himself and his parachute.

I arose cautiously, picking up the chute and draping it over my head and body, using it as an excellent camouflage against the white background of the snow. I could see now that the black area which had puzzled me earlier was a large clump of evergreen trees. I could hear the wind rustling through their foliage – they were quite close.

So I headed in that direction for cover as I felt very exposed in the middle of a field. I had only gone a few yards when I heard men talking directly to the front of me somewhere in the darkness. I stopped in an instant and strained my eyes. There was a group of low buildings, which looked like barracks, hidden against the background of a forest, only a few yards ahead.

At once Deck turned around and headed in the opposite direction. He tried to place his feet quietly in the snow to avoid any crunching noise, hoping anxiously that he was not heard.

The parachute was damn awkward and heavy to lug around, so I decided to ditch it – leaving it hidden as best I could in a ditch surrounding a small haystack. I now started making my way up a hill in a westerly direction. As I reached the top of the hill a powerful searchlight started scanning the countryside from another hilltop and illuminated me in its beam. I threw myself down and waited for it to swing the other way or else go out. Meanwhile I could hear dogs barking and the talking of young people.

It was most likely that these were only local civilians, seemingly just walking home down a road. In his tense frame of mind Deck, however, imagined the whole population to be out with their dogs searching for the crew of the downed Halifax, and him in particular.

In the sky above I could hear hundreds of bombers on their way home, and it made me a bit homesick, and disgusted that such a thing should happen to us on our last trip. More than that, I was worrying about the rest of the crew, and what they were thinking because it came to me that it was my fault that we got shot down. It was playing on my mind a lot.

He felt that he must have guided their pilot, Biddell, to take them out of the main stream, so that predicted flak had been able to pinpoint them. After a few minutes, when the searchlight went out, Deck rose from his prone position and walked on.

From this hilltop I could see around a little bit. There was a ravine running north and south in front of me and, further south, there was a road running south-east and north-west. I took to the ravine until I hit the road, and then went parallel with the road, as I didn't want to break onto the road where my footprints in the snow would show. I walked for some time, then broke away and headed for the woods, where I wanted to hide until the hunt blew over.

The forest was a plantation with the trees all in rows, and with little or no undergrowth Deck was able to walk in easily.

I sat down and rested for a while, and decided the forest wasn't big and thick enough to hide away in. So I continued on out of it at a different angle to that I had entered, and made my way towards some more woods. After a few hours I was satisfied, and prepared to spend the day in a good-sized forest. When daylight came I wandered about in the woods and found water, and a hiding spot where I spent the day. I got out my map and escape aids, and summed up the situation. I figured it would take me at least a month to reach Switzerland, and I could live on my rations for about twenty-four days.

Deck's optimism in thinking he could walk to Switzerland, over 500 miles, in the depths of a German winter was driven by a desperate fear of being captured or worse.

> The first day I had one square of York chocolate, and a fruit drop candy. I cut the wings and hooks off my battle-dress, but left my flying-boots on. Time seemed to go fairly quickly and soon it was night again. Trying to sleep in the snow was pretty cold and miserable.
>
> Next morning at dawn I walked down to where I could see onto the road again, as I wanted to have a look at it before I took off. I walked a few yards inside the edge of the wood leading down to the road. I thought that I was hidden, but it wasn't long before a flashlight was turned on me by one of two Jerries, who were patrolling on the road below.

The Germans searching for Deck had found his parachute, and followed his tracks which led into the forest. However, rather than entering the woods too, they had merely waited for him to emerge towards the road.

> Well, they'd seen me now, and were making their way towards me. So I just high-tailed it back into the wood a short distance, and squatted down in a dark spot and prayed for the best. I could hear them coming, walking through the forest, and thought my time was up. But they must have picked up my tracks of thirty-six hours previously, because they passed me by, and went on into the next wood where I had been the day before.

Deck stayed where he was, waiting for darkness to descend. Then he moved, walking away in another direction.

> It was hard trudging, and my feet were soaking wet from the snow. Before dawn came, I found an empty caboose where men had been doing roadworks or something. I pried the door open and got in. The next day broke stormy, and a regular blizzard came on, making it very cold even in the caboose. I was glad in one way as my tracks would be extinguished. The caboose was almost blown off its wheels many times by the wind. By nightfall it had died down, and I got out and walked towards a wood near a road that ran into a village. I decided to go to ground in the wood, and waited there for three days, thinking I would have to take a chance and walk through the village in daylight.

Deck hoped to brazen his way through the village, so the evening before he planned to take this risk, he went down to a stream for water so that he could shave, and try to tidy up his appearance. On the way, he saw a log cabin and approached it to see if it was uninhabited for if so, there might be some food and clothes he could use.

Luckily, just before he got to the cabin door, he noticed fresh footprints and quickly backtracked. His deteriorating physical condition was making him more and more desperate. In the face of hunger, physical exhaustion and hypothermia, subconsciously the fear of being taken prisoner was dissipating.

A little before dawn I was all ready to strike out. When I did and reached the road, I killed a little time by walking in the opposite direction to the village, and then walked back again. I didn't want to be seen in the village too early in the morning. The road was very open and, coming up behind me, I heard several men also walking towards the village. I paid no heed but soon they were close on my heels.

However, before they actually overtook me, they branched off and took a short cut into the village and got there before me. The inhabitants were up and about when I got there. I passed several as they led teams of oxen with snow sleighs laden mostly with manure. I greeted them with 'Guten morgen', and they responded likewise. But I couldn't help the feeling that they all turned and stared for a moment or two before proceeding.

In the centre of the village there was a bridge over a stream and, as Deck came to it, a number of geese waddled out of the stream screeching at him. The noise brought a man out of a nearby large house, and he called out to Deck who did not understand his shouts.

I had passed him by, so I made out I didn't know who he was yelling at, and so paid no heed to his cries. Then a woman whom I was passing at the time, called something back to me. I thought that I could not walk on and ignore them both, so I gingerly turned. The man waved at me to go over to him.

He jabbered something at Deck, who was unable to respond. It presumably convinced him that Deck could not understand and was not a German.

This man ushered me into his house, and into his office, which was the house's front room. He was no doubt the town burgomaster and had that official air about him. To be inside the warm room, and to then have his daughter bring me coffee and bread, made me wonder why I hadn't got myself captured sooner. Anyway, being so cold and hungry as I was, I was actually glad to get captured. But I didn't tell them so!

After I'd relieved my captors of the fear that I was either 'Russki' or 'Polski' they relaxed, and seemed to marvel at their great victory in capturing a Canadian flyer. The burgomaster phoned up the Luftwaffe, who had some men in the vicinity and, after a while, a young air office officer arrived. He showed about as much excitement as a man who comes in after a day's work.

The Luftwaffe officer stood looking at Deck and lit a cigarette.

> By this time of course all the families in town had heard what had happened in their sleepy village. I guess that for once I had the honour of being the centre of attention. The old burgomaster was having to tend to his usual business. Women were coming in with their ration books to be checked etc. Every time a man came in they'd 'Heil Hitler' a couple of times, and then jabber on. The women were looking at my flying suit, which I had rolled into a bundle, and were admiring all the material and the zippers on it.

After a time, a rotund older Luftwaffe officer arrived. His appearance was clearly why the younger officer was waiting patiently with Deck.

> Shortly after this the three of us, the fat officer on one side of me and the young one on the other, set off walking through the outskirts of the village. Soon we came to a gate leading into the railway yards, and there was a Luftwaffe sentry on guard. There were a number of passenger carriages on a side track, and these were now in use as a camp for these Luftwaffe men. They led me to one of them, where I was handed over to another officer, who was all ready to interrogate me, and to relieve me of everything I had in my pockets.

What followed for Deck was typical of the experiences of other downed airmen on capture – interrogation and transfer to one or more PoW camps. Eventually he was a PoW in Stalag VIIA Moosburg, until liberation by General Patton's US Third Army. He had survived the war.

* * *

On his return to No. 429 Squadron, Deck learned that their flight on 16 January to Magdeburg had been unnecessary. In respect of the aborted operation on the 12th, which at the time did not count as a completed operation, there had been a subsequent decision to credit it retrospectively as a completed operation. In hindsight, it meant that they need not have gone on that fateful Magdeburg operation. For pilot Biddell, having completed two other operations with other crews, the Magdeburg operation was his thirty-second. Nevertheless, for the rest of the crew the squadron's operations record book still shows each other member as having completed twenty-nine operations.

In 1990 Deck met with Biddell, Streatfield and Bourne in a reunion. Biddell finally put to rest Deck's concern that 'predicted flak' had shot them down. Biddell told him that it was not flak that hit the aircraft. It was fire from a night-fighter with the upward-firing *schräge Musik* cannon, which attacked from underneath the Halifax in its blind spot, where there was no gunner for protection.[4]

Chapter 36

'I shot upwards like a bullet!'

Sergeant R.F. 'Ricky' Dyson, Rear Gunner[1]

In the sixth year of the war Sergeant 'Ricky' Dyson was still flying operations as a rear gunner in a Lancaster. Since his lucky escape in the evacuation from France in May 1940, he had sustained his motivation over those years to 'do his bit'. More recently he had made a rapid recovery from injuries and burns suffered in November 1944 when, in a crashing Lancaster bomber, he and his turret were ripped away from the aircraft's fuselage.

On the night of 2 February 1945 Dyson was in one of the nineteen Lancaster bombers of No. 189 Squadron, based at Fulbeck near Newark-on-Trent in Lincolnshire, that were rostered to attack Karlsruhe in Germany. The previous night he and his crew had flown a seven-hour round trip in an operation raiding Siegen, landing back at Fulbeck at 23.55 hours.[2] Taking into account the debriefing on the Siegen raid, snatched sleep, and then briefings and preparation during the day for the Karlsruhe operation, it was a rapid, debilitating turnaround for aircrew.

> On this occasion in an operation to Karlsruhe, I was rear gunner again in my own crew, flying in Lancaster PB840 K-King. After take-off time was twice delayed, we eventually 'got off' at about 20.00 hours.[3]

In addition to Dyson, the rest of his crew members in K-King were:

Crew Member	Role
Flying Officer W.D. 'Ned' Kelly	Pilot
Flying Officer R.J. Webb	Navigator
Flight Sergeant A. James	Bomb Aimer
Flight Sergeant F.A. Fox	Mid-upper Gunner
Warrant Officer J.H. Grubb	Wireless Operator
Sergeant J. 'Jack' Haworth	Flight Engineer

The total force comprised 250 Lancasters and eleven Mosquitoes, all of No. 5 Group, in an operation to attack the railway yards and factories of Karlsruhe, the capital of Germany's Baden state.

Sergeant Ricky Dyson, (back row second from right) No. 189 Squadron RAF prior to Karlsruhe raid February 1945. (*Private collection M. Dyson*)

Weather conditions on the outward flight were worse than forecast and, over France, they experienced quite severe icing and electrical storms, to which Dyson in his rear turret was most exposed.

On reaching the target we found we were sandwiched between two cloud formations. There was black stuff below obscuring the target, and layers of alto-stratus above. It made us a sitting target for Jerry night-fighters, which were out in force. As we approached our run in, to bomb on green markers on the aiming point, there was a blinding flash and a terrific explosion.

The next thing I remember was being shot upwards like a bullet, and at the same time I felt my head and neck being forced down into my stomach. Then I think I blacked out, before recovering seconds later to find myself in mid-air somersaulting earthwards.

I thank God and the 'powers that be' at the Air Ministry that I was wearing the adapted pilot-seat-type parachute attached to the harness, which saved many rear gunners' lives. I pulled the ripcord and landed safely in a snow-covered ploughed field. Except for slight burns and a few bruises, I was virtually uninjured! My elation at having survived yet again was soon to disappear as I thought of the other members of my crew.

Dyson wondered if miracles can happen twice in one night, or if all six other crew members were killed in that one awful moment of time. Having made a safe landing, he soon became aware that he was trudging about in a snow-covered field in bare feet. Lancaster K-King had crashed at around 23.00 hours between the two villages of Untcrocwishcim and Obcrocwishcim.[4]

> My boots and socks had been sucked off during my descent. After hiding my 'chute as best I could, I went in search of some kind of footwear whilst it was still dark. I came upon an old barn, but was surprised by a German soldier who took me prisoner. With his bayonet fixed on his rifle he escorted me to a farm house, and introduced me to two elderly ladies who looked as scared as I felt. They were very kind and gentle, and gave me some lumps of sugar soaked in cinnamon. These had the wonderful effect of settling my stomach, which had been feeling very queasy.

After a while two German officers came to the house and spoke to Dyson in German.

> I assumed they were trying to interrogate me despite their lack of English. I was then taken to a German army detention barracks, where I met up with another Lancaster rear gunner. We were interrogated, placed in separate cells, and given some black bread, sausage and rosewood tea. I complained about my lack of footwear, and was eventually handed a pair of suede fur-lined flying boots. As grateful as I was to have them, I was saddened at the names I saw written inside.

One boot had belonged to the mid-upper gunner, Flight Sergeant F.A. Fox, and the other to the flight engineer, Sergeant Jack Howarth, of K-King. It meant that Fox and Howarth would no longer be in need of those boots. About three hours later, Dyson and the other RAF gunner were taken together from the cells.

> We were wrapped around with paper bandages, splashed with red ink in appropriate places, and taken to a courtyard. There we were ordered to get on board the front of a lorry. We were then each tied with a rope, wedged between a wing above the front wheel and the engine bonnet, and driven around the town and outlying villages.

How was this going to end? Dyson was terrified. Were they going to be hanged or shot by firing squad, as some downed airmen had been at the hands of enraged civilian mobs or the Gestapo?

> We were exhibited as 'British Terror Bombers'. We were jeered at, spat upon and had garbage thrown at us by the local population, whom we had bombed the night before.

It was an ordeal that both airmen thought could have only one ending. At the end of a terrifying tour around local streets, that evening they were taken to a local village jail, where they stayed for four days in unsavoury conditions. All the time they had no idea what their fate might be, or when the unthinkable might happen.

> We were fed reasonably well, which improved our morale somewhat. On the fifth day we were allowed to shave and have a brush-up before we boarded a train with two guards to Frankfurt. This was en route to the 'sweat-box' of Dulag Luft at Oberusel, where we were subjected to the usual process of interrogation, and the bogus Red Cross forms which we had been warned about.
>
> After about eight days we travelled again, first by train and then on foot to Vetzler, which was a transit camp for all PoWs being sent south into southern Germany. The onward journey from there was not without incident as we travelled by train in cattle trucks or on foot in all weathers. While imprisoned in a cattle truck one day, we were inadvertently shot up by rocket-firing RAF Typhoons, from which there were a large number of casualties.

Yet again Dyson's good fortune had held and he was unscathed from the Typhoons' attack. On another day in early April after they had been walking all day, Dyson was lucky to be allowed with some other PoWs to spend the night in the shelter of a barn, sleeping on straw on a platform above sheltered cattle.

> I was soon asleep when I suddenly awoke to a rustling noise in the straw. Thinking I was about to have my Red Cross parcel stolen, I sat bolt upright with a stick across my knees ready to strike the would-be thief. It was then that I saw two eyes gleaming brightly in the darkness. There was a swish and the 'thing', about the size of a cat, landed on my lap.
>
> Its rat face with tusk-like teeth petrified me. I believed I screamed out in terror, waking up about thirty of us in the barn. As we all went in search of the rat, beating the straw to find it proved useless, and luckily we didn't see it again. As you can imagine, further sleep for me, anyway, was out of the question that night! It has given me nightmares ever since.

Eventually, on 15 April, Dyson and his fellow PoWs arrived at Stalag Luft VIIA, Moosburg. It was not for long, as on the 29th, the camp was liberated by the US Third Army under the command of General Patton. The first to enter Stalag Luft VIIA and free the PoWs was the 4th Armoured Division, also sometimes known as 'Patton's Wild Cats'.

We remained at Moosburg until 7 May, and [were] then flown out via Rheims to England. We landed at RAF Tangmere and were given a marvellous homecoming by their reception committee.

Of the seven crew who had taken off in Lancaster K-King on the night of 2 February 1945, only Ricky Dyson survived the crash. The other crew members – Kelly, Webb, James, Fox, Grubb and Haworth – did not have Dyson's luck, and died either in the aircraft or in the crash. Their bodies were found and buried locally at Unteroewisheim, Karlsdorf and Ubstadt.[5]

For No. 189 Squadron, the raid on Karlsruhe on the night of 2/3 February 1945 was a horrendous operation. Of the nineteen Lancasters despatched, four aircraft and their crews were lost, and listed as 'Missing without trace'. It was a loss rate of 21 per cent, far above the maximum acceptable rate of 5 per cent.

* * *

During more than five years of war service, good fortune certainly accompanied Ricky Dyson. He had been transferred from the Fleet Air Arm's ill-fated HMS *Glorious*, survived the chaotic evacuation from France in May 1940, and twice been blasted out of his rear gun turret of a crashing Lancaster, followed by perilous captivity as a PoW. Even more remarkable was his resilience and spirit to come through all the trials and sufferings that he encountered and remain unbroken.

On 24 April 1942 it was announced in the *London Gazette* that the King had approved the award of the George Medal to Sergeant Richard Frederick Dyson, in recognition of his act of great bravery, and his selfless efforts on 26 November 1944 to rescue the other members of his crew from the crashed Lancaster. Referring to the conflagration of the destroyed aircraft, its fuel and exploding bombs, the citation stated:

> The danger was at times so great that members of the rescue parties were obliged to park vehicles 200 yards away and wait until the explosions and fires had moderated. Sergeant Dyson showed outstanding gallantry by his persistent efforts to help his comrades and undoubtedly saved the life of his pilot.[6]

On his return to the UK, Ricky Dyson was presented with the George Medal by King George VI at an investiture at Buckingham Palace. Dyson was accompanied by his sister, Miss Mary Dyson, and his aunt, Miss Olive Dyson. However, the three family members were in shock at the investiture since, just two days earlier, Ricky and Mary's father, Mr Arthur Cecil Dyson, had passed away.[7]

Although Dyson was honoured with the award of the George Medal, his war service of more than five years, like that of many others, also left a legacy that will never die.

Chapter 37

Engine gone – jump into the sea, or crash land behind German lines?

Flying Officer John Ulm[1]

In the winter of 1944–45 in northern Italy Allied Armies came to a standstill at the Gothic Line. After a year's hard slog fighting their way north from amphibious landings at Reggio, Salerno and Anzio, the Allies' Fifth and Eighth Armies ground to a halt, confronted by the mountains, the onset of winter and the long-prepared German defences. For more than a year the Germans had been using the Tuscan Apennines to build their Gothic Line, which in their minds would be a final defence to guard the River Po valley and Italy's industrial north.[2]

From the beginning of January the Allies' intention was that around 75 per cent of air operations in Italy were to be of an interdiction nature, to starve German forces of supplies. In late January winter intensified, with heavy snow and freezing temperatures curtailing all air operations until improved conditions arrived in early March. Once spring brought drier weather and longer days, a massive ground and air assault, Operation GRAPESHOT, would attempt to break through the German defences.[3]

* * *

Over the Adriatic coastline of northern Italy, not far north of Venice, on 6 March 1945 it was a beautiful sunny morning. A flight of four Spitfires of No. 145 Squadron RAF, led by Flying Officer Bill Hughes, with his number two, Warrant Officer Harry Clifton, and Australian Flying Officer John Ulm, with his number two, Sergeant Alan Stacey, took off at 10.00 hours from their airfield at Bellaria. Each Spitfire carried a 500lb bomb.

Flying Officer John Ulm, a twenty-three-year old from Sydney, Australia, had joined the RAAF in April 1942, after which he was transferred to Britain for further training at Eshott OTU in Northumberland before being posted to No. 145 Squadron in Italy.

The operation on this March morning for Ulm and his three fellow pilots was to attack an enemy military train which was travelling in German-held territory. Most Axis transport moved at night to avoid attack by Allied aircraft, so when the four Spitfire pilots sighted the heavily-armed train moving in daylight, they recognised their designated target. Flying Officer Ulm thought the train's protection meant that it was of some importance.

The train was protected by five railcars with triple-mounted flak cannon. We dived into attack, reaching 400mph or more in our approach down to around

Flying Officer John Ulm, No. 145 Squadron RAF. (*Private collection, John Ulm*)

fifty feet, and bombed and strafed the train. I could see my cannon shells exploding on the locomotive.

At about twenty feet, right on top of the locomotive, I collected a godawful thump to starboard in the Spitfire's Merlin engine, jamming the throttles open at over 350mph. I immediately called up our flight leader Bill Hughes, 'Bill, I am hit!' He responded, 'Bale out! Bale out!' I ducked behind some trees to avoid any more flak. Then thinking that the engine will burn out, I headed to the heavens.[4]

He needed to be at 1,500 feet at least to bale out safely. To Ulm, the cockpit dials looked good, the aeroplane was still flying, and he gained height while he could. At around 9,000 feet, and once more over the sea, the engine seized. It seemed that he must take Hughes' advice and bale out. In an instant the dire options available in his situation confronted him. He had previously thought that in this situation he would try to land on the beach. With the Spitfire's engine gone, that was no longer realistic.

Now I felt I had only two other options. One was to bale out and come down in the sea. But by the time the squadron's Walrus seaplane came out to look for me, I would have drowned. I decided the better alternative was to try to glide the aircraft inland and crash land hopefully in an area of Italian partisans friendly to the Allies.

In a matter of split seconds, Ulm committed himself to gliding the aircraft back over the land. It would be touch and go whether the Spitfire would glide the distance back to the shoreline. Rather than opting for the dire risk of baling out over the sea, he thought that trying to find somewhere back from the beach to make a crash landing might give him a better chance of coming out alive.

It was on his mind that he had already nearly 'bought it' on three previous occasions in perilous situations in northern Italy. It meant, of course, that he would be crash-landing into German-held territory. If he was unable to glide the distance to reach land, at least he could ditch in the sea closer to the shore.

> I glided the Spitfire down, and luckily back over the land at around 150mph, and I could see flat farmland, where I hoped to make a wheels-up belly landing. I picked a field, going in fast, keeping flaps up in reserve. I flicked them down to lift through a line of trees, but still touched some of the topmost branches.

Like most pilots in this situation Ulm had never done a belly landing before, and had to hope that there were no rocks or other obstacles where he managed to put down. Wherever he picked, there was no way of knowing that.

> To be ready to get out of the cockpit fast, I had pulled on the toggles opening the perspex canopy, and slid it backwards. At the last moment before hitting the ground I grabbed hold of the gunsight in front of my face with both hands, to prevent my head from being smashed into it on impact. The aircraft landed heavily but flat. Unfortunately, the cockpit canopy had not jettisoned as it should have when I slid it back. Possibly blocked by the aerial behind, it slammed forwards into the back of my head, leaving a bad cut.

As soon as the Spitfire came to a shuddering stop, on one of his intercom channels Ulm radioed his compatriot Harry Clifton, to say that he was down on the ground and still in one piece, and about to leave the aircraft. It would mean that his mother would hear that he had survived. Then he clambered out in something of a daze from his head injury. Ulm stood beside the aircraft clutching a Very flare in his hand. A pilot's standard instruction on making a forced landing in enemy territory was to fire a two-star red cartridge into the aircraft to destroy it. As he stood there some Italian farmworkers came across the fields towards him. He had to hope they were partisans friendly to the Allies.

> Among these farmhands was an Italian civilian, a city type in a crumpled suit. As he looked around he said, 'Tedeschi! Tedeschi!', meaning there were German troops close by. I had two Dunhill cigarettes on me and gave him one, rather than risk it being taken off me by Germans. He was possibly a member of the Italian Resistance, and he wanted to hurry me away. But, before we could do so, two German soldiers appeared, peering at us over a nearby hedge.
> With that he nicked off quick smart, and straight after the two Jerries picked me up. As they led me away I pointed to my head, which was bleeding and aching, and I tried saying in Italian 'Mal de testa', that my

head was wounded. They found an Italian doctor to treat me, who drove some staples into my head before bandaging it. For the pain he gave me a brandy with woodchips swimming in it!

When I sat down at the side of the road, one of the soldiers went off on his own. He came back with a small dray cart pulled by a mule. With me in the cart we set off again, until we reached a small village.

From there a small German army unit took Ulm to Camposampiero where interrogation sessions began. He found this questioning included countless and most tedious observations. 'One very boring remark was, 'For you the war is over,' to which I responded, 'And so say all of us!'

While lying in a bunk next to the orderly room, Ulm reflected on how military services of all countries must have similarities in many things.

I could hear the Orderly Sergeant shouting over his crank-phone to an opposite number in the Luftwaffe at Mestre. It was words to the effect, 'I've got a bloody airman here.'

The German army wanted rid of him. As he anticipated, he was now transported in a German VW 'Jeep-type' vehicle to the Luftwaffe HQ at Verona where he got to know two SAAF Spitfire pilots, and an American, S.E. 'Eddie' Hausner, from Linden, New Jersey.

Eddie and I got to know each other by scratching matching finger holes in the hollow plaster walls of our 'cells'. While flying a Thunderbolt at dusk over Florence, Eddie had his own very lucky escape. He sneaked up on a Fw190 and blew it out of the sky. But its bomb exploded, which blew him up too.

From Verona, Ulm and his fellow pilots were marched with an estimated 7,000 other Allied PoWs through the Brenner Pass to Germany. They walked at night and Ulm noted how the traffic was heavy, nose to tail, whereas during the day there was none to be seen. In the Brenner Pass the convoy and column of marching PoWs was bombed by Allied aircraft, and once again Ulm came through unscathed.

Later in Germany, marching through the Black Forest in a column of *Kriegsgefangener* troops, we were momentarily strafed by a Thunderbolt, but at least he waggled his wings in an apology. And how we exulted on seeing from a few miles away, the shock waves in the cumulo-nimbus clouds at 30,000 feet, rising from the bombing of Nuremberg. There was smashed-up destruction in the main cities, and one's main impression of the population was of a dull resignation under stress.

We had lots of waiting around for trains, and we had to get out of a wood-fuelled half-track to push it up hill. To German civilians we were curious, but some of them had a bad attitude, understandably. In Augsburg, a tall executive type in immaculate black suit and hat, and polished shoes, put down his attaché case on the footpath and marched past several times, spitting at us and snarling, 'Schweinhunde, terrorfliege!' We were lucky our guards never took their gunsights off him.

It was another reminder that surviving being shot down was not the end of it. In the custody of the enemy death could come in many guises.

When we went through Schweinfurt, which was still smoking from a big USAAF raid the previous day, I experienced a very chilling, nerve-racking moment. Picking our way through the wreckage, one of our German guards, while adjusting his rucksack, handed his beautiful Schmeisser sub-machine gun to a wild-eyed twelve-year-old boy, who pointed it distressingly at my nose!

The boy did not pull the trigger, and the guard reclaimed his Schmeisser. Yet another heartstopping scare had passed. Ulm and the three other pilots eventually reached a PoW camp, Stalag VII at Moosburg near Munich. There Ulm and his fellow PoWs survived until liberated by an American tank unit in May 1945.

*   *   *

John Ulm is the son of Charles Ulm, the legendary Australian civil aviation pioneer of the 1920s and 1930s. Charles Ulm and Charles Kingsford-Smith made a number of record-breaking flights, notably the record for a UK to Australia flight of six days, seventeen hours and fifty-six minutes, and the first ever trans-Pacific flight. On 3 December 1934 flying between San Francisco and Hawaii, Charles Ulm's plane, *Stella Australis*, disappeared. No trace of the aircraft was ever found.

At the end of the war John Ulm continued his father's work in the aviation industry, and made a new life. He joined *The Sun* newspaper as a war correspondent and, in 1946, went to Japan to cover the Allied occupation and after that the Korean War. He subsequently became the Aviation Editor of *The Sun*, before taking on a senior management role with the Qantas airline in Sydney. John married Val in 1954, bringing up three sons and two daughters. Now approaching their centenary John and Val Ulm live independently in Sydney.

And So Many More

Because of the unexpectedly high number of contributions that were received from veterans and their families, time and space has only allowed for those stories selected. So many more could not be included. A number of those exclusions are summarised below:

Emergency surgery at Liège: Bender, Flying Officer Clifford A. 'Cliff', DFC
On 25 February 1945 Lancaster NG364 of bomb-aimer Flying Officer Bender was on a return flight from a daylight raid on Kamen in Germany when, in heavy flak, a shell exploded very close to the aircraft. Shards of metal penetrated the Lancaster, severing the brachial artery of Bender who also suffered wounds to his arm and chest. With Bender bleeding profusely and appearing certain not to last until their return to base at RAF Mildenhall in Oxfordshire, the pilot, Flight Lieutenant Noble, in desperation found, and landed at 15.34 hours, at an airfield at Liège in Belgium. At once Bender was rushed to an American army tent hospital where he was given immediate blood transfusions and surgery that saved his life. Noble took off again at 16.02 and flew the Lancaster and the remaining crew safely back to Mildenhall.[1]

Forced landing behind Japanese lines: Bowles, Flight Lieutenant Percy, DFC
During April to June 1944 pilot Flight Lieutenant Bowles flew Wellington transport aircraft of No. 357 Squadron RAF out of Jessore in north-east India, ferrying bombs and ammunition to British forces besieged by the Japanese in Imphal. In December 1944 Bowles took a Dakota transport plane 400 miles into Japanese-occupied Burma to deliver supplies to Allied forces. After a forced landing he spent three days and nights grounded before Japanese attackers were driven away and his aircraft was sufficiently airworthy to take off and make the return flight.[2]

Walking wounded through occupied France: Coates, Sergeant E. 'Ted'
Sergeant Coates was the pilot of a Wellington shot down in November 1942 near Lyons in France. He and his crew baled out but Coates was the only one to avoid capture on the ground. Although wounded in one leg, he walked for fifty-three days in winter weather, assisted by French villagers, all the way to Spain

and eventual safety. He believed that he was the first airman to escape through France and over the Pyrenees without help from the French Resistance.[3]

Oxygen lines severed by flak: Harvey, Wing Commander D.C. 'Doug', DFC and Bar
On 21 January 1944 pilot Doug Harvey's Lancaster of No. 467 Squadron RAF, while on a bombing run at over 20,000 feet over Berlin, was coned by searchlights and hit by flak. In the damage to the aircraft a severed oxygen line rendered some crew members unconscious. Only by throwing the bomber into a corkscrewing dive to below 10,000 feet to evade the flak, and also enabling the crew to breathe again, was Harvey able to fly the Lancaster out of danger and save their lives. [4]

Wireless Operator joins the French Resistance: Hawken, Flight Sergeant Stanley A., OBE
On the night of 18/19 July 1944 Flight Sergeant Hawken, a wireless operator, was in one of ten Lancaster bombers of No. 630 Squadron RAF which took off at 21.50 hours from RAF East Kirkby in Lincolnshire. They were part of a force of 115 bombers on an operation to bomb the railway yards at Revigny, 141 miles east of Paris. At the beginning of his aircraft's bombing run, Hawken was concentrating on his listening watch when they were hit by fire from a night-fighter. Both inboard engines were damaged and at once ablaze, so that the bale-out order from the pilot came immediately. Only Hawken and two other crewmen got out. After landing on his own, Hawken evaded capture with the help of a French family. Later he joined the French Resistance and took part in sabotage operations in France until liberation by American forces.[5]

Five crew are still missing: O'Brien, Sergeant John
At 10.00 hours on 20 June 1942 Sergeant Pilot O'Brien of No. 49 Squadron lifted Manchester L7387 into the summer skies above RAF Scampton, Lincolnshire. The operation was a patrol over the North Sea off the Grimsby coast. O'Brien's aircraft failed to return. The Manchester bomber had a high incidence of mechanical failure, and O'Brien's plane may have been lost for that reason. Two crew members' bodies were later washed ashore and subsequently buried in Sweden and Holland. John O'Brien and the other four crewmen are listed as missing to this day. For many years their families may have harboured hopes that they might have escaped a watery grave, and either be PoWs or in hiding somewhere. [6]

Ditched in Indonesia: Roberts, Warrant Officer Ross K.
While flying a patrol operation in a Beaufighter of the 1st Tactical Air Force RAAF near Amboina Island (Ambon), Indonesia, Warrant Officer Ross

Roberts and his navigator, Sergeant Basil Phillips, were forced to ditch the aircraft in the sea and take to a dinghy. Three hours later a Catalina flying boat, which was despatched to their rescue, touched down close by their dinghy. It took only three minutes to take Roberts and Phillips on board. But in that time, the rescue rendezvous having been spotted by Japanese forces on shore, enemy fire hit the Catalina and wounded one of the crew. Another Beaufighter sent to provide cover was also hit but both aircraft were able to return to base safely.[7]

Arctic Circle Air Sea Rescue: Sommerville, Flying Officer Robert M. 'Bob'
On 18 July 1944 at 14.02 hours Liberator F-Freddie (F/86) of No. 86 Squadron left RAF Tain in Ross-shire, Scotland. The pilot, Squadron Leader Nelms, and co-pilot, Flying officer Sommerville, were setting out on a search patrol for U-boats in the Arctic Ocean west of the Lofoten Islands, off the coast of Norway. Around 100 miles west of the Lofotens they attacked a U-boat, but enemy anti-aircraft fire from the U-boat hit the Liberator, forcing Nelms and Sommerville to ditch the plane in the sea. Six of the crew got out before the aircraft sank, and they managed to launch three one-man dinghies, with two men sharing each dinghy. Despite their drenched clothes and exposure to the freezing temperatures of the Arctic Circle, they stayed together in the three dinghies and hung on. Four days later, they were found by a Catalina flying boat, remarkably still alive, and flown back to RAF Sullom Voe in the Shetland Islands. It is thought that it was the most northerly air sea rescue of the Second World War.[8]

Hellcat crash leaves a hell of burns: Worner, Sub-Lieutenant Gerald W.
After taking off in a Grumman Hellcat on a training flight on 3 September 1945 from RAF Nutts Corner near Belfast, Sub-Lieutenant Worner crashed the large fighter. On impact it overturned and caught fire. Worner survived the mangled wreck but suffered extensive burns and fractures which required him to spend a year in the Queen Victoria specialist burns hospital at East Grinstead, Sussex.[9]

Chased by jet fighters: Watson, Flight Lieutenant W.K. 'Ken', DFC
The Mosquito weaved violently from side to side, varying its height, as it tried to stay barely above the tree tops of a Bavarian pine forest. At one point the plane clipped a branch sending a shower of pine leaves into the air. On a return flight from a raid on Munich, Flight Lieutenant Watson was running for his life, with two of the Luftwaffe's latest Me.262 jet fighters chasing his Mosquito. For around thirty minutes, he sustained desperate evasion

manoeuvres, hugging the terrain before escaping the two jets and eventually landing safely at an Allied air base in Italy. [10]

Beating the odds, and the Second Pilot jinx: McManus, Flight Lieutenant John B., DFC

Between August 1944 and January 1945 Flight Lieutenant John McManus, pilot of a Halifax bomber with No. 466 Squadron, completed thirty-two operations. He began with an operation to Homberg as a second pilot, known as 'Second Dickey', and subsequently also flew in that role on four training flights in 1944–45. On one of these training exercises he took the position of the rear gunner for experience, and was lucky to survive a crash on take off. On one raid over Germany when McManus was accompanied by a second pilot, an 88mm flak shell exploded close to the aircraft, sending shrapnel straight through the cockpit windscreen. It missed McManus but, seconds earlier, it would have hit his 'Second Dickey' if he had not luckily been bending down. Nevertheless, McManus attributed much of the credit for completion of his tour of operations, to the rigorous training he received from former experienced bomber pilots. [11]

Favourable Fortune: Wright, Flight Lieutenant Frederick R. 'Fred', DFC

Flight Lieutenant Fred Wright was one of those aircrew who appeared to make his own luck. As the pilot of a Halifax during 1944–45 with No. 78 Squadron RAF at Breighton in East Yorkshire, he completed one operation as a second pilot, and thirty as captain. On those missions he was a close witness of many of his fellow aircrew as their aircraft were shot down by flak or enemy fighters. In the recommendation for the award of his DFC, the Station Commander said:

> During his operational tour this officer has never failed to display the highest standard of personal courage, determination and leadership. On several occasions his aircraft has been damaged by flak or enemy fighters, and he has always carried through his mission with a cool determination regardless of the danger.[12]

Like so many flyers Wright became well aware of how *Fortuna*, the Roman goddess of fate, of good or bad luck, had watched over him favourably. After the war he summed up well a common and fatalistic view of Bomber Command aircrew.

> In these operations the loss ratio in the first five operations was usually about 90 per cent, and if you were lucky to survive the first five, then you had a 30 per cent chance of reaching ten ops. After that you had a reasonable chance of reaching twenty ops, and after that the survival rate reduced dramatically. If you had done twenty-five ops, the chances of reaching your thirty, and completing your tour of operations was given as 5 per cent.[13]

As another veteran of Bomber Command reflected, flying on operations in the Second World War was 'dicing with death'. Day after day, night after night, airmen of Allied air forces took off into a lottery of death, each time knowing all too well that they might not return.

Epilogue

The extraordinary stories of escape and survival by aircrew recorded in this book display the amazing resilience of the human spirit in extreme adversity. While the air wars against Germany and its Axis allies in Europe, and the militaristic regime in Japan, comprised the predominant theme of these accounts of survival, there was another foe that airmen had to fight and keep at bay.

Aircrew, particularly those based in Britain, experienced a unique double life, very different to servicemen in front-line units of the army and navy. When not on duty airmen were free to socialise in the community near to their base, often with family and close friends. Yet they were continually leaving that normality of civilian life to fight to the death against an enemy in the sky. Within hours of leaving a convivial social gathering, they would be in a life-or-death struggle in the air, often shot down over enemy-occupied territory, where at times they were summarily executed.[1]

Their life was split between attempts to develop normal relationships with civilians, and flying operations which led to adrenalin-pumping encounters with enemy aircraft and anti-aircraft fire that, on so many occasions, ended their lives. For aircrew two personalities fought for dominance of their psyche – in varying degrees it brought about split personalities, and in essence these were not dissimilar from a 'Dr Jekyll and Mr Hyde' effect.

Many airmen who did survive the war carried chronic physical injuries into their subsequent lives. Perhaps they even more suffered long-term psychological conditions, once termed war neuroses, which today are diagnosed as Post Traumatic Stress Disorder (PTSD). In many cases, such psychological effects were undiagnosed, or just not spoken of, but in this book's stories some such consequences were recognised.

When Eric Maher's Wellington was hit by flak, he was seriously wounded in both legs and his body peppered by shrapnel. Helped by other crew to bale out, Maher landed in the sea off the Dutch coast. He carried the disabling effects on his legs, and the embedded shrapnel wounds in his head, for the rest of his life. The resulting trauma meant that he was never able to get on a plane again.

As a pilot of a bomber, Jim Comans completed over 100 operations, yet at the end of the war he threw away his uniform. He never again wanted to take the controls of an aircraft, and never did.

At only twenty-two years old, Alan Peart, a Spitfire fighter ace in North Africa, Italy and Burma, returned home to New Zealand near the end of the war physically drained, suffering from tropical health ailments and mental stress. It took him several years to recover, although he never forgot that turbulent time.

After the war Harry Howard remained a gregarious personality, yet his ordeals in Bomber Command, his severe injuries, and deprivations as a PoW, left their legacy. He was susceptible to bouts of depression, and was sometimes introverted for days at a time.

Bryan Good survived thirty operations in Bomber Command, but like so many he would pay a price. Those life-or-death raids left him with insomnia for many years, and recurring nightmares related to those times.

When an aircraft was shot down, if aircrew survived baling out, or a crashed landing, life or death remained a lottery. They became desperate to evade being captured by enemy forces. An unknown number, while floating down by parachute, were machine-gunned to death by enemy fighters. Many who were taken prisoner on the ground were summarily executed by enemy forces or their civilian supporters.

Yet amidst the hate, death, destruction, and worldwide misery of the Second World War, humanity's instinctive kindness, care and selfless generosity towards fellow human beings still thrived and was found in some most unlikely places. Aircrew brought down in enemy territory were only able to survive with assistance from either local civilians or enemy forces.

After baling out and wandering for seven days lost and near delirious in the jungle of New Guinea, Gene Rehrer had reached the point of total collapse when tribesmen from the Brown River village came upon him. They carried him back to their village by donkey, gave him water and food, then on to a European settlement. Without their instinctive help he had been doomed.

On a Dutch beach Eric Maher lay supine, soaking wet, critically wounded and unable to walk; he would soon freeze to death. Rather than allowing their troops to finish him off, or leave him to die, two German officers took off their winter greatcoats, covered him to keep him warm and alive, and with two of their men took him into custody and a hospital for emergency surgery.

Shot down over Japanese territory and into the mangrove swamps of the Burmese jungle, Barney Barnett had wandered on bare feet that were ripped and ragged. After four days without food or water, he was close to total collapse when he was found by some local villagers. At risk of certain death and their village being destroyed by the Japanese, they gave Barnett water, bathed him, then carried him across a river and handed him over to an advance party of British troops.

Herbert Penny parachuted into German–occupied Holland and, in need of shelter, took a chance by knocking on the door of a house in a Dutch village. He was lucky. The occupants sympathised with the Allies and hid him in their home. Then he was helped under a false identity to travel by civilians ('Helpers') of various resistance groups through Holland, Belgium, France and Spain to Gibraltar and escape back to Britain. His 'Helpers' in each country risked their lives and their families. If caught it meant torture at the hands of the Gestapo to provide information on other resistance members; then, if they survived the torture, they and their families would be either sent to a concentration camp or executed.

To evade capture by the Japanese, Allan Liedl and three other aircrew of a Catalina flying boat spent nearly two months walking, then stumbling and staggering around in circles in the jungle of New Britain. Living solely off local vegetation, they had become almost too weak to move any more until by chance a local villager came upon them. Despite the close proximity of Japanese troops, and if caught certain death and destruction of their village and families, the tribesmen gave them shelter, food and water, and then guided them over the mountains to a friendly European settlement.

Lloyd Leah, having been shot down near Gelsenkirchen, and captured by German troops, was deliberately shot in the neck, and left to bleed to death. Only merciful intervention by a German officer, who arranged for him to be rushed to hospital, saved his life.

Having parachuted down near the Dortmund-Ems canal in Germany, Harry Howard lay bleeding in a ditch. With a lacerated and near-severed arm, hip and back injuries, he was unable to walk and likely to bleed to death. By chance, a sympathetic German farmer found him, took him back to his farmhouse, and arranged for his transport to hospital.

Richard Deck baled out into snow-covered terrain close to Magdeburg in Germany in the severe winter of January 1945. After a few days on the run and in freezing temperatures living in the open, he was recognised and confronted by a village burgomaster. He was taken into the burgomaster's home, where his daughter served Deck coffee and bread.

It made him made wonder why he had not let himself be captured sooner.

The stories in this book of airmen's incredible escapes are astounding, each one in many and different ways. Perhaps the most remarkable and wonderful aspect is that so many airmen owed their survival to the help and kindness of perfect strangers, many who gave their help knowing that if found out, it would bring death to themselves, their friends and families.

The 'Helpers' in all countries knew the risks they were taking. Like the airmen they, too, were hostage to fortune and their courage was just as incredible.

Notes

Foreword
1. Middlebrook, *The Bomber Command War Diaries*, Location 13520

Prologue
1. NA Kew, AIR 27-1322-21/22, Operations Record Books (ORB) No. 214 Squadron RAF, November 1943.
2. Ibid.
3. Middlebrook, *The Berlin Raids*, pp. 112–18.

Chapter 1
1. Richey, *Fighter Pilot*, pp.14–31.
2. Terraine, *The Right of the Line,* pp. 96, 122–3.
3. National Archives (NA) UK, AIR 27-1-40, ORB No. 1 Squadron, October 1939.
4. Chant, *Aircraft of World War II*, p.161, and p.249.
5. Richey, op. cit., p. 32.
6. Ibid., p.143.

Chapter 2
1. Mackersey, *In the Silk,* pp. 70–2.
2. *Traces of World War 2* – No. 218 Squadron RAF, www.epibreren.com/ww2/raf/218_squadron
3. Mackersey, op. cit., pp. 64–6.
4. Ibid.
5. Mackersey, op. cit., pp. 70–3.
6. Terraine, op. cit., p. 127.
7. *Traces of World War 2*, op. cit.
8. *History of No. 218 Squadron RAF*, Harrington Aviation Museum, www.harringtonmuseum.org.uk/history-of-no-218-squadron-raf

Chapter 3
1. Veteran's Account, Ricky Dyson.
2. Collier, *The Sands of Dunkirk*, pp. 60–1.
3. Terraine, op. cit., p. 153.
4. Veteran's Account, Ricky Dyson.
5. Private collection, M. Dyson.
6. Veteran's Account, Ricky Dyson.
7. Ibid.
8. NA Kew, AIR 27-554-14, ORB No. 59 Squadron, May 1940.
9. Ibid.

Chapter 4
1. Masters, *So Few*, pp. 21–7.
2. NA Kew, AIR 27-149-10, ORB No. 10 Squadron RAAF, June 1940.

3. Masters, op. cit. pp. 21–7.
4. Australian War Memorial (AWM), Wing Commander Julian Allan Cohen (aka Richard Kingsland) AO CBE DFC.
5. NA Kew, AIR 27-149-10, op. cit.
6. *Daily Telegraph*, Biography (John Edwards), www.telegraph.co.uk/news, 14 October 2012.
7. Chant, *Aircraft of World War II*, p. 291.
8. NA Kew, AIR 27-149-10, op. cit.
9. *Daily Telegraph*, op. cit.

Chapter 5
1. Veteran's account, F/Lt Bevis.
2. Evans, *The Decisive Campaigns of the Desert Air Force 1942–1945*, pp. 11–15.
3. Veteran's account, Bevis, op. cit. (and all subsequent direct quotes).
4. Evans, op. cit., pp. 11–15.

Chapter 6
1. Veteran's account, P/O Allan Simpson, No. 108 Squadron RAF.
2. Ibid.
3. NA Kew AIR 27-849-4, ORB No. 108 Squadron, October 1941.
4. Terraine, op., cit., pp. 333–4.
5. Ibid.
6. Veteran's account, Simpson op. cit. (and all subsequent direct quotes).

Chapter 7
1. Beevor, Anthony, *The Second World War*, p. 436.
2. Terraine, op. cit., pp. 492–4.
3. NA Kew, AIR 27-449-6 ORB No. 44 (Rhodesia) Squadron, April 1942.
4. *The Comprehensive Guide to the Victoria and George Cross*, www.vconline.org.uk)
5. NA Kew, AIR 27-449-6 op. cit., Combat Report, S/Ldr Leader John Nettleton, and Air Ministry, *Bomber Command Continues*, p. 26.
6. *London Gazette*, 28 April 1942.
7. NA Kew, AIR 27-449-6, op. cit., Combat Report, S/Ldr John Nettleton, and Air Ministry, *Bomber Command Continues*, p. 26.
8. *London Gazette*, 28 April 1942.
9. Terraine, op. cit., pp. 492–4.
10. Ibid.
11. *London Gazette*, 28 April 1942.
12. *The Comprehensive Guide to the Victoria and George Cross*, www.vconline.org.uk)

Chapter 8
1. Veteran's account, Lt/Col H.E. 'Gene' Rehrer.
2. Ibid. (and all subsequent direct quotes)
3. Larry Rehrer, 'Nothing more than Dust in a Jar – The Jungle Journey of 2nd Lieutenant E Rehrer' (unpublished article), private collection.
4. 39th Pursuit Squadron Association.
5. Pacific Wrecks, www.pacificwrecks.com

Chapter 9
1. Veteran's account, F/Lt Eric Maher.
2. Ibid.
3. Ibid (and all subsequent direct quotes).

4. NA Kew, AIR 27-1907-08, ORB, No. 460 Squadron, June 1942.

5. Bull, Gp/Capt, RAF Bomber Command Commemoration (RAAF), No. 460 Squadron, 26 May 2019.

Chapter 10

1. Veteran's Account, Lt/Col Sponenbergh.

2. Moreton Bay Council, *Redcliffe Remembers the War Years 1939–1945*, pp. 66–7.

3. Ibid.

4. Veteran's Account, op. cit., Sponenbergh.

5. Ibid.

6. Ibid.

7. Ibid.

8. Ibid.

9. Ibid.

10. Ibid.

11. Moreton Bay Council, *Redcliffe Remembers the War Years 1939–1945*, op. cit., pp. 65–6.

12. Hart, Duane, *Redcliffe Pictorial History*, Vol. 2 1824–1949.

13. Veteran's Account, op. cit., Sponenbergh.

Chapter 11

1. Veteran's account, S/Ldr McRae (and all subsequent direct quotes).

2. Middlebrook, Martin, and Everitt, Chris, *The Bomber Command Diaries*, Location 13510 (eBook).

3. Evans, *The Decisive Campaigns of the Desert Air Force 1942–1945*, pp. 20–4.

Chapter 12

1. Veteran's account, F/Lt J.V. Comans DFC and Bar.

2. Ibid.

3. Scott Coleman, Historian, Marist Brothers High School, Darlinghurst, Sydney, NSW, Australia, *Flight Lieutenant J.V. Comans DFC*.

4. Chris Whiteman, private collection.

5. NA Kew, AIR 27/126/37, ORB No. 9 Squadron, July 1942.

6. Ibid.

7. Bending, Kevin, *The History of 97 (Straits Settlements) Squadron in the Second World War* (unpublished), Index to Aircrew 1941–1945 – A-J, Comans, J.W. (pilot) p. 66.

8. *Sydney Daily Mirror*, Australia, February 1971.

9. *The Sun Herald*, Australia, 2 August 1992.

Chapter 13

1. Veteran's account, F/O Barnett.

2. Evans, *Air Battle for Burma*, op. cit., p. 86.

3. Day, AWM, p. 190; and Evans, op. cit., pp. 192–4.

4. Ibid.

5. Veitch, *Fly*, pp. 174–8; and Evans, op. cit., pp. 192–4.

Chapter 14

1. Veteran's account, F/O Bert Hollings.

2. NA Kew, AIR 27/1234/16 ORB, No. 207 Squadron, August 1943.

3. Geoff Hollings, private collection.

4. Brotherton, *Press on Regardless*, pp. 128–9.

5. Veteran's account, F/O Bert Hollings.

6. Ibid.
7. Brotherton, op. cit., pp. 128–9.

Chapter 15
1. Veteran's account, F/O Albert Hollings.
2. Brotherton, op. cit., pp. 127–9.
3. Middlebrook, op. cit., Introduction Summary (back cover).
4. Ibid., pp. 26/7.
5. Geoff Hollings, private collection.
6. NA Kew, AIR 27-1234-15/16, ORB No. 207 Squadron, August 1943.
7. Veteran's account, F/O Albert Hollings.
8. Geoff Hollings, private collection.
9. Middlebrook, op. cit., pp. 29–76.

Chapter 16
1. Veteran's account, F/O Penny.
2. Ibid.
3. Middlebrook, op. cit., p. 1.
4. Veteran's account, F/O Penny (and all subsequent direct quotes).
5. Middlebrook, op. cit., pp.78–84.
6. Cheshire, *Bomber Pilot*, p.23.
7. Meyerowitz, *The Lost Airman*, p. 60.
8. Ibid, p.210.
9. Ibid.
10. Middlebrook, op. cit., p.84.
11. Penny, Nick, private collection.
12. *The Royal Air Forces Escaping Society 1945 – 1995*, www.ww2escapelines.co.uk
13. Veteran's account, F/O Penny.

Chapter 17
1. Veteran's account, P/O Peart.
2. Evans, op. cit., pp. 115–16.
3. Veteran's account, P/O Peart (and all subsequent direct quotes).
4. Ibid., and Peart, *From North Africa to the Arakan*, pp. 11–19.
5. Ibid.

Chapter 18
1. Veteran's account, F/Lt Vern Scantleton.
2. John Scantleton, private collection.
3. NA Kew AIR 27-1322-21 and AIR 27-1322-22, ORB No. 214 Squadron, November 1943.
4. Veteran's account, F/Lt Vern Scantleton (and all subsequent direct quotes).

Chapter 19
1. Vincent, David, *Catalina Chronicle – A History of RAAF Operations*, pp. 47 and 50.
2. Interrogation by MIS-X Section, HQ Allied Airforces, South West Pacific Area, 15 April 1944 (E&E Report No 44/408 – Secret).
3. Chant, p. 87.

Chapter 20
1. Veteran's account, F/O Bryan Good.
2. Holland, *Big Week*, pp. 98–106.

3. Veteran's account, F/O Bryan Good.
4. NA Kew, AIR 27-2137-14/16 ORB No. 622 Squadron, February 1944.
5. Ibid.
6. Middlebrook, *The Nuremberg Raid*, pp. 138–40.
7. Ibid., pp. 274–81.
8. Bryan Good private collection (Suellyn Everett).

Chapter 21
1. Veteran's account, F/Lt Vern L. Scantleton.
2. Ibid (and all subsequent direct quotes).
3. John Scantleton, Private Collection.

Chapter 22
1. Veteran's account, F/O Peart.
2. Shores, *Aces High*, p. 490, and Evans, *Air Battle for Burma*, pp. 145–9.
3. Veteran's account, F/O Peart (and all subsequent direct quotes), Franks, *The Air Battle of Imphal*, pp. 28–30, Thomas, *Spitfire Aces of Burma and the Pacific*, p. 42.
4. Veteran's Account, F/O Peart, and Peart, *From North Africa to the Arakan*, p. 157, and Evans, op. cit., pp. 145–9.
5. Franks, op. cit., pp. 28–30.
6. Ibid, and NA AIR 27/678, ORB, No 81 Squadron.
7. Thomas, op. cit., pp. 42–3.
8. Veteran's Account, F/O Peart, and Peart, op. cit., pp. 155–63.
9. Shores, *Air War for Burma*, p. 185, and Thomas, op. cit., pp. 42–3.
10. Veteran's Account, F/O Peart, and Peart, op. cit., pp.155–63
11. Ibid.
12. Shores, op. cit., p. 185, and Evans, op. cit., pp. 145–9.
13. Franks, op. cit., pp. 32–5, and NA AIR 27/678, ORB, No 81 Squadron RAF, March 1944.
14. NA AIR 27/678, op. cit.
15. Veteran's Account, F/O Peart, and Peart, op. cit., pp. 8–10.

Chapter 23
1. Veteran's account, F/O Fischer.
2. Ibid. (and all subsequent direct quotes).
3. Private collection, Geoff, Bruce and Janet Fischer (John Fischer's letter to G.J. Fleming).
4. Middlebrook, *The Berlin Raids*, p. 279.
5. Private collection, Geoff, Bruce and Janet Fischer.

Chapter 24
1. Veteran's account, F/Sgt Lloyd Leah.
2. Log Book, Flight Sergeant Lloyd Leah.
3. Veteran's account, F/Sgt Lloyd Leah (and all subsequent direct quotes).
4. Private Collection, Peter Leah.

Chapter 25
1. Veteran's account, F/Sgt Keith Campbell.
2. NA Kew, AIR 27/1928/13, ORB No. 466 Squadron RAAF, 24 July 1944.
3. Veteran's account, F/Sgt Keith Campbell (and all subsequent direct quotes).
4. NA Kew, AIR 27/1928/13, op. cit.
5. Veteran's account, F/Sgt Keith Campbell.
6. *Sydney Morning Herald*, Obituary 20 July 2019.
7. Ibid.

Chapter 26

1. Veteran's account, P/O K.E. Tanner.
2. Terraine, *The Right of the Line,* pp. 665–6.
3. Saunders, *RAF 1939–45 Vol III The Fight is Won,* pp. 190–1.
4. NA Kew, AIR 27-1922-2, ORB No. 463 Squadron RAF, September 1944
5. Ibid.
6. Saunders, op. cit.

Chapter 27

1. Veteran's account, F/O Dyer.
2. Saunders, op. cit., pp. 192–4.
3. Private collection, Stephen Dyer.
4. Veteran's account, F/O Dyer (and all subsequent direct quotes).
5. Private collection, Stephen Dyer.

Chapter 28

1. Veteran's account, F/Sgt Harry Howard.
2. NA Kew, AIR 27-1922-1/2 ORB, No. 463 Squadron, September 1944.
3. Gretta Howard, private collection.
4. Veteran's account, F/Sgt Harry Howard.
5. Middlebrook, *The Nuremberg Raid,* op. cit., pp. 69–72.
6. Veteran's account, F/Sgt Harry Howard.
7. Gretta Howard, private collection.

Chapter 29

1. Brotherton, op. cit., pp. 161–2.
2. Ibid.
3. Korda, *Alone,* p. 435
4. NA Kew, AIR 27-451-22, ORB No. 44 (Rhodesia) Squadron, November 1944.
5. Ibid.
6. Brotherton, op. cit.
7. NA Kew, AIR 27-451-22, op. cit.
8. Brotherton, op. cit.

Chapter 30

1. Veteran's account, WO Richard Nairn.
2. Ibid. (and all subsequent direct quotes).
3. NA Kew, AIR 27-816-22, ORB No. 103 Squadron, November 1944.
4. Ibid.
5. Ibid.
6. Andrew Nairn, private collection.

Chapter 31

1. Veteran's account, Sgt Ricky Dyson.
2. Doherty, *Irish Men and Women in the Second World War,* p. 118.
3. Ibid. (and all subsequent direct quotes).
4. *London Gazette,* 24 April 1945.
5. Ibid.
6. Ibid., and Mavis Dyson, private collection.

Chapter 32
1. Veteran's account, P/O W.G. 'Bill' Taylor.
2. NA Kew, AIR 27-457-18, ORB No. 45 Squadron, December 1944.
3. Veteran's account, P/O W.G. 'Bill' Taylor (and all subsequent direct quotes).
4. Commendatory endorsement – Group Captain, F.O. Whiteley, AOC 221 Group RAF, 24 January 1945.
5. NA Kew, AIR 27-457-18, op. cit.
6. Private collection, Sue Cox.

Chapter 33
1. Veteran's account, F/O M.G. Bache DSO.
2. Veteran's account, F/Sgt John 'Jim' Jay.
3. NA Kew, AIR 27-1931-25/26, ORB No. 467 Squadron, January 1945.
4. Ibid., and F/O M.G. Bache DSO – Combat Report.
5. Veteran's account, F/Sgt John Jay.
6. F/O M.G. Bache DSO – Combat Report, op. cit.
7. Ibid.
8. Veteran's account, F/Sgt John Jay, op. cit.
9. F/O M.G. Bache, DSO – Combat Report op. cit.
10. Veteran's account, F/Sgt John Jay, op. cit.
11. Ibid.

Chapter 34
1. Veteran's account, F/Sgt Russell Stinson.
2. NA Kew, AIR 27-2044-20, ORB, No. 571 Squadron, January 1945.
3. Middlebrook, *The Berlin Raids*, op. cit., p. 327.
4. Veteran's account, F/Sgt Russell Stinson (and all subsequent direct quotes).
5. Private collection, Geoff Baldwin.

Chapter 35
1. Veteran's account, F/Sgt R.A. Deck.
2. Veteran's account, F/Sgt R.A. Deck (and all subsequent direct quotes).
3. NA Kew, AIR 27-1854-1/2, ORB No. 429 Squadron, January 1945.
4. Alan Deck, private collection.

Chapter 36
1. Veteran's account, Sgt Ricky Dyson.
2. NA Kew, AIR 27-1152-7/8, ORB No. 189 Squadron, February 1945.
3. Veteran's account, Sgt Ricky Dyson (and all subsequent direct quotes).
4. RAF Investigation Report (Abschrift), Pilot Officer D.S. Bassett, 3 NREU, BAFO.
5. Ibid.
6. *London Gazette*, 24 April 1945 (Supplement No. 37054).
7. Private collection, M. Dyson.

Chapter 37
1. Veteran's account, F/O Officer John Ulm.
2. Evans, op. cit., p. 171.
3. Ibid., p.193.
4. Veteran's account, F/O John Ulm (and all subsequent direct quotes).

Postscript

1. Bender, F/O Clifford A. 'Cliff', DFC (Shirley Bender, private collection).
2. Bowles, F/Lt Percy, DFC (Ralph Bowles, private collection).
3. Coates, Sgt E. 'Ted' (private collection, Rosemary Wright).
4. Harvey, Wg/Cdr D.C. 'Doug', DFC (private collection, Jim Harvey).
5. Hawken, F/Sgt Stanley A. (Des Leavey, private collection).
6. O'Brien, Sgt John (Jenny Priestley, private collection).
7. Roberts, WO Ross K. (Colin Lamb, private collection).
8. Sommerville, F/O Robert M. 'Bob' (Lesley Sommerville, private collection).
9. Worner, Sub/Lt Gerald W. (Colene Taylor, private collection).
10. Watson, F/Lt W.K. 'Ken' DFC (private collection, Ian Campbell).
11. McManus, F/Lt John B., DFC (private collection, John McManus).
12. Wright, F/Lt Frederick R. 'Fred', DFC (private collection, Annette Wright).
13. Ibid.

Epilogue

1. Mann, *And Some Fell on Stony Ground*, pp. 7–8.

Glossary and Abbreviations

General

AA	Anti-Aircraft
AASF	Advanced Air Striking Force, of the RAF in France 1939/40
ACM	Air Chief Marshal
AI	Airborne Interception radar
AM	Air Marshal
Angels	Height (or altitude) in thousands of feet, used in airborne radio communication
AOC	Air Officer Commanding
AOC-in-C	Air Officer Commanding-in-Chief
AVM	Air Vice Marshal
Bandit	Enemy aircraft (identified)
'Big City'	Berlin (pseudonym used by Bomber Command aircrew)
Bogey	Unidentified aircraft (suspected enemy)
Boozer	Sensor to activate an alert flashing light in the cockpit when enemy radar locks on to the aircraft
Chaung	inlet from the sea or a river (usually tidal)
C-in-C	Commander-in-Chief
CO	Commanding Officer
'Dinah'	Mitsubishi Ki-46 Army Type 100 two-seat high-altitude interceptor fighter and command reconnaissance aircraft
Ditch	Come down in the sea or other water
Flamer	aircraft shot down in flames
Flap	excitement or some especially chaotic event
GOC	General Officer Commanding
Hang up	Bomb(s) not released from the bomb bay (or other equipment) of an aircraft
HE	High Explosive bombs
Helper	civilian in Nazi-occupied Europe who assisted Allied airmen to avoid capture and escape back to Britain
IFF	Identification Friend or Foe, airborne radio identification device
IJAAF (or JAAF)	Imperial Japanese Army Air Force
KIA	Killed in action
LG	Landing Ground
LNSF	Light Night Striking Force
Mae West	Lifejacket for ditching in water

Ops	Operations
ORB	Operations Record Book
'Oscar'	Nakajima Ki-43 Hayabusa (Peregrine Falcon) Army Type 1 single-seat fighter/fighter-bomber
OTU	Operational Training Unit
Pancake	Emergency landing with undercarriage retracted
PR	Photographic Reconnaissance
PRU	Photographic Reconnaissance Unit
RA	Royal Artillery
RAAF	Royal Australian Air Force
RAF	Royal Air Force
RCAF	Royal Canadian Air Force
RDF	Radio Direction Finding (later known as radar)
Recce	Reconnaissance
RNZAF	Royal New Zealand Air Force
R/T	radio traffic (communication)
Scramble	Take off urgently, usually in response to detection of a bandit or bogey
'Second Dickey'	A newly-trained pilot taken as a second pilot to gain experience on an operation
Sortie	one aircraft doing one trip to target and back
Through the gate	Maximum engine revs to give emergency power
U/S	unserviceable, or not available
USAAF	United States Army Air Forces
Vector	Direction to steer
Vic	aircraft formation in the shape of a V (three aircraft or more)
W/T	Wireless Telegraph (communication)

Bibliography and Sources

Air Ministry/Kark, Wing Commander Leslie, and Central Office of Information, *Wings of the Phoenix-The Official history of the Air War in Burma*, HMSO, London 1949.

Allied Air Forces HQ, South West Pacific Area, Interrogation by MIS-X Section.

Bauer, Lieutenant Colonel E., *The History of World War II*, Lifetime Distributors, Sydney, Australia, and Amber Books Ltd, London 2009.

Beevor, Anthony, *The Second World War*, Back Bay Books, Hachette Group, New York, USA 2012.

Bending, Kevin, *The History of 97 (Straits Settlements) Squadron in the Second World War* (unpublished), Index to Aircrew 1941–1945 – A-J, Comans, J.W. (pilot)

Brotherton, Joyce M., *Press on Regardless* (unpublished), Imperial War Museum (Cat. No. 6649 97/25/1)

Chant, Chris, *Aircraft of World War II*, Amber Books Ltd, London 1999.

Cheshire, G/Capt Leonard VC DSO DFC, *Bomber Pilot*, Hutchinson & Co., Ltd, London, 1954

Collier, Richard, *The Sands of Dunkirk*, Collins, London, 1961.

Crosby, Francis, *A Handbook of Fighter Aircraft*, Imperial War Museum, Hermes House.

Doherty, Richard, *Irish Men and Women in the Second World War*, Four Courts Press Ltd, Dublin, 1999.

Eastern Air Command, *Burma Air Victory*, SEAC, Calcutta, June 1945.

Evans, Bryn, *Air Battle for Burma*, Pen & Sword Books Ltd, Barnsley, UK, 2016.

——, *The Decisive Campaigns of the Desert Air Force 1942–1945*, Pen & Sword Books Ltd, Barnsley, UK, 2014.

Franks, Norman, *Images of War, RAF Fighters over Burma*, Pen & Sword Books Ltd, UK, 2014.

Grehan, John, & Mace, Martin, *Far East Air Operations 1942–1945*, Pen & Sword Books Ltd, Barnsley, UK, 2014.

Hart, Duane, *Redcliffe Pictorial History*, Vol 2 1824–1949, Ocean Reeve Publishing, Brisbane, Queensland, Australia 2017.

Hawken, Stanley A. OBE, *Missing Presumed Dead*, Hill of Content Publishing, Melbourne, Australia, 1989.

Herington, John, *Air War Against Germany and Italy 1939 -1943*, Australian War Memorial, Halstead Press, Sydney, 1954.

Holland, James, *Big Week*, Bantam Press, Penguin, London, 2018.

Korda, Michael, *Alone*, Liveright Publishing Corporation, New York, 2017.

Mackersey, Ian, *Into the Silk*, Granada Publishing Ltd, London, 1978.

Mann, Leslie, *And Some Fell on Stony Ground*, Icon Books Ltd, London, 2014.

Masters, David, *So Few*, Eyre & Spottiswood Ltd, London, 1945.

Meyerowitz, Seth, *The Lost Airman*, Atlantic Books, London, 2016.

Middlebrook, Martin, *The Nuremberg Raid*, Cassell & Co, London, 2000.

——, *The Battle of Hamburg*, Cassell & Co., London 2000.

——, *The Berlin Raids*, Cassell & Co., London, 2002.

——, and Everitt, Chris, *The Bomber Command War Diaries: An Operational Reference Book 1939–1945*, Midland Publishing, UK, 1998.

Odd Bods UK Ass, *ODD Bods at War 1939–45*, Veritage Press Pty Ltd, Gosford, NSW, Australia

Peart, Alan McGregor DFC, *From North Africa to the Arakan*, Grub Street, London, 2008.

Redcliffe City Council, *Redcliffe Remembers: The War Years 1939–1949*, Redcliffe City Council, Queensland, Australia, 2014.

Richey, Paul, *Fighter Pilot*, Cassell Military Paperbacks, London, 2001

Rickard, J. *No. 571 Squadron RAF: Second World War*, www.historyofwar.org/air/units/RAF/571_wwII.html

Sarkar, Dilip, *Spitfire Manual 1940*, Amberley Publishing, Stroud, 2010

Saunders, Hilary St George, *RAF 1939–45 Vol. III The Fight is Won*, HMSO, London, 1954.

Shores, Christopher, *Air War for Burma*, Grub Street, London, 2005.

——, & Williams, Clive, *Aces High*, Grub Street, London, 1994.

Terraine, John, *The Right of the Line*, Pen & Sword Books Ltd, Barnsley, 2010.

Thomas, Andrew, *Spitfire Aces of Burma and the Pacific*, Osprey Publishing, Oxford, 2009.

Time-Life, *China-Burma-India*, Time-Life Books, Inc., 1978.

Time-Life, *Rising Sun*, Time-Life Books, Inc., 1977.

Veitch, Michael, *Fly*, Bolinda Publishing Pty Ltd, Australia.

Vincent, David, *Catalina Chronicle – A History of RAAF Operations*, Printed by LPH, Adelaide, South Australia.

Wright, F.R. DFC, *My Life in the RAAF*, F.R. Wright, Gerrigong, NSW 2534, Australia.

National Archives, Kew, London, UK
AIR 27-1322-21/22 ORB Nov 1943, No. 214 Squadron RAF

AIR 27-1-40 ORB Oct 1939, No. 1 Squadron RAF

AIR 27-554-14 ORB May 1940, No. 59 Squadron RAF

AIR 27-149-10 ORB June 1940, No. 10 Squadron RAF

AIR 27-849-4 ORB Oct 1941, No. 108 Squadron RAF

AIR 27-449-6 ORB April 1942, No. 44 (Rhodesia) Squadron RAF

AIR 27-1907-08 ORB June 1942, No. 460 Squadron RAF

AIR 27-1234-15/16 ORB August 1943, No. 207 Squadron RAF

AIR 27-678-35/36 ORB September 1943, No. 207 Squadron RAF

AIR 27-1322-21/22 ORB November 1943, No. 214 Squadron RAF

AIR 27-2137-14/16 ORB February 1944, No. 622 Squadron RAF

AIR 27-678-39 ORB March/April 1944, No. 81 Squadron RAF

AIR 27-1928-13 ORB July 1944, No. 466 Squadron RAF

AIR 27-1922-1/2 ORB September 1944, No. 463 Squadron RAF

AIR 27-451-22 ORB November 1944, No. 44 Squadron RAF

AIR 27-816-22 ORB November 1944, No. 103 Squadron RAF

AIR 27-459-18 ORB December 1944, No. 45 Squadron RAF

AIR 27-1931-25/26 ORB January 1945, No. 467 Squadron RAF

AIR 27-2044-20 ORB January 1945, No. 571 Squadron RAF

AIR 27-1854-1/2 ORB January 1945, No. 429 Squadron RAF

AIR 27-1152-7/8 ORB February 1945, No. 189 Squadron RAF

Veterans' Accounts
Bache, Flying Officer M.G. 'Merv', DSO.

Barnett, Flying Officer D.J.

Bender, Flying Officer Clifford A. 'Cliff", DFC.

Bevis, Flight Lieutenant Lewis S., Pilot, RAF transport, Hurricane fighters.

Bowles, Flight Lieutenant Percy, DFC.

Campbell, Flight Sergeant Keith, OAM.

Coates, Sergeant E. 'Ted'.

Comans, Wing Commander J.L.V. 'Jim'.
Deck, Pilot Officer R.A. 'Dick'.
Dyer, Flying Officer F.S. 'Fred'.
Dyson, Sergeant Ricky, GM.
Fischer, Flight Sergeant John B.
Good, Flying Officer Bryan, DFC.
Harvey, Wing Commander D.C. 'Doug'.
Hawken, Flight Sergeant Stanley A., OBE.
Hollings, Wing Commander Albert, DFC.
Howard, Flight Sergeant H. 'Harry'.
Jay, Flight Sergeant John 'Jim'.
Leah, Flight Sergeant Lloyd.
Maher, Flight Lieutenant Eric.
McManus, Flying Officer John B., DFC LdH.
McRae, W.W. 'Bill', DFC AFC LdH.
Nairn, Warrant Officer Richard.
O'Brien, Sergeant John.
Peart, Flight Lieutenant Alan, DFC.
Penny, Group Captain Herbert A., OBE.
Rehrer, Lieutenant Colonel H.E. 'Gene'.
Richey, Wing Commander Paul, LdH.
Roberts, Warrant Officer Ross K.
Scantleton, Flight Lieutenant V.L. 'Vern', DFC.
Simpson, Allan, Group Captain.
Sommerville, Flying Officer Robert M. 'Bob'.
Stinson, Flying Officer Russell.
Tanner, Pilot Officer K.E.
Taylor, Pilot Officer W.G. 'Bill'.
Ulm, Flying Officer John.
Watson, Flight Lieutenant W.K. 'Ken', DFC.
Worner, Sub Lieutenant Gerald W.
Wright, Flight Lieutenant Frederick R. 'Fred', DFC.

Private Collections
Bowles, Flight Lieutenant Percy, DFC (Ralph Bowles)
Campbell, Flight Sergeant Keith, OAM.
Comans, Wing Commander J.L.V. 'Jim' (Chris Whiteman).
Deck, Pilot Officer R.A. 'Dick' (Alan Deck).
Dyer, Flying Officer F.S. 'Fred' (Stephen Dyer).
Dyson, Sergeant Ricky, GM. (Ian Campbell and Mavis Dyson).
Fischer, Flight Sergeant John B. (Geoff, Bruce and Janet Fischer).
Good, Flying Officer Bryan, DFC (Suellyn Everett).
Hollings, Wing Commander Albert, DFC (Geoff Hollings).
Howard, Flight Sergeant H. 'Harry' (Gretta Howard).
Jay, Flight Sergeant John 'Jim'.
Leah, Flight Sergeant Lloyd (Peter Leah).
Liedl, Flying Officer Allan B. (Scott Carmock).
Maher, Flight Lieutenant Eric (Kate Schafer).
McManus, Flying Officer John B., DFC LdH.
McRae, W.W. 'Bill', DFC, AFC LdH.
Nairn, Warrant Officer Richard (Andrew Nairn).

Peart, Flight Lieutenant Alan, DFC.
Penny, Group Captain Herbert A., OBE (Nick Penny).
Rehrer, Lieutenant Colonel H.E. 'Gene' (Larry Rehrer).
Scantleton, Flight Lieutenant V.L. 'Vern', DFC (John Scantleton).
Stinson, Flying Officer Russell (Geoff Baldwin).
Taylor, Pilot Officer W.G. 'Bill' (Sue Cox).
Ulm, Flying Officer John.

Miscellaneous Sources

Australian War Memorial (AWM), Wing Commander Julius Allan Cohen AO CBE DFC (biography).
Bull, Group Captain, *RAF Bomber Command Commemoration (RAAF)*, No. 460 Squadron, 26 May 2019.
Coleman, Scott, *Flight Lieutenant J.V. Comans DFC,* Marist Brothers High School, Darlinghurst, Sydney, NSW, Australia.
Daily Telegraph, Biography Wing Commander 'Jim' Comans (John Edwards), www.telegraph.co.uk/news, 14 October 2012.
Harrington Aviation Museum, *History of No. 218 Squadron*, www.harringtonmuseum.org.uk.
London Gazette, 24 and 28 April 1942.
Pacific Wrecks, www.pacificwrecks.com.
Sydney Daily Mirror, Australia, February 1971.
The Adelaide Advertiser, 30 April 2016.
The Comprehensive Guide to the Victoria and George Cross, www.vconline.org.uk.
The Sun Herald, Australia, 2 August 1992.
The Sydney Morning Herald, Obituary *Keith Campbell OAM*, 20 July 2019.
Traces of World War 2, No. 218 Squadron RAF, www.epibreren.com.

Every effort has been taken to attribute to each of the above veterans the final rank attained, as well as their awards and other decorations.

Index

PART 1: MILITARY, AIR AND NAVAL FORCES

PART 2: GENERAL

Notes

1. Every effort has been taken to attribute the appropriate rank as the last known and as used in the text. However, this may not be the final rank attained of those mentioned in the index.
2. It has not been possible to research the final rank, or full name, of some participants.